The Evergreen Portfolio

The Evergreen Portfolio

TIMELESS STRATEGIES TO SURVIVE AND PROSPER FROM INVESTING PROS

Martin Truax
Ron Miller

WILEY

John Wiley & Sons, Inc.

For general information on our other products and services or for technical support, please contact our Customer Care Department within the United States at (800) 762-2974, outside the United States at (317) 572-3993 or fax (317) 572-4002.

Wiley also publishes its books in a variety of electronic formats. Some content that appears in print may not be available in electronic books. For more information about Wiley products, visit our web site at www.wiley.com.

Library of Congress Cataloging-in-Publication Data:

Truax, Martin.

The evergreen portfolio: timeless strategies to survive and prosper from investing pros / Martin Truax, Ron Miller.

    p. cm.

Includes index.

ISBN 978-0-470-56008-2 (hardback); 978-0-470-89026-4 (ebk); 978-0-470-89027-1 (ebk); 978-0-470-89028-8 (ebk)

   1. Investments. 2. Hedge funds. 3. Finance, Personal. I. Miller, Ronald E. II. Title.

HG4521.T694 2010

332.6–dc22

2010018284

Printed in the United States of America

10 9 8 7 6 5 4 3 2 1

Contents

Preface

For the past 20-plus years, a group of individual investors, advisors, and writers has been gathering together in the spring for a tradition of exchange of investment outlooks and ideas. Starting in Atlanta, the meeting moved midway to the North Georgia Mountains to a private estate known as Chota Falls. Thus, what started as the Atlanta Investment Conference began to transition into the Chota Forum, where the number of speakers stayed about the same but the size of the audience became more limited. One of the advantages of this revised forum size was the greater ease of one-on-one exchange and interaction.

Over the years, the "elves" from Louis Rukeyser's *Wall Street Week*, national political representatives including the former Speaker of the House, Hon. Newt Gingrich, major brokerage firm analysts, investment newsletter writers, and business executives (future billionaires included)—have participated as speakers and presenters. Although not everyone saw the future the same, they gave our attendees a heads-up about what was happening in our country and the world, and an opportunity to perhaps *position their investments more advantageously.*

At the Chota Forum in the spring of 2009, the speakers were individually interviewed by the Master of Ceremonies after their specific presentations. In each taped interview, Gary Alexander asked them five specific questions:

1. How did we get in this mess?
2. What will the recovery cycle be like?
3. What is your suggested solution to the problems?
4. What is your longer term outlook?
5. How should one invest in this environment?

As you will read in Chapter 2, those speakers participating in that year's personal interviews were:

- Bob Barr, former Congressman and Libertarian Party presidential candidate
- Robert Bishop, longtime editor of *Gold Mining Stock Report*
- Roger Conrad, editor, *Utility Forecaster* and *Canadian Edge*
- Adrian Day, CEO, Adrian Day Asset Management
- Neil George, former editor, *Personal Finance*
- Elliott Gue, editor, *Personal Finance* and associate editor, *Energy Strategist*
- Dr. Alan Keyes, former Republican presidential candidate
- Ian McAvity, editor, *Deliberations*
- Rick Rule, CEO, Global Resources Investments Inc.
- Ben Sheperd, editor, *Louis Rukeyser's Mutual Funds*
- Mark Skousen, editor, *Forecasts & Strategies*
- Frank Trotter, president, Everbank.

Soon after the 2009 Conference, we were contacted by publisher John Wiley & Sons about putting these thoughts into book form. Many of the presenters agreed to put more extensive thought and advice into a single chapter for this combined contribution project.

When informed of it, other financial experts agreed to join this project. Robert Prechter and Alexander Green, editor of the Oxford Club, quickly agreed to add their thoughts. In addition, *U.S. & World Early Warning Report*'s editor, Richard Maybury, gold guru Duane Poliquin, rare-coin experts Van Simmons and David Hall, and estate planning attorney Gary Kashdan agreed to contribute.

The Friends for Autism Foundation, Inc., has been the organizer and beneficiary of the 20-year conference event.* It will also be the recipient of the royalties of this book. Over the years, all of the speakers have contributed their time, and in most cases, their expenses of being at the conference, in order to help the cause of autism. When the event was first organized in 1987, it was estimated that 1 in 10,000 were affected by this condition. Now the Centers

---

* For information on the Friends for Autism Foundation and its partner, Childhood Autism Foundation (CADEF), you can go online to *CADEF.org*.
For information on the Atlanta Investment Conference/Chota Forum, please e-mail: *atlinvestconf@mindspring.com*.

for Disease Control and Prevention (CDC) estimate this number at *1 in 105* (1 in 70 for boys). The Friends for Autism Foundation appreciates the generosity of all the forum speakers and attendees over the years. The Atlanta Investment Conference/Chota Forum has raised substantial sums for the cause. These funds have contributed to an autism center at Emory University Medical School in Atlanta, and toward model schools and training programs. Again, we thank all those who have made this and other efforts benefiting this cause both meaningful and worthwhile.

What you are about to read contains the condensed wisdom of more than 15 seasoned investment pros in a very unique gathering of contributions never before brought together in written form. We believe you will find it a most valuable and useful guide in helping you build the tools necessary to successfully invest and profit even in the most tumultuous times. In compiling these selections, our goal is to help you meet your financial challenges with more of your assets intact and with an appreciation and a better understanding of what is happening, and most importantly, of how to prepare and adjust accordingly.

With our best wishes and expectations,
Martin Truax, Conference Co-Chairman

CHAPTER 1

The Evergreen Portfolio

THE BIG PICTURE

Martin Truax

Our planet had a close call with financial fate in the fall of 2008. The dominoes began to fall as nontransparent hedge funds rejected redemption requests and aggressively yielding money funds were about to do the same. As investors' emotions switched from greed to fear, a classic run on the alternative and shadow banking system began. Some of the most savvy were transferring bank balances to Treasuries only. Complacency had suddenly become concern, and capitulation soon followed. We had a financial panic, the worst in 70-some years. The banking system froze and deleveraging ensued, bringing on a deflationary adjustment in almost all classes of global assets, with the exception of the highest quality of liquidity.

Government financial intervention became the most aggressive in modern times. Liquidity, low interest rates, purchases of doubtful debt, cash to consumers, incentives to buy cars and homes, anything that might slow the speed of the falling dominoes was attempted. *Less bad* was soon seen as *better* than *more bad*. Liquidity went mostly into the financial markets, into stocks and all levels of bonds, from the government's short-term debt to corporate junk paper. With direct correlation, most of the global financial markets had a significant rebound. The intervention appeared to be successful for the time being.

Now we have what many are describing as a *new normal.* It's become a different world with higher unemployment, excess manufacturing and housing capacity, and difficult-to-obtain credit. Consumers hesitate to buy beyond the necessities. Their hopeful expectations for the prime collateral of the world, real estate, are forced to be adjusted. Buyers look for bargains and wait until prices are actually further reduced. It's a classic deflationary scenario that ushers in a *self-feeding deflationary trend.*

The Long Cycle

Extending over the life expectation of the average adult, the long-term economic/financial cycle repeats about every 70 to 80 years. Our human errors are revisited as memories formed by experience fade away. The financial lessons of history are forgotten. Beginning the long cycle, from a conservative mindset of debt *avoidance*, debt steadily is sought and extended until it becomes unmanageable. In the first decade of the new millennium, we arrived at the unmanageable level again. We have employed debt instruments created by financial engineers that are so convoluted that even the engineers aren't sure what, where, or how much exists. Rules put in place some 70 years ago to prevent recurrences of past mistakes were changed and abandoned. Gone were the Glass-Steagall Act, which separated commercial banking from investment banking; the stock lending rule for shorting; and the uptick rule. Gone, too, were the more conservative bank leverage caps, and the regulation on the largest financial markets—derivatives. These safeguards were all abandoned or ignored to allow *greed* to once again overwhelm the system. And the system broke. Can it be put back together once again?

For the U.K., the U.S., and most of the developed countries, it will probably take a long time for the deleveraging side of the long-term cycle to unwind—perhaps a decade *or more.* And depending on who's in charge, our social structures could be significantly altered during this transition. Americans' expectations are high. Y2K proved to be beatable and a nonevent. We continually want and expect quick financial fixes. But Americans have promised themselves *what cannot possibly* be delivered in their future. As I heard the late John Templeton (1929–2008) say simply in one of his final presentations, "American industry and government have overextended themselves in retirement and health benefit promises." It has become our expectation to be taken care of in our senior years. Historically, the family took care of the family. Elections and labor negotiations were won with promises that someone besides our family might provide for us instead. The means are just not there. Any further deflation and destruction of the value of what remains (of our nest eggs) will further extend the time for potential financial recovery. We've arrived at that point in the cycle where the ammo for quick fixes is getting low and the incoming opposing forces loom overwhelmingly.

Our Future

In our personal battle for financial survival, plans for our retirement or legacy may need to be adjusted. Certainly our investment strategy will need to be different when we're in the deleveraging/deflationary back end of the long-term cycle than when we're in the early inflationary/leveraging expansionary stages of the cycle. In round one of the deleveraging process from 2000 to 2009, the average global investor lost about a quarter of his overall asset values in stocks, bonds, and real estate—probably more if leverage (debt) was employed. Round two, a carryover of the unfinished first round, could be even more destructive. We can expect the governments of the world to attempt to further delay the natural cycle. They've done so already, but only by expanding debt even more. This increasing debt will have to be dealt with again at a future time.

As Ludwig von Mises said: "There are no means of avoiding the final collapse of a boom brought on by credit expansion. The alternative is only whether the crisis should come sooner as a result of voluntary abandonment of further credit expansion, or later as final and total catastrophe of the currency system involved." The writer of possibly the longest-published investment newsletter in the United States, Richard Russell, observes: "There have been other debt bubbles in history, but this one is by far the greatest ever and definitely more international in scope. The outcome when previous bubbles have fallen apart has always been a deflationary depression." My own thought is that eventually renewed inflation will be the alternative of choice, whether we experience a depression or somehow manage to avoid that potential social changing event.

From the book *This Time It's Different*, authors Carmen M. Reinhart and Kenneth Rogoff say:

> Perhaps more than anything else, failure to recognize the precariousness and fickleness of confidence—especially in cases in which large short term debts need to be rolled over continuously—is the key factor that gives rise to the "this-time-it's-different" syndrome. *Highly indebted governments, banks, or corporations can seem to be merrily rolling along for an extended period, when bang!—confidence collapses, lenders disappear, and a crisis hits.* [Italics added for emphasis.]
>
> Economic theory tells us that it is precisely the fickle nature of confidence, including its dependence on the public's expectation of future events, that makes it so difficult to predict the timing of debt crises. High debt levels lead, in many mathematical economics models, to "multiple equilibria" in which the debt level might be sustained—or might not be. Economists do not have a terribly good idea of what kinds of events shift confidence or how to concretely assess confidence vulnerability. What one does see, again and again, in the history of financial crisis is that when an accident is waiting to happen, it eventually does. When countries become too deeply indebted, they are headed for trouble. When debt-fueled asset price explosions seem too good to be true, they probably are. But the exact timing can be very difficult to guess, and a crisis that seems imminent can sometimes take years to ignite.

Just as the economists, politicians, and majority of investors didn't anticipate round one, or at least its timing, we can probably expect that round two's long-term impact will be at least equally surprising, and probably at least as destructive. I might expect it could be even more so, as much of the means to defend or counterattack have been depleted. Interest rates can't go below zero for too long—or can they? To what asset categories will be the next flight to safety?

Is there a round three out there as well? Probably so. It might well be the "unintended consequence" of rounds one and two. What will rounds two and three look like? Biblically speaking, we're not given to know our fate, but that doesn't mean that we do nothing in preparation for the possibilities. Some of our colleagues have addressed potential preparations in the following chapters of this book. Personally, I feel that we need to respond as the events occur. But we need to have in place a plan that we can quickly implement as the future unfolds. The best investors will seize the opportunities as the present affords them. As the late financial manager Peter Bernstein remarked, "Look at your wealth as a loan. It can be called at any time." By employing a diverse strategy, we'll hope to survive and maybe even prosper. By all things we can consider, we'll certainly plan on it.

Asset Placement

The average investor has accumulated real estate (30%), business interests, cash reserves (12%), bonds (7%), and stocks (25%), as well as life insurance policies and pension plans.* Most investors use some kind of management for these more liquid assets, be it comingled funds or separately managed accounts. And most have also bought into both the *efficient market theory* and the *modern portfolio theory*. The first theory states that it's tough to beat the market indexes over time. The second states that you diversify through different styles of management. Different styles can include big cap, small cap, mid-cap, international cap, value, and growth (*cap* is short for the *capitalization* size of the companies).

My response to this is:

Rule #1. If you want to survive and hopefully prosper during the back side (the deleveraging) of the long cycle, forget both of those theories.

Rule #2. Remember Rule #1.

If you have so much big cap, small cap, mid-cap, and international cap and the market declines, it means that, overall, you're going to have *so much less cap*. I've never had an investor tell me that's what he wants and expects from his assets—less cap. But most investors have bought into these themes when they were presented to them. It's what the financial industry teaches its people in training and through continuing education programs. It's repeated over and over again. Financial advisors and management have no doubt believed it and have certainly bought into it.

Barron's 9/14/09—David Rosenberg.

There are certain periods when these theories can work: when the market goes up over a decade or two, such as the two periods of 1949 through 1966, and again from 1982 to 1999. Both were approximately 17-year periods of continually higher markets with periodic corrections (declines). But the three periods of 1966 through 1982, 1929 through 1949, and 1999 through whenever, were not periods of upward-trending markets with periodic corrections. Rather, these were periods when we experienced extended declines with periodic upward corrections. These periods, too, can last 17 to 20 years. The only way for your equity assets to survive and possibly prosper in such a period is for you to become a tactical asset allocator. *Tactical* means: There's a time to increase equity asset exposure, and a time to decrease equity asset exposure. Yes, there should be a timing to be fully invested. There should also be a timing to cause us to be less so. In my opinion, we are in a period for the latter. To think and act otherwise could be destructive to your capital—like a loan, callable at any time.

Most financial advisors will tell you that it's just time in the market. But for the first decade of the new millennium, 2000–2010, the Dow Jones Industrial Average crossed 10,000 approaching 30 times. The index investors didn't make a dime, even with their dividends, for their time in the market. That's 10 years of negative return, with the S&P (including dividends) down approximately 10 percent. In addition to the actual losses, there is also the opportunity loss of the income that could have been received from Treasuries or money market funds had one stayed on the sidelines. Even at the end of that decade, the market was still at a historically expensive multiple to earnings.

We can also look at the results of some of the timing of tactical investors, individuals who used a successful method of adjusting equity exposure during this past decade. Some more than tripled their equity assets during that same 10-year period. We have to choose which drummer we want to march with. Do we go with those who say, "You can't time the market; you can't beat the market"? Or do we march with those who have been successful at doing just that? According to investment manager Ron Arnott, a study shows that annually rolling over 20-year Treasury bonds since 1966 has beaten the S&P during that same period. That's right: For 42 years through December 2008, government-guaranteed bonds have beaten the stock market indexes.

Bonds

Bonds also need management and adjustment. We can just choose to roll over varied laddered maturities. For example, we can invest in 2-, 4-, 6-, 8-, 10+-year bonds and, when each matures, we just roll to the 10-year period. In 8 years you'll have all the money at more favorable 10-year rates. You'll also have liquidity every 2 years. You could also create a similar ladder going out as far as 20 years. And maybe that's okay for the *first* 70 years of the long-term cycle. But remember, the current cycle was artificially stretched to avoid the pains of recessions. It started when Federal Reserve Chairman Greenspan reacted after the crash in 1987 with, "not on my watch." Presidents learned that *it was the economy* that most impacted their ability to stay in office. Whatever it took to keep the economy growing and the markets hitting new highs became the priority of the past 25 years.

Each economic slowdown of the past quarter-century has been met with lower interest rates and monetary stimulation (called *quantitative easing*). We became accustomed to the "Greenspan Put." The Maestro could turn it around. He could defy the unpleasant deleveraging/deflationary part of the inevitable long-term cycle. We postponed the unpleasant, just as we can postpone a trip to the dentist. Regular trips will keep us healthier. Extended avoidance will eventually allow a small cavity to rot the tooth to the core. At some point, through postponement, it will give way and be lost.

Quantitative easing (money printing or computerized expansion of available cash or bonds) by a government with immunity from writing checks without sufficient funds can be useful in emergency situations. Most of us have overdraft protection on our personal accounts for such occurrences. But when debt is not paid back, how much and how long can it go unaddressed? We'll find out, for sure. Most would agree that we're past the point of being able to repay. We can't raise taxes high enough. We can't cut expenditures low enough (much of the expenditure is interest on the debt). So what can be done? The answer is that eventually we'll probably have to deflate the relative value of debt. Remember your first mortgage or auto loan? If you had to borrow, it probably seemed big at the time. But now most of us look back at that debt as small in comparison to some potential asset financing today. That's a lot of creeping inflation. Just accelerate that inflation of the assets and the current fixed debt, too, can look smaller and more manageable.

We must remember, however, should inflation reappear as a solution to excessive government debt, that interest rates would likely adjust upward. Investors expect to get the inflation rate plus 2 or 3 percent of earnings on their money. If rates go up, previously issued longer term bonds adjust downward to compensate for the new higher rates. So, longer term bonds could leave us with less purchasing power when they mature after inflation, and less principal if we cashed them in early to get the new higher rate. Meanwhile, the short-term rates during ZIRP (zero interest rate policy) leave us little or no return after taxes.

By law, states, counties, and municipal governments cannot run deficits. These governments are not able to write checks against insufficient funds. So, greater care must be exercised in selection of which regional entities will have the sufficient funds in times of state and local government financial shortfalls. Some state budgets are already short almost 50 percent in their tax receipts to their budgeted expenditures. Taxes can't be raised enough to offset these deficits. Budgets can't be easily cut in half without social consequences. Something has to give. How much of it will be from the repayment of bond principal?

Fixed Returns

All this is to say that a guaranteed rate of return might be nice for planning retirement and legacy purposes during the first 60 or 70 expansionary or milder asset-inflating years of the cycle. It might be just as nice in a normal, longer-term backside or deflating side of the cycle as well. But our current cycle was not allowed to be normal on the Maestro's watch. Election considerations were prioritized. So, rolling a large portion of our assets to a guaranteed return during a period of artificially low rates could be devastating if inflation becomes the ultimate answer to debt excess. Since lowering expenditures and raising taxes don't win elections, what do you think the other solutions might possibly be? Investors need to plan accordingly and not get overly fixated on a guaranteed return at this time. And remember, in round one, many of the guarantors had to get guaranteed themselves. That was just in round one. Unfortunately, most individual investors were choosing to place their investable assets into fixed returns (cash and bonds) as this first decade, or round one, was closing out.

Stocks

Most investors expect history to repeat in terms of long-term performance of equities. Over the long term, 10 percent has been the
average. As discussed earlier, there are cycles of approximately 17
years when the returns have substantially exceeded 10 percent, and
periods of approximately 17 to 20 years when they have substantially
fallen short of the average and actually been negative. The years
2000 through 2009 are an example of an entire decade with negative returns. Over the long term as well, about one third to a half of
the 10 percent return has come from dividends.* With the 80 million or so Baby Boomers wanting to retire soon, or having already
done so, they will need income. Total return investing (a combination of dividends and appreciation) yielded unsatisfactory results
for the past decade. The biggest problems that caused the financial
crisis, panic and a negative performance (overextension of debt and
use of derivatives), have only gotten more unmanageable. My expectation for the remainder of this current potential (minimum) 17-year
period, which began in 2000, is for more of the same.

I feel that high-dividend stocks will be in strong demand. Combined
with hedging techniques that follow the market direction, these "cash
cows" can help preserve principal while providing spendable income.
As the collection of Social Security and Medicare premiums (taxes)
from the working generation falls short of promised distributions to
the retired or semiretired Boomers, something has got to give. Will it
be "means testing" that lowers our benefit payments, or will it be higher
premiums or taxes? Those with "other means" (other income, assets, or
both) might even see both a higher tax and a lower benefit payment.
To maintain the lifestyle to which we have become accustomed, and
want, and expect, Boomers will need to become more self-sufficient—
as in having spendable (bird-in-the-hand) income from our investable
assets. I feel any time can be a good time to be accumulating high-
dividend stocks, but only when combined with a defensive, disciplined,
hedged approach to investing.

The *hedged approach* should be transparent (with no secrecy
of what you're investing in), liquid (to be able to get your money
on a day's notice) with no "lockups," without leverage (with no
margin), and guaranteed against theft by government-sponsored

---

* One-third since 1926 for the S&P 500; half since 1919 for the Dow Jones
Industrial Average.

insurance. If I am right that retirees will need income to live, what better/easier source than passive, inflation-adjusting high dividends from well-chosen equities to help meet our needs? I believe that future demand for a limited number of higher-dividend company stocks could be strong, allowing for potential future appreciation through participation in secular and cyclical rallies, in addition to the income. But without the disciplined hedge program (tactically adjusting to the market down waves), your assets will be subject to "less cap" and potential capitulation (panic selling at the bottoms of market declines). The transparent, liquid hedged program is essential to your financial well-being for the foreseeable future.

Cash

Cash is king in *normal* deflationary cycles. But again, the old Maestro and the new Maestro remain determined not to have that normalcy on their watch. So, we'll need continued low interest rates and economic stimulation, as well as somebody to buy *existing* debt as it matures. Somebody will also have to be willing to buy the *new* debt to finance the 10 years of *forecasted* trillion-dollar deficits. And why would the deficits just disappear after the next 10 years? Is the picture getting somewhat more unpleasant, but realistically clearer?

The U.S. dollar has been the reserve currency of the world since World War II. In recent years, the United States has been *importing more than we're exporting* as our manufacturing capacity continually moves to lower-wage-rate countries. The net foreign purchases (imports we've bought with dollars) have been stacking up in foreign hands faster than they can be respent. *At our higher production costs*, there are not a lot of *U.S. goods* that can be exchanged for these stored dollars. If the dollar goes down relative to other currencies, that will make our goods more price attractive. But then, our foreign competitors don't like losing market share, and they, too, will try to weaken their relative currency value. They can do this by creating more of their own currency in order to buy more dollars (to attempt to push the dollar back up). So all countries most likely will continue to resort to money creation to remain trade competitive.

Money creation has been attempted by the ruling parties throughout history. It has eventually destroyed *every currency ever created* with the exception of those still in use, for the time being. A currency is ideally a means of exchange as well as a store of value.

The only currency still used as a store of value after 5,000 years is gold bullion and coinage. That store of value is still alive and well, and also accepted as a medium of exchange for any other paper currency today.

In a time of currency revaluations, ideally we'd like to be in a relatively appreciating currency. This, too, takes active management. Currencies will be up and down as "flights to safety," trading by speculators and large holders of currencies to diversify in order to adjust their allocation of paper to different assets or exchange expectations. So even our cash asset allocation should not be purely passive, unless it's a less significant part of our asset structure. Some currencies with higher interest rates also experience relative appreciation against the dollar as money seeks higher returns.

Real Estate

Why should a used home or commercial building appreciate? If the replacement costs of a structure rise due to inflation, then the old building may become more valuable as an alternative to building anew. Limited location can also be a major factor. For example, there's only so much waterfront property, and water and extended hilltop/skyline-type views seem to add to the tranquility of the living experience. But besides inflation and the emotional appeal of style and location, there is the income factor. Can a building be purchased for either cash or even all debt, where the rents will cover all the costs: interest costs, taxes, maintenance and repairs, insurance, and utilities? Is there any cash flow remaining? What return would I expect on my cash invested? That tells us the potential desirability of real estate as an investment. We may choose to live in our investment and forgo the cash returns. But if it were rentable, what would the return be? That is the value question, when the issue is not emotional (limited location/style).

Otherwise, if it doesn't give a good return on cash, we're hoping that someone with less economic sense will buy it for a higher price than we paid. In an inflationary environment, that can work. In a deflationary part of the cycle, that doesn't work as well. Again, that's considering the emotional appeal aside. It's strictly business. Potential investors should ask, Is the rental income expected to go up or down? Do we want the maintenance, repair, and leasing problems associated with real estate to occupy our time, or lessen our return if delegated to management? Is passive income investing preferable through financial assets? What are the comparative rates of expected return for the efforts?

Reality

Is much real today? Are statistics believable? Most (70–80% of daily volume) of the trading balance today is done by computers close to the exchanges. It's called "fast trading" and it's done in split-second timing by large professional investors, often ahead of other real buys and sells. The exchanges like the fees it generates and insist it adds to liquidity of the market. But do we remember the *program trading crash* of 1987? Safeguards were put in place to prevent a recurrence, but most of those safeguards have recently been reduced, removed, or no longer enforced.

A large Wall Street firm had a computer and program stolen by an employee in 2009. The firm told the judge that in the wrong hands, that program could destroy the markets. Should we assume that in that large firm's hands, it was in good hands? We see that some large investment firms report in-house trading profits almost every day. We all know that independent day traders doing it the old-fashioned way on their own are lucky to get it right even half the time. They stop their losses quickly and let their profits run to make their returns. Now, are we to believe that the computer traders are in and out in a second and get it right over 90 percent of the time? Go figure. Is it an accident waiting to happen? Or does it have to be an accident? Remember, "the wrong hands" could possibly destroy the market.

It's good to have experienced people in oversight positions to help prevent or solve problems. But how close are the experienced people to those whom they oversee and regulate? All of this adds to the heightened difficulty of expecting old-fashioned returns from buy-and-hold investing. Are we in a time of the fox guarding the hen house, letting the foxy buddies get away with most of the chickens, and the eggs as well?

Perhaps 5 percent of investors understand the potential implications and are staying on top of the changes. Another 10 percent or so are informed enough to follow some of the 5 percent. But the other 85 percent or so probably don't have a clue what's happening. They watch the excited commentators talk about beating earnings guidance expectations (almost all companies do). The commentators then slump in their chairs at the bottom of a market decline and lean forward with excitement at market tops. It takes a steady view of the big picture to keep our investment heads while most around us are losing theirs. That's not always easy.

What Can We Do?

When it comes to retirement and legacy planning, what matters is the preservation of both asset value and purchasing power. We'd like (and may need) some growth, too. But gone for now are the easy days of the buy and hold, efficient indexed, and simple asset-style diversification that worked in that much easier expansionary leg of the long-term cycle. We're now deleveraging and deflating, as assets depreciate and debt is reduced. Will it change? Sure, but we have to let the long-term cycle complete, now or a little later. It's not as much fun and frankly it is more work. Buy and hold, reinvest or spend the dividend, and total return is nice stuff, when you can get it. For now, indications are that our world has not solved its financial problems nor found a way to deleverage without pain. Some time, some place, the tooth will eventually fall out.

We will get to better days, when it's not just less bad that seems better. It will probably happen first in countries that are just emerging from the dark ages and getting past the hunting, gathering, and farming for the necessities stage and have begun to industrialize. These are countries where the citizens are anxious to work, save, and invest. They are just starting to consume more and respond to demand creation through commercialization. They, too, will want and eventually expect more immediate gratification, and will most likely begin to borrow to meet their consumer wants. These countries will grow and prosper, and probably reach a bubble point of debt over time as well. The developed world has already been there and done that, for now.

Our elected and appointed officials are trying desperately to reinflate as quickly as possible to avoid the pain of further deflation and economic collapse. ("Please, God, give us one more bubble" is the bumper sticker *du jour.*) Can they do it? If so, for how long? And what will be the future unintended consequences? Nobody can know for sure. We just can't anticipate who will decide what. Political uncertainty also enters into our risk management now. A benevolent dictator may ultimately become desired. Let's hope it's a friend and even someone we can trust, just so long as he or she promises to take care of our problems. Isn't that what we all prefer?

Back to Reality

Let's get more real. We want to survive, and maybe even prosper a little, right? We certainly have preservation of assets in mind, as well as some growth as the opportunities present. We've got retirement plans, and maybe some extra legacy surplus to do something with, if Peter Bernstein's observation, "our assets are only on loan" doesn't get to us first. So we need a workable plan, one that we might expect to accomplish our goals, despite an anticipated struggle with the back-deleveraging side of the long-term cycle. Our dreams were partially burst and reduced in round one. What should we do now to prepare for a possible second and third assault wave?

The Investment Plan

First we'll *diversify*, because we know we can't guess the next financial event's exact nature or timing. The black swans (unexpected events) are circling, and where they may land, nobody knows. Sleeper cells (terrorists in hiding) could suddenly awaken. So, we'll diversify with cash into varied currencies (including the more enduring 5,000-year variety), bonds, equities, and maybe some real estate and private business holdings we may have chosen to acquire. We'll deal here with just the first three, the more-liquid-asset portion.

All of our liquid assets should be *actively* managed. Blindly buy and hold only at your peril. Do you think the 545 nationally elected will be able to suddenly figure out how to deleverage without pain and live up to the promises that got them there? The *only buy and hold* I can think of for the foreseeable future is that 5,000-year-old currency that has glittered and endured and tends to hold its purchasing power over the longer term. What other asset has *gone up every year* for the past decade?

Currencies, bonds, and stocks need to be in a *disciplined sell system*. We need a seat near the theater exit, maybe even one foot out the door. We should expect some false alarms. *Nobody* gets it all right all of the time. *Nothing wrong with being wrong.* It's part of the investment process. *But staying wrong is what can destroy us.* So we'll be nimble.

Sooner or later (probably near the end of the long wave), the investment industry will come up with a *new* "modern theory" of *tactical allocation* (shifting levels of financial commitment in response to what is happening). It took a lot of investors 40, 50, or 60 years to accumulate the assets they have, and maybe longer if an inheritance came from ancestors. But let's actively plan and implement a strategy to survive and hopefully even prosper over our remaining years, and to also help benefit those people and causes we most care about as well.

In round one, we had two warning shots from 2000 to 2002 and again from 2007 to 2009. The first hit hard and the second hit harder. We're still alive. But *the problems have not gone away*. The causes (deleveraging debt and derivatives) are just getting bigger. We'll need to plan to retreat from time to time. The financial markets will always try to confuse us and do the unexpected. So let's be prepared as events and timing unfold. We may hope everything turns out just fine. But, hope is not a strategy. We'll also plan on a round two and possibly round three just in case. The debt and derivative clocks are ticking. That benevolent dictator is not yet in place. He most likely does not exist. In the words of Lord Acton, "Power tends to corrupt; and absolute power corrupts absolutely."

We'll wait with suspense, expectation, and a counterplan. We'll want to minimize any further significant destruction of capital. We'll hopefully be part of the 5 to 15 percent who understand that the big picture still looks very stormy. We and our designees will want some wherewithal to participate in the next rebuilding process. But first we will most likely revisit the consequences of our past. We'll just have to get through the completion of this cycle, clear the massive debt burden, check the uncontrolled greed, and start anew. That may take awhile, but it's just like we've read about all those years: "This time it's different" need not apply here. *Preservation through preparation* is our working mantra. Our former slogan, "Make it, keep it," should perhaps be modified to, "Made it, keep it, for now."

CHAPTER 2

How Did We Get into This Mess? And What Is the Best Way Out?

Gary Alexander

At the Atlanta Investment Conference in late April 2009, I was able to interview over a dozen of our main speakers in a private televised taping room during the breaks between the conference's general sessions.

After speaking at nearly every Atlanta conference since its founding in 1988, and serving as co-emcee when not speaking, I had already heard these gentlemen speak many times before, including their podium time at the similar New Orleans conferences, held in the fall. In recent years, many of these speakers had been predicting an event something like what we saw in late 2008, yet all we usually hear in the popular media is that "nobody saw this crisis coming." That's why conference organizer Martin Truax thought it would be a good idea to ask those who did, indeed, see this mess coming, about what might happen next.

Martin requested that I ask five key questions (with follow-ups) of each speaker, asking first about the market malaise that was then attacking the nation and the world. The other questions led toward long-term outlook and the best long-term solutions. Bear in mind that at the time of these interviews, we had just come off the market bottoms in March 2009. There was still a haunting sense of "another shoe to drop" (i.e., another big bank or car company to fail, another market correction, another big spending bill—in short, more pain ahead). Most of the speakers were by no means certain that the current "baby bull market" recovery was anything more than a normal bear market rally.

With the firm understanding that nobody knows the future, especially short-term developments, I asked these 13 speakers their views on five key questions. Here are their names and major affiliations:

- **Bob Barr**, former Congressman and Libertarian Party presidential candidate
- **Robert Bishop**, long-time editor of *Gold Mining Stock Report*
- **Roger Conrad**, editor, *Utility Forecaster* and *Canadian Edge*
- **Adrian Day**, CEO, Adrian Day Asset Management
- **Neil George**, former editor, *Personal Finance*
- **Elliott Gue**, editor, *Personal Finance* and *Energy Strategist*
- **Alan Keyes**, former Republican presidential candidate
- **Ian McAvity**, editor, *Deliberations*
- **Robert Prechter**, editor, *The Elliott Wave Theorist*
- **Rick Rule**, CEO, Global Resource Investments, Inc.
- **Ben Shepherd**, editor, *Louis Rukeyser's Mutual Funds*
- **Mark Skousen**, editor, *Forecasts and Strategies*
- **Frank Trotter**, president, Everbank

Question 1: How Did We Get into This Mess?

There is no more elegant word than *mess* to describe the financial situation in early 2009. We had seen the fastest 50 percent market decline since 1929–1930, along with bankruptcies (or shotgun weddings) at Bear Stearns, Lehman Brothers, Indymac Bank, Washington Mutual, Merrill Lynch, Countrywide Financial, and other financial firms, plus two of the Big Three car companies.

After 25 years of market gains, we were facing the worst bear market of our lives. How did we get into this mess? There was a surprising consensus among our speakers:

Frank Trotter expressed the majority opinion well: "As a nation, we've been over-borrowing to fuel consumption. The Fed held interest rates too low for too long a period of time. This process bid the price of risk down, so that nearly everyone was taking cheap risks, in the belief that most markets would go in one direction—up—forever." He referred to similar once-in-a-decade bubbles like gold in the 1970s, Tokyo stocks in the 1980s, tech stocks in the 1990s, "and now real estate."

Adrian Day agreed: "At the base, this is about excessive government credit, encouraging people to be greedy and excessive in their consumption and investments, masking risk (by not punishing risk sufficiently). We are, in a sense, being punished for our excesses, and we are reverting to the mean after past excesses. I believe we are in a bear market now, and it could last for a long time, but bear market rallies can be extremely strong. Being up twenty-five percent in the last six weeks is wonderful. But the market is still selling well above its traditional valuations from past bear market lows."

How long has this mess been in the making? **Ian McAvity**, who has been writing about global markets in his newsletter since 1972, said, "We've seen the end of a major secular trend that dates back to the late 1970s—or 1982, at the latest. This trend was characterized by a massive addition of debt. By the peak, in 2006, people were 'consuming' their houses, one brick at a time, through refinancing schemes. Then, the collapse in housing prices weighed down the stock market."

Why didn't academic economists see this coming? **McAvity** adds: "Academic economists are not really market oriented. They're not 'in the game.'" **Adrian Day** adds, "Many people saw this crisis coming, so it annoys me a bit when government officials say that nobody saw it coming."

Mark Skousen offered this contrarian viewpoint: "Those who predicted the current mess tend to be perma-bears, who have predicted a crisis for a long time." For his part, economist **Skousen** says this mess was largely caused by the "complexity of the once-simple home mortgages being packaged into exotic derivatives." After the tech stock crash and 9/11, he explained, "people began to wonder if they wanted all their money in one asset class—in a single market that can fall so sharply. After all, the stock market closed for one full week in September 2001. So, people started moving their money into real estate, prompted by low interest rates and teaser rates."

Rick Rule resurrected an old bromide about debt: "When your outgo exceeds your income, your upkeep becomes your downfall." The latest crisis arose, he said, because "people have lived beyond their means for a long time. That will work just fine, as long as prices rise, but the market fell apart when housing prices fell, then stock prices followed." In America, he said, we have to realize that a 56-year-old unionized auto worker in Detroit isn't really worth $60 an hour more than a 22-year-old college-educated auto worker in India." This reality will take time to sink in.

Robert Bishop echoed the majority position: "As a country and as a people we have lived far beyond our means for a long time, exacerbated by a legislative and regulatory framework that encouraged risk. We exported this toxic debt and overspending habit to the world in the form of weak dollars held by overseas nations, and now we are reaping the logical outcome."

Robert Prechter added a socioeconomic viewpoint: "There are predictable waves of social mood, vacillating between optimism and pessimism. People buy more stocks in up cycle. They attend more sports events and listen to more upbeat music. They also lend and borrow more money, which leads to overextension. This current crisis came after the end of a major uptrend and may be the once-in-a-century bust the likes of which we've only seen in 1720–1722, 1835–1842, and 1929–1932."

Even though the market fell 55 percent in nominal terms, **Prechter** reminds us that "the market is down eighty-three percent in terms of gold since 2000." The Dow traded at 40 ounces of gold in 1980. Now the ratio is less than 10-to-1. As a result, "we are now in the extremely pessimistic wave of sentiment, with banks afraid to lend, and consumers and businesses afraid to borrow." He said we will likely see a burst of positive sentiment later in 2009, as the bear market rally surges up through the summer. We will see "excitement from coming off the bottom. We will see optimism in the stock market and in the lending business. We will hear that the Fed's program of re-liquefying the market is working, that government stimulus plans worked. This positive second-wave bull market rally could last six months or more, with the destructive third wave yet to come."

Elliott Gue agrees: "There was a confluence of a number of things, but the main problem was too much leverage, with hedge funds leveraged up to thirty times. There was too much faith in the monetary authorities and their power to curb any market excesses through intervention." His compatriots at *Personal Finance* echoed the same strain: **Ben Shepherd** said, "This crisis has been brewing for well over two decades, beginning with the mandate for universal home ownership for Americans. It's a noble and idealistic goal, but it's not practical." **Roger Conrad** added: "Congress was very easily persuaded to change the rules and encourage crazy leverage," but "the market is not buying a lot of the rhetoric out of Washington, like they did in the past."

Turning to the political angle, our past presidential candidates added a moral and philosophical tone. **Alan Keyes** said this crisis is "a reflection of the overall breakdown of discipline, the death of the expectation that others will act with reasonable responsibility. There was a breakdown in the process of promise keeping. There used to be a process that connected action to outcome."

Keyes added that "politicians were trying to be hometown heroes, claiming that they brought the glories of home ownership to more of their constituents. But you can't have rights (like home ownership) divorced from responsibilities. A right implies that someone else is responsible to provide you with that right. That's slavery, isn't it? Why would I be obligated to deliver a home to you, or to vote for someone else to take money from a third party on your behalf? Yes, there are a lot of advantages to owning a home, but that is the end result of many years of savings."

Bob Barr added, "The problem is not Republicans or Democrats, but government, which exists for one purpose only—to acquire and retain power. The founding fathers concocted a system of government that divided powers. That's because they could not guarantee that politicians could not circumvent the system. They tried to make single-party control difficult to maintain. But now we have a population that is largely ignorant of what government does, should do, and has done."

Question 2: Where Are We Now in the Recovery Cycle?

To start discussion about the inevitable recovery, I used common short-hand for the shape of the recovery: A "V"-shaped recovery is a sharp decline, followed by a sharp recovery. A "U"-shaped recovery has a longer bottoming-out process before recovering, gradually at first, then sharply. A "W"-shaped pattern implies a double-dip recession, the look of a V but cut off in mid-recovery by another sharp drop, then a final recovery. And the worst possible scenario is an

"L"-shaped future, in which there is no bright sunshine on the horizon "for as far as the eye can see."

Bear in mind that this question refers to the *general economy*, as reflected by the gross domestic product (GDP). It does not refer to the stock market, which might indeed shoot back in a V.

The general consensus was for an L (non-recovery), but that only means that our eyes can't see very far, for now. I'll start with the super-bears and work up to some more hopeful positions.

Ian McAvity says, "I believe we're in an L that hasn't reached its ninety-degree bottom yet. That's several quarters away. Right now, the powers that be are trying to patch the economy together with airplane glue, but I don't believe we will see our past standard of living—overconsumption, like we saw in 2005 into 2006—for many years, maybe decades. I'm not convinced that this market has seen its bottom yet, even though everyone's very anxious to declare a bottom."

Robert Bishop agrees: "I see an L ahead, even though we've seen a V in the stock market. As a resource investor, I'm used to seeing the stuffing kicked out of my assets in down cycles, but millions of people who have never known general market adversity don't know how to handle such a reversal. We're on the other side of that hump now, and it's going to take a while to recover. The ripple effect is still rippling. People take a long time to adjust to any new reality."

Neil George says, "I foresee a flat-line, an L. This is very much like 1976, following the last major general market crash of 1974. There is general hope in a new president (Carter then, Obama now), but our leaders are merely flailing away at a wide variety of issues." He sees "a malaise for the next five to six years," but with many interim ways to profit (as discussed in the following).

Elliott Gue says, "We're more in the lines of an L, a very long recession. We're still declining, but at a lower rate. We may have slow growth by the end of the year, but the economy will be very flat for the whole year. Next year might not be as positive as the pundits are now saying."

Robert Prechter looks for a sharp recovery off the ultimate bottom: "We're very likely to have a V bottom. The collapse has been relentless and it will continue, until the bottom, but then the recovery will also be rapid. Before the bottom happens, we may see more social conflicts, more anger, more protests. People were very afraid in 1932 and 1982, at those long-term market bottoms, and they will be again."

Alan Keyes adds that "there is a real potential for a catastrophic failure in our system. It is being exploited by some to aggregate power. A crisis could impel us to either rediscover our moral and spiritual capacities, or fly apart socially. But I don't believe our moral capacity is beyond recall."

Adrian Day sees something like a U: "Recessions can be shallow or deep; short or long. This is not a normal recession: We have not seen high inflation, high interest rates, or tight money, so we can't get out of it by lowering interest rates, which are already low. So far, this has already been a longer recession, since the regular tools aren't working or aren't even available."

Roger Conrad also sees "some kind of a U recovery," but he also sees "a lot of positive things that are not reflected in the market yet. Twenty years ago, we had a Berlin Wall and nuclear missiles pointed at us, with a Chinese uprising in Tiananmen Square. The world is a lot safer place now than it was then." He cited other hopeful signs: "Many companies that did not leverage up are doing nicely. People who controlled their personal debt are grabbing up bargains in properties, businesses, and stocks. This could be the start of some very great fortunes."

Turning to the W crowd, **Rick Rule** sees lots of ups and downs, with "quite a few Ws, perhaps a WWW, like the World Wide Web." He thinks that there will be some positive quarters, but a long succession of Ws as part of "a recession that will last certainly longer than five years."

Ben Shepherd also sees a W double-dip, citing the bull-versus-bear surveys by the AAII, which now show "an extremely pessimistic view, the most bearish levels in decades. You can't maintain a strongly pessimistic or optimistic view for too long, so there will be some recovery."

Mark Skousen was the most positive analyst in our group, saying, "I am by nature more of an optimist than some of your other participants on this program. I believe we are at the beginning of the end. If GDP is calculated by adding C + I + G (consumption + investment + government), we have G growing strongly, while consumption and private investment are weak." However, not all G spending is counterproductive: "Within the G factor, we have C or I, meaning that government can either consume (bad) or invest in infrastructure, which is more positive."

Frank Trotter threw up his hands and said, "I wish I could create a Chinese character to picture this crash and recovery, because it is more complex than your U-V-W-L options." Nevertheless, he rejected the L scenario, saying it implies an "open-ended depression, which I don't buy."

Question 3: What Is Your Favorite Solution to This Problem?

I prefaced this question with a litany of the favorite solutions being tossed around in the media at the time: the end of "mark-to-market" accounting, a reinstallation of the "up-tick" rule, stricter financial regulatory laws and agencies, and several other cosmetic changes. Those suggestions did not go over well, so I followed up by asking our speakers about their favorite solutions.

Favorite Solutions of the Media

First, some comments on the favorite solutions of that time:

- *On the uptick rule,* **Ian McAvity** said, "Commodity markets have functioned more efficiently than stock markets without an uptick rule. If we have an uptick rule, let's have a 'down-tick rule' to prevent 'irrational buying.'" **Mark Skousen** said the uptick rule "fuels too much speculation." **Ben Shepherd** added that it is "a silly game which traders can easily circumvent." **Bob Bishop** disagreed, saying that "the uptick rule helps discipline shorts from piling on in a bear market."
- *On repealing mark-to-market accounting,* **Ian McAvity** said that the Accounting Standards Board (FASB) "has changed the rules virtually every quarter since this crisis began. The rules for the first-quarter reporting, for instance, change on April 2." **Mark Skousen** added, "We need more transparency in accounting, in place of a rather simplistic mark-to-market rule." **Rick Rule** said, "Let the market work, and let speculators be punished by excesses, or rewarded if they bet right."
- *On drafting tighter regulation,* **Adrian Day** spoke for many other regulated advisors in the room when he said, "For twenty years, the SEC visited Bernie Madoff's operation and found nothing wrong, yet now we're going to trust the same gang of regulators to protect us better than they already have. We have

all the regulation we want or need, but they failed. Now the government wants new systems to identify bubbles before they happen, while they are pouring more money and easy credit into the system—more excess liquidity, which caused the crisis in the first place."

- *On political reforms in general,* **Rick Rule** quoted H.L. Mencken, who said, "An election is an advance auction of stolen goods," by which he means, "Legislators operate for their own interest, so more legislation is not the solution. All government can do is take from one person to give to another, minus their take." **Elliott Gue** agreed: "Changing the names of the politicians doesn't change the system." **Frank Trotter** added that "we need to get rid of the idea of federal czars running every type of business." **Bob Bishop** cited a specific conflict of interest: "The conflicts of interest in Washington are astonishing. Henry Paulson ran Goldman Sachs and he put the TARP program together to save his compatriots, among others. This does not pass the smell test."

Our Favorite Solutions

But here were some of our favorite solutions.

Mark Skousen recommended that U.S. banks imitate the Canadian banking system. Canadian banks seldom fail, operate nationally, and have much stricter rules on real estate loans. The bailout of large U.S. banks, by contrast, has created a moral hazard problem, with the concept that the biggest financial institutions have been protected by Congress, because they have been deemed "too big to fail." Also, "our tax system should be simplified, perhaps with a modified flat tax with no tax on dividends, interest, and capital gains. We don't have a stable enough monetary or fiscal policy, either. We run from one extreme to another in both areas: easy money, tight money. Stability is what generates a willingness to invest for the long term."

Alan Keyes agrees: "Stop centralized income taxes. Let citizens spend their first dollar and then tax on the consumption. We won't have a long recession if we abolish income tax and install a national sales tax. We would cut costs by abolishing cabinet offices and Congressional bills that defy the clear constitutional mandate for limited powers. This crisis might be a good time to bring the power grab in Washington to a crashing end, and then tell people, 'No more handouts.'"

Rick Rule says, "We should let big financial firms fail, if they deserve to fail. The sun will come up tomorrow. The assets don't go away. The price changes and the ownership changes, but the assets remain. So far, big business has wanted to privatize profits and socialize debts or losses."

Turning to political realities, Rick added: "I'm in favor of split government, between one party controlling Congress and the other in the White House. These are like warring gangs, and when one is in total power, as now and under Bush and the Republican Congress, we are in danger."

Adrian Day favors opening up a free market in ratings agencies: "So far, the SEC only approves three agencies to rate debt, and they have failed us. There is a conflict of interest in consulting with a company and rating its debt. They rated nearly everything AAA, until things went wrong."

Roger Conrad favors "more trade agreements, more free trade between nations, and an end to protectionism." Likewise, "the cap-and-trade bill, as currently proposed, would be an economic disaster." Also, "we have to restore faith in the banking system, perhaps more like the Canadian model. Canadian banks have capital ratios two to three times our own. The worst thing you can do is take over big banks and try to run them, showing favoritism in loans—the China model."

Question 4: What Is Your Long-Term Outlook for the Market?

Our speakers agreed that the short-term is anyone's guess, but we wanted to know the outlook for markets one year, two years, or five years from today. Are we—as **Martin Truax** proposed—in the midst of a 15- to 20-year market malaise, as we were back in 1929–1949, or 1966–1982? That theory implies another 5 to 10 years of sideways markets. Or is there hope for a quicker resolution to our problems than this historical parallel implies? Our speakers were skeptical:

Robert Prechter points back to the 16-year period of malaise from 1966 to 1982, which we have generically called "the Seventies." There were plenty of bear market rallies during that time span. In 1976, he pointed out, the market was rising but it was too early for a more permanent bullish change. By 1980, he said, the nation was ready for a revolution: Reagan's election in 1980 paralleled FDR's rise in 1932, and perhaps that will happen again in 2012 or 2016.

"If you're a politician," he said, "you want to run when the market is approaching a bottom. Then, you will get credit for the recovery that follows." Prechter leans toward a 2016 bottom: "another seven years of difficulty." But "if we go down hard enough, fast enough, the bottom could come sooner than that." How hard is "hard"? Prechter said, "The Dow could go under 1000 before it's all over."

Adrian Day agrees that there is a lot more unwinding of debt to come. "There are a lot more problems to surface—credit card debt, commercial debt, as well as massive budget deficits. If a business has a five-year lease and can't pay the rent, landlords will need to lower rents. There is excess commercial inventory and empty space is going begging." Why do we have too many office buildings and malls? "Because it was too easy to build more buildings with easy money."

Ian McAvity said, "Governments are making the same mistakes they made in the early 1930s, by blaming the rich, who had suffered just as much as the middle class from this market crash." Put more colorfully, "Eating the rich is not a very rich meal. We will run out of rich people very fast." The political mistakes of 1930–1931 sowed the seeds for the bottom in 1932. "The Dow was very low, and unemployment was still very high into the early 1940s, before Pearl Harbor. We may indeed have a rally from our lows, but that does not mean the structural problem is over."

Roger Conrad says the depth of this bear market depends on political actions taken now: "With protectionism, we would enter 'The Dark Tunnel' of the 1930s again. The dangerous opposite of globalization is trade war and nationalism." The same is true of deregulation versus reregulation.

Alan Keyes postulated that a new attack on America could generate a greater level of fear and defensiveness than it did in 2001, and then "people with a centralizing tendency will act on that fear, saying, 'Let us take control and protect you.' I fear that we could surrender to a mindless, security-based social order." But on the positive side, "We are likely to see a future as wonderful to us in 2009 as today's prosperity of America would look to those suffering through the 1930s." The future is positive unless we have a "psychotic episode," to which government fails to adapt.

Mark Skousen was once again the most positive voice. He predicted a record-high Dow above 14,280 within two years, by 2011. He had just polled people in the hardest-hit real estate areas— Florida, California, Las Vegas, and so on—and "I found a lot of optimism, now that house prices are so low once again. The U.S. entrepreneurial spirit has not been killed, although it was severely wounded in the last year. Obama is a bright man and he's adapting to reality. I think he's going to work within the system. My biggest fear is a tax increase, or the cap-and-trade bill."

Question 5: How Should We Invest in This Environment?

For the final question, I asked the speakers to be general, about asset categories, without naming specific stocks or other opportunities, which they will mostly outline in their separate chapters. Given all that you see for the future, how would you plan to invest right now?

Mark Skousen likes well-chosen stocks and closed-end funds: "I'm very bullish on good growth companies that are making good profits and beating analyst expectations. I like dividend-paying stocks and closed-end funds with dividend-paying stocks."

Frank Trotter looks more to currencies: "I see a drop in the dollar over the next three to ten years, so I focus on foreign currencies. For starters, look at Norway, with its great fiscal management, or Australia, which doubles as a China/commodity play."

Ian McAvity agrees: "Look at commodities. The world is now heading toward a generalized commodity standard, not just a gold standard. The Chinese are already moving in this direction. Currencies among the resource-based English-speaking nations are strongest: the Canadian dollar, Australian dollar, and New Zealand dollar. Since we still have freedom to invest overseas, we have the choice of investing in resource-rich nations with more open markets. Eventually, politicians will overregulate the U.S. market, opening up the opportunity to invest overseas."

Adrian Day expands on the same theme: "Overseas markets offer better opportunities, but you must be nimble. You can find value in specific opportunities, but you can't say anything as general as 'I like European stocks now.' For instance, Nestle is a rock-solid company that just raised its dividend to 3.6 percent, but that does not mean you can buy just any Swiss stocks. Likewise with Asian selected stocks, like HSBC or Swire-Pacific. For a financial base, remain liquid with a high percentage in cash, while holding some gold as a hedge against the decline of the dollar. After that, there are tremendous bargains in the gold stocks, which are selling at record low multiples."

Rick Rule: "Resource stocks are a moving target. The resource market is much more volatile and cyclical than the general market. In a grand washout, resources will be the best investment, since demand returns before supply. We're not there yet. Turning to specific commodities, Gold is catastrophe insurance, and I don't necessarily want a payoff on that insurance. I hold gold, but I trade silver, since silver bugs are like gold bugs on steroids. For now, silver is overextended."

Rick continues, in more detail: "The no-brainer in resources is alternative energy, especially hydro and geothermal. This is politically correct energy. The powers-that-be want this stuff, so there are no political restraints and some political benefits, despite the terrible private credit markets. In the longer run, water conservation is vital. The arbitrage between agricultural and urban water use will cause a temporary repricing of water, and perhaps nationalization of water. Buy water now. Sell when the shortage of water finally reaches the cover of *Time* magazine."

The *Personal Finance* team also likes energy: **Elliott Gue** says, "You have to be a more nimble trader now and not ride long-term investments. Energy is necessary, and developing markets are growing faster." **Ben Shepherd** says "we must all become contrarians now," while **Roger Conrad** likes the Canadian energy plays, nuclear power plants, and other utility opportunities.

Bob Bishop likes rare minerals as the next big play. For gold and silver stocks, "upgrade your portfolio, sell some of the juniors. People find it easy to buy, but harder to sell in a bear market. Go for the higher-quality names in your portfolio, unless you just enjoy 'playing in the space.'"

Robert Prechter counsels safety, but what is safe? "The FDIC backs bank accounts, but is FDIC backing safe during a time of massive bank failures? Also, municipal bonds, including counties and states, may be forced to default. U.S. Treasury bonds will be the last to default, so they're relatively safe, but if you want real money with no counterparty risk, you have to look at gold."

Neil George sees a long sideways general market, but "you can profit from cash flow—bonds and income vehicles yielding seven to nine percent—even if we have a slow- or no-growth environment." He mentioned AT&T bonds or bonds from the big power utilities.

"Go for income. Don't worry about what doesn't work. Turn away from them and invest in sure, safe things."

Alan Keyes is not an investment advisor, but his common sense makes for a fitting conclusion: "Folks with sufficient capital always have more choices, but those with limited means need to keep with permanent 'rainy day' savings. On the other hand, I don't think we should neglect funding America's future. We must be working on bigger solutions. Hunkering down in a bunker won't develop the next new technologies we need. Responsible people of surplus need to invest in a better future, and if you back something that brings us needed solutions, you will prosper."

CHAPTER 3

Know the Signs of the Times

Mark Skousen

"There is much ruin in a nation."
—Adam Smith

"We have outlived the short-run and are suffering from the long-run consequences of [Keynesian] policies."
—Ludwig von Mises

"There are disturbing trends: huge imbalances, disequilibria, risks—call them what you will. Altogether the circumstances seem to me as dangerous and intractable as any I can remember, and I can remember quite a lot. The United States is skating on increasingly thin ice."
—Paul Volcker, former Fed chairman, 2005

As a free-market financial economist, my investment approach is largely influenced by government policies, both good and bad.

If we lived in a society with sound money, low taxes, free trade, balanced budgets, limited government, the rule of law, and peace abroad, we would witness a never-ending higher standard of living, and investors could pursue a buy-and-hold strategy without fear of losing their hard-earned savings. Gold and silver would be low and stable. The dollar would be strong.

Adam Smith's Ideal Model

Adam Smith called this laissez-faire model a "system of natural liberty." By adopting this policy, a country could achieve economic nirvana. As Adam Smith wrote, "Little else is required to carry a state to the highest degree of opulence from the lowest barbarism, but peace, easy taxes, and a tolerable administration of justice."

Unfortunately, we have moved gradually away from Adam Smith's system of natural liberty. Today, we face an activist government bent on promoting easy money and inflation, high deficit spending, unlimited government, and pursuing wars abroad.

Not surprisingly, the impact for traditional investors is largely negative. They must abandon buy-and-hold strategies and become short-term speculators. As the dollar weakens abroad, gold and other commodities rise.

The Return of Depressing Keynesian Economics

The fact is that *Obamanomics* (Keynesian economics in disguise) is counterproductive and making matters worse. That's because business and Wall Street recognize that there is no free lunch—government spending is piling up huge debts that will need to be paid back, probably through the printing presses.

Keynes is famous for the line, "In the long run we are all dead." And that's what Wall Street fears—that financially we are all going to be killed by excessive debt.

Lack of confidence in Obama, Geithner, and Bernanke is why gold is becoming a haven again and is moving back up. The problem is Keynesian-style policy, the darling of the establishment politicos and media giants.

The Big Three in Economics

Earlier this year I walked into the largest Barnes & Noble bookstore in New York and saw a big display table up front with all kinds of books on John Maynard Keynes and Keynesian economics. One book, *The Return of Depression Economics*, (W.W. Norton, 2000) was written by Paul Krugman, the *New York Times* columnist who just won the Nobel Prize. Another book was called *Keynes, Return of the Master*, (Public Affairs, 2009) by Lord Robert Skidelsky.

Another book was called *The Case for Big Government*, (Princeton University Press, 2009) by Jeff Madrick, the editor of *Challenge* magazine. I can understand writing a book in support of good, efficient, strong, and productive government, but "big" alone? Most Americans prefer the motto "cheaper and better."

The biggest surprise at Barnes & Noble was to see my own book, *The Big Three in Economics* (2007; available at Amazon.com), prominently displayed alongside all the Keynesian and Marxist books. It has suddenly become my most successful book.

But mine was the only book there that took a dim view of Keynes and Marx, and their solutions to the financial crisis (always more government, more taxes, and more regulations). For my money, Adam Smith and his followers (Ludwig von Mises, Friedrich Hayek, Milton Friedman, Murray Rothbard) deserve to be at the top of the Totem Pole of Economics.

Unfortunately, Keynes is all the rage now. The British economist became famous in the 1930s for advocating going off the gold standard, running deficits, and bailing out troubled banks with easy money as a way to end the Great Depression.

Today's politicians, from George Bush to Barack Obama, have suddenly become Keynesians during this financial crisis, spending money they don't have in a vain effort to right the ship. Even *Newsweek* has gone so far as to say, "We are all socialists now." Alan Greenspan, the ex-student of Ayn Rand, now favors nationalization of the big American banks Citibank and Bank of America.

Every investor and gold bug should know the enemies—Keynes, the advocate of big government and the welfare state, and Karl Marx, the radical who advocated outright state socialism and total central control of the means of production.

After World War I, Randolph Bourne observed, "War is the health of the state." Today he might say, "A financial crisis is the health of the state."

It looks like modern-day statists are getting their wish. We're getting big government, good and hard. Adam Smith and Milton Friedman are out of favor, while John Maynard Keynes, the patron saint of bailouts, inflation, and the welfare state, is making a comeback with a vengeance.

Leviathan is the only real growth industry today, and the trend is truly shocking. With Obama in office, we can expect the G in GDP to exceed 25 percent, actually close to 40 percent if you count transfer payments, such as Social Security and Medicare. Various Washington bailouts could push the federal deficit to $1.5 trillion or more, and some estimate the costs of the bailouts will eventually reach 60 percent of GDP.

The tentacles of the state are growing by leaps and bounds. In 2009, global governments will be the largest shareholders in commercial banks, reversing 20 years of retreat by the state. The costs of entitlements are exploding upward, and Congress hasn't had the courage to address future liabilities. Social Security and Medicare are government-sponsored Ponzi schemes that will make Bernie Madoff's embezzlement look like a picnic.

The late management guru Peter Drucker said, "Government is better at creating problems than solving them." In fact, wrote a cynical Drucker, government has gotten bigger, not stronger, and can do only three things well—taxation, inflation, and making war. According to Drucker, the state has become a "swollen monstrosity. . . . Indeed, government is sick—and just at a time when we need a strong, healthy, and vigorous government." (He said all this in 1969!) If you want to solve problems, he counseled, you must turn to business and the private sector.

But where does one get the straight scoop on Keynes, Marx, and their nemesis, Adam Smith and the followers of free-market capitalism? I have no apologies for where I stand on the issue. In writing *The Big Three*, I commissioned a Florida woodcarver, James Sagui, to create "The Totem Pole of Economics."

Clearly, my hero is Adam Smith, the author of *The Wealth of Nations*, published in 1776, who made a declaration of *economic* independence. Adam Smith, the eighteenth-century philosopher, is at the top of the Totem Pole for his advocacy of a revolutionary new doctrine that he called a "system of natural liberty," what we might call *laissez-faire* or *free-market capitalism*. He used the "invisible hand" to symbolize how the private actions of individual entrepreneurs would lead to the public good.

Keynes is ranked below Adam Smith, because he supported big government and the welfare state as a way to stabilize the crisis-prone capitalist economy, the "middle ground" between laissez-faire and totalitarian socialism. But as we have seen, Keynesian activism has led to much mischief in the world today, and countries that have adopted his bureaucratic, regulated mindset have witnessed "slow growth" and "stagflation"-style economies.

Marx is the low man on the Totem Pole. His radical solution, government ownership and control of the production, distribution, and consumption of goods and services, would be, as Hayek says, "the road to serfdom."

Is the Global Economy Depression Proof or Accident Prone?

Recently, I was in Stockholm, Sweden, for the Mont Pelerin Society meetings, where 300 top experts gathered from around the world. At this meeting, I organized a special ad-hoc session reassessing Milton Friedman's famous lecture, "Why the American Economy Is Depression-Proof." Friedman gave this optimistic lecture in Sweden in 1954, at a time when some prominent economists and financial advisors were predicting another crash on Wall Street and a collapse in the economy. Then, 55 years later, in the face of the worst financial crisis since the Great Depression, everyone at the meeting wanted to know if Friedman, one of the founders of the international society, would have changed his mind.

Nobody knows for sure, since Friedman died in late 2006, before the crisis started. I do know that until his death, he had always defended his bold prediction. From 1954 until his death in 2006, the United States suffered numerous contractions in the economy, an S&L crisis, a major terrorist attack, and even a few stock market crashes, and still it has avoided the "Big One," a massive 1930s-style depression characterized by an unemployment rate of 15 percent or more (Friedman's definition of a depression).

In his lecture, Friedman pointed to four major institutional changes to keep another Great Depression from happening: federal bank deposit insurance; abandonment of the international gold standard; the growth in the size of government, including welfare payments, unemployment insurance, and other built-in stabilizers; and most importantly, the Federal Reserve's determination to avoid a monetary collapse at all costs. Because the public and officials are petrified by the possibility of another depression, Friedman predicted that any signs of trouble would lead the Federal Reserve to take "drastic action" and shift "rapidly and completely to an easy money policy." Consequently, according to Friedman, rising inflation would be far more of a threat to postwar America than another Great Depression.

So far, so good. But now, following the financial crisis of 2008, I suspect Friedman would be forced to revise his views if he were alive. Admittedly, Friedman is still technically correct. There has still been no Great Depression. The Fed and the federal government appear to have averted disaster once again. Yet, they were able to do so only by taking on unprecedented powers and trillions of dollars in debt that may so weaken the government and the public's trust in its financial capacity that a deflationary collapse, hyperinflation, or centrally planned economy sometime in the future may be unavoidable.

Clearly, bank failures are not a thing of the past, and there have been runs on commercial banks and other financial institutions (money market funds), although Friedman is right that most banks are now either taken over by the FDIC or the Treasury, or forced to merge with a bigger, safer bank.

Friedman said, "There has been no major depression that has not been associated with and accompanied by a monetary collapse. . . . Monetary contraction or collapse is an essential conditioning factor for the occurrence of a major depression."

Yet, the United States came awfully close to an economic collapse in 2008 without any monetary contraction. In fact, during 2008, the money supply (M2) grew every month and 9 percent for the year. Clearly, monetary contraction isn't the only source of instability in the economy. Economic disaster can also be precipitated by too much monetary inflation, irresponsible banking practices, or perverse tax and regulatory policies. One of the weaknesses of the Friedman/Chicago school approach is their belief that inflationary asset bubbles only have microeffects on the economy and can be defused without having a debilitating macroeconomic impact. The real estate crisis of 2007–2009 demonstrated otherwise. Keynesian-style inflation can have unintended consequences and can create economy-wide unsustainable imbalances that can lead to disaster. As Ludwig von Mises once said, "We have outlived the short-run and are suffering from the long-run consequences of [Keynesian] policies."

Few Agree with Friedman Anymore

At the end of our special session, I asked members of the Mont Pelerin Society how many of them still agreed with Friedman, that the American economy is "depression proof." Only a handful raised their hands, and they were all American economists. The rest of the crowd, mostly from abroad, pointed out that most other countries did not suffer a banking crisis. The financial crisis was largely American-induced. They agreed that until the United States adopts a stable monetary and banking system, it can no longer be considered depression proof.

Is the Dollar Going to Collapse?

My biggest concern right now is a dollar crisis, the kind that Paul Volcker predicted in 2005. It reminds me of Harry Browne's 1970 bestseller, *How to Profit from the Coming Devaluation.*

For over a year now, the Fed has adopted a *zero interest rate policy* (ZIRP). It comes right out of Keynes's playbook, *The General Theory,* written in 1936.

John Maynard Keynes (1883–1946), the British economist, favored a permanent cheap money policy as the key to economic nirvana. Recently, I had dinner with Lord Robert Skidelsky, Keynes's authoritative biographer, in New York, and he confirmed it: "He wanted interest rates to be zero."

ZIRP can be successful for a while, but there's a dark cloud within this silver lining—higher commodities prices, especially oil and gold. Oil, gold, and most commodities are priced in dollars. If the price of oil gets too expensive, it will impact the U.S. economy, and cause a secondary economic crisis and downturn. Higher oil prices, more than gold, are the danger.

Rumors are flying that secret meetings are taking place between Arab states, China, Russia, Japan, and France, to dump the dollar and replace the U.S. currency's role in the pricing of oil. Is there any truth to the rumors that the dollar is being replaced by a basket of foreign currencies, and what will be the impact on your investments and the U.S. economy?

The U.S. dollar is still the world's currency, but a crisis is looming. Oil, gold, and other commodities have to be conveniently priced in some currency, and the dollar has traditionally been the currency of choice for a variety of reasons: The United States remains by far the world's largest economy and trading partner. It remains the only military superpower. And the Federal Reserve is the most powerful central bank.

Despite all the talk of pricing oil in another currency, the dollar reigns supreme. Russia has been talking about doing an oil contract in rubles for years, but it hasn't happened. The Arabs lost out to the New York Merc in the early 1980s in setting the price of crude.

Crude oil is the world's most actively traded commodity and the NYMEX light sweet crude oil futures contract is the world's most liquid form for crude oil trading, as well as the world's largest-volume futures contract trading on a physical commodity, and the pricing is in dollars. So far, changing the pricing to a basket of foreign currencies has proven unworkable.

The Treasury securities market is the world's largest liquid market. Where else is China going to keep its foreign exchange reserves of $2.1 trillion? As of July 2009, foreigners owned the following amounts in U.S. Treasuries (see Table 3.1).

But the Chinese and other foreign countries are looking to diversify their holdings into euros, yen, Swiss francs, and British pounds, as well as stockholding gold and other commodities. That's just prudent diversification.

And it could cause a run on the dollar. In 2009, the IMF reported that the dollar's share of total reserves had fallen to its lowest level since 1995. And for the first time in decades, central banks are no longer selling their gold, but are net buyers.

The biggest risk is a massive crash or run on the dollar, and that's always conceivable if the Federal Reserve continues to engage in a reckless irresponsible monetary policy. The dollar fell sharply in 2009, losing over 20 percent against the euro, but so far it's been an orderly decline.

In order for the dollar to rally, the Fed needs to abandon ZIRP and return to a natural rate of interest (3–4%), and the U.S. economy needs to recover sharply from the Great Recession. So far, neither event has happened. Until these two events occur, it would be wise for investors to keep buying gold and silver, especially silver. Gold has hit new highs, but silver at $17 an ounce is still way below its all-time high of $50 an ounce, set in 1980.

Table 3.1   Foreign Holdings in U.S. Treasuries

Holder	Total
China	$800.5 billion
Japan	$724.5 billion
United Kingdom	$220.0 billion
Caribbean banks	$193.2 billion
Oil exporters	$189.2 billion
Brazil	$138.1 billion

Source: United States Treasury.

When the Rich Get Poorer, Look Out Below

In August 2009, the *New York Times* had a cover story: "After 30-Year Run, Rise of the Super-Rich Hit a Sobering Wall." One line that stood out at me was:

> Any major shift in the financial status of the rich could have big implications. . . . Over the last century, the worst years for the rich were the early 1930s, the heart of the Great Depression.
> (*New York Times*, August 21, 2009)

The financial crisis has hit the rich hard—the net worth of rich Americans dropped by an average of 24 percent in 2008, according to a new Merrill Lynch Wealth Management report. The number of people with investable assets over $1 million has fallen from 3 million to 2.5 million. They have lost big money in real estate and stocks, their two biggest holdings. Even the price of the Mei Moses Art Index fell 32 percent during the credit crisis.

The real question is, what is the impact of less wealth on the average American? The answer is: serious.

The wealthy, a category that includes business entrepreneurs like Bill Gates and independent investors like Warren Buffett, have led the global economy to astonishing new heights over the past generation.

The *New York Times* doesn't want to admit it, but over the past 50 years, the rich have gotten richer and the poor have gotten richer, too. If you look at average real income figures, the wealthy have benefited more from the growth economy since the Reagan Eighties, but many critics argue that income inequality has worsened in the United States.

But wage income does not tell the whole story. If you look at actual goods and services used by Americans over the past 30 years, middle and poor income earners may have done much better, and may have even done as well as the rich in terms of the quality and variety of life. According to a recent study by the Dallas Fed, the poor and middle class are enjoying substantially more and better-quality cars, food, housing, education, and entertainment since 1980. If you look at the average size of a new home, and households with a computer, cable TV, microwave, and washer/dryer, the indicators are all higher for all income levels. (See Chapter 1 of my book, *Economic Logic*; Capital Press, 2001, available from www.amazon.com.)

The positive effects of market capitalism have been felt around the world. Even in countries like India or Brazil, the number of poor people has declined markedly since 1980. Worldwide, the number of extreme poor has fallen by 50 percent.

As Andrew Carnegie once said, "Capitalism is about turning luxuries into necessities."

But what about the future? The answer is simple: When times are good, the rich get richer and the poor get richer, too. When times are tough, the rich get poorer—and so do the poor and middle class.

And times are tough. When you tax the rich, you get less wealth and fewer rich people. When you regulate successful corporations, you get less profits and less retained earnings. That means fewer job opportunities for everyone, rich and poor, and less income.

It's all a cycle of wealth and poverty. Do you want to return to prosperity? Encourage the rich to invest, hire, and spend more. You don't do that by taxing, regulating, and attacking the rich.

Calvin Coolidge said it best: "Don't expect to build up the weak by pulling down the strong."

Investment Strategy in Uncertain Times: Know the Signs of the Times

What is the best strategy in today's crisis-prone global economy? It can be summed up simply as, "Know the signs of the times." As Jesus said in the New Testament, "Take heed that no man deceive you" and "Discern the signs of the times."

We live in times of fair weather and foul weather. During fair weather, be invested in stocks, bonds, and real estate. I especially like income-producing stocks and mutual funds that pay high and sustainable dividends. This has been my most successful strategy during the 30 years I've been writing my newsletter, *Forecasts & Strategies.* (See also my book, *Investing in One Lesson*, Regnery, 2007.)

In foul weather, take refuge in gold, silver, commodities, cash, and even, when appropriate, "safe" government securities (assuming the government survives).

Be your own money manager as much as possible. Nobody cares more about your hard-earned money than you do.

Ending On a Positive Note

I end on an optimistic note. Adam Smith and his "system of natural liberty" have come under attack many times by arch enemies, the Marxists and Keynesians. But Smithian economics has nine lives, and has always managed a comeback. With your help, Adam Smith will return. The Scottish professor was an optimist. He wrote in *The Wealth of Nations* (1776):

> The uniform, constant, and uninterrupted effort of every man to better his condition ... is frequently powerful enough to maintain the natural progress of things toward improvement, in spite both of the extravagance of government, and of the greatest errors of administration.

Long live Adam Smith and his system of natural liberty.

How Fed Policy Fuels
Market Cycles

Gary Alexander

S*ince 1913, we've seen five 17-year market cycles. We've just seen a decade-long bear market. What's next?*

The Federal Reserve Board is nearing the end of its first century. Its track record consists of a rollercoaster ride of artificial booms, mega-busts, and a collapsing currency. More often than not, Fed policies extended the periods of market decline from a brief but painful natural cleansing process to a 15-to-20-year downward arc. The U.S. dollar is another casualty. Except for the Civil War, the dollar's value was stable for the 125 years before the Fed was created. Since 1913, however, the dollar has fallen by 98 percent.

The Birth of the Modern Federal Financial System

On March 31, 1913, J.P. Morgan, Sr., died at age 76. He had been a one-man Federal Reserve Board over the previous generation, single-handedly rescuing the nation from the panics of 1894 and 1907.

Morgan's death ironically came in the same month that Woodrow Wilson was inaugurated as only the second Democratic President since 1860. In the same fiscal quarter, the 16th Amendment authorized federal income taxes. Later in 1913, the Federal Reserve Act was signed into law. So, 1913 was the birth of the modern financial order—and the start of a series of six long-term bull and bear markets in stocks.

World War I soon intervened and global stock markets were closed for most of the second half of 1914. During that timeout, the Federal Reserve was officially launched on November 16, 1914. Then, when the stock market reopened in December, the Dow sank to a low of 53.17 on Christmas Eve. But over the next 15 years, the first big bull market of the 20th century lifted stocks a whopping 617 percent to 381 in 1929.

The majority of that sevenfold market gain came as a result of the laissez-faire policies of presidents Harding and Coolidge in the 1920s, as engineered by their free-market secretary of the Treasury, Andrew Mellon. Their biggest success was a tax cut that opened the gates to the Roaring Twenties' prosperity, but underneath it all, the Federal Reserve was having growing pains, leading to alternate waves of inflation and deflation.

In short, the Fed created a huge, overblown credit boom and then slammed on the brakes way too hard. An institution that was designed as a passive observer, charged with preventing future bank panics (like the one in 1907), the Fed fueled credit inflation, and then severe deflation. First, it fueled wartime liquidity and postwar inflation, flooding the system with too much money and credit for its first 15 years, through 1929. Then, in a morning-after repentance, it drastically cut money supply by fully one-third, from 1929 to 1932, making the Great Depression far deeper and longer than any panic in previous years.

The Five 17-Year Bull and Bear Markets since the Birth of the Fed

Market cycles are not carved in stone for any demographic or mystical reason, but the past 95 years of Fed-fueled finances have shown us that the stock market has swung in very wide bull and bear market trends. The trend only changes when public policy changes in a dramatic way. (This is not a partisan statement. The bad choices have come from both major political parties, and so have the good choices.)

In brief, here are the six (five-and-a-half, really) 15-to-20-year cycles since the birth of the Fed in 1913 (as per the Dow Jones index)

1. The 1914–1929 bull market (+617%) was fueled mostly by tax cuts and credit expansion.
2. The 1929–1949 bear market (–57%) was exacerbated by tariffs and credit contraction.
3. The 1949–1966 bull market (+516%) was largely created by free trade policies under GATT.
4. The 1966–1982 bear market (–22%) was deepened by profligate fiscal and monetary policies.
5. The 1982–1999 bull market (+1,409%) was inspired by tax cuts and a war on inflation.
6. The current bear market (–30% so far) is due to a return to profligate spending policies.

What follows is a thumbnail sketch of those alternating bull and bear markets since 1929.

The 1929–1949 Bear Market: Caused by Government Policies, Not Wall Street

The stock market crash of October 1929 gets all the headlines and most of the blame, but the market was recovering nicely six months later, until politics destroyed that recovery. On April 17, 1930, the Dow climbed all the way back to 294.07, almost 50 percent above its mid-November 1929 panic low. But then came a chilling 86 percent drop in the next 27 months. The main cause of the collapse was a trade bill working its way through Congress that spring. In desperation, on May 4, 1930, 1,028 leading economists signed a petition that protested the tariff. Their plea didn't work. The Smoot-Hawley bill was signed into law on June 17. That day, the Dow Jones index fell by a massive 19.64 points (–8%), from nearly 250 to 230.

The 1,028 economists were right. Their warnings proved prophetic, as foreign nations retaliated against Smoot-Hawley by passing their own tariffs, which deepened into a global depression, and then World War II.

In addition to that mistake, the Fed cut money supply by one-third in three years, causing deep deflation. President Hoover tried to keep wages artificially high during a deflation, leading to 25 percent unemployment.

Price Deflation, 1930–1932

1930	– 6.4%
1931	– 9.3%
1932	–10.3%

The 1949-1966 Bull Market was Mostly Fueled by a Revolution in Free Trade

In a mirror image of the protectionist Smoot-Hawley trade bill of 1930, the advent of the General Agreement on Tariffs and Trade (GATT) in 1947 opened the door to postwar prosperity. Politically, after learning lessons from the punitive 1919 Treaty of Versailles, the United States and the rest of the world helped rebuild Germany and Japan with the Marshall Plan and other relief measures. It all began in mid-1947, with the Dow languishing in the 160 range— less than half its value at the peak of the 1929 bubble.

Here's a sample of the liberating events in the middle of 1947, while the GATT meetings took place:

- May 7, 1947: General Douglas MacArthur approved a new, liberalized Japanese constitution.
- May 17: The Dow sank to 163.21, marking the end of a 23.2 percent one-year postwar bear market.
- June 5: In a commencement speech at Harvard, Secretary of State George C. Marshall outlined a proposal to provide massive U.S. aid to postwar Europe. Between 1948 and 1951, the Marshall Plan poured over $13 billion into Europe, sparking economic recovery and, in the process, saving the U.S. economy from a postwar recession by providing a greater market for U.S. goods.
- October 30, 1947: 23 countries signed the General Agreement on Tariffs and Trade (GATT) in Geneva, lowering 45,000 tariffs in the first of several GATT rounds over the next 60 years.

And don't forget the role of technology: On December 23, 1947, the transistor was invented by John Bardeen, Walter Brattain, and William Shockley, of Bell Labs. The computer revolution was born.

Investors weren't impressed. They were scared. The Dow sank to a slightly lower low (161.6) in 1949. A 1949 Federal Reserve Board survey found that 69 percent of American families with incomes over $3,000 a year (an above-average income then) were opposed to investing in stocks. Another 1949 survey found that 90 percent of the richest residents of St. Paul (MN) had never purchased a share of a stock or bond in their life. Most Americans thought the "stock market" referred to the beef market in Chicago. Americans spent $9 billion a year on cars but $540 million on stocks. Just when stocks were set to soar, few were buying.

The 1966–1982 Bear Market Was Mostly Fueled by Bad Fed and Fiscal Policies

The 17-year bull market of 1949–1966 was fueled by global trade, a lack of punitive wartime reparations, the Green Revolution, and a dollar partially backed by gold. The long bull market came to an end on February 9, 1966, when the Dow hit 1001, inter-day, but then closed at 995. That's as close as the Dow got to 1000 for seven years. The Dow fell 25 percent over the next eight months of 1966 and didn't close above 1000 until early 1973, when Dow 1000 was eroded by inflation and economic stagnation ("stagflation").

The cause of the peak and subsequent decline was a series of three profligate fiscal policies and Federal Reserve inflation:

1. A fiscal policy of "Guns and Butter" under LBJ, as he escalated the war in Vietnam while promising great increases in all facets of domestic spending
2. Raising taxes shortly after cutting taxes
3. A profligate Federal Reserve, bending to political pressure to inflate the dollar

In addition, two consecutive presidents removed all remaining silver and gold backing to the currency. On July 23, 1965, President Johnson signed a bill to remove all silver from U.S. coinage, and on August 15, 1971, President Nixon closed the gold window and instituted wage and price controls.

These presidential measures removed all restraint from money supply increases from a compliant Federal Reserve under political appointees Arthur Burns (Fed chairman from 1970 to 1978), and G. William Miller (in office only 17 months, 1978–1979). Not until the appointment of Paul Volcker in late 1979 did the Federal Reserve's monetary spigots come under control, whipping inflation, but at great cost.

One other cause of the 1966–1982 bear market was the repeal of the Kennedy-Johnson tax cuts, which had fueled great economic growth in the early 1960s. After a booming 1964–1965, due in part to tax cuts, on the day after Christmas, 1965, H. Gardner Ackley, chairman of the President's Council of Economic Advisors, issued a report calling for massive tax increases "to prevent the economy from overheating." That report was admittedly lost in the holiday cheer and stock market euphoria in the push to Dow 1000, but Ackley kept beating the drum in 1966 for higher taxes, in an overt attack on high corporate profits.

Ackley's basic proposal (with the blessing of LBJ) was for tax "surcharges" (a euphemism for raising taxes) amounting to 5 percent more on capital gains, 7.5 percent more on income, estates, and trusts, and 10 percent more on corporations, plus some new excise taxes on cars. Bear in mind that personal income tax rates were already astronomically high, at 70 percent, recently down from 92 percent before the Kennedy-Johnson tax cuts.

In March 1966, right after the Dow first touched 1000, President Johnson gave a speech to 150 leading business executives asking their support for higher taxes. Not one corporate leader applauded or in any way supported him. But Congress was then more than two-thirds Democrats, so LBJ eventually got his tax increases in June 1968, after two years of struggle. In the meantime, investors knew what was coming and they sold stocks at the lower (pre-1968) capital gains rates. The stock market peaked right at the time President Johnson and his tone-deaf chief economist were calling for punitive tax increases, just two years after doing the right thing by lowering the 90 percent-plus tax rates that funded the 1942–1963 defense buildup.

Along the way to passing those tax increases, on March 30, 1968, President Johnson announced that he would not run for reelection (and the market staged a 4% one-day rally). Historians blame his self-inflicted retirement on the failed Tet invasion in Vietnam, but 20/20 hindsight shows that Tet was a defeat for the Communist north and there was still widespread national support for the war in early 1968. Perhaps LBJ's foolhardy tax increases were responsible for a greater part of his sagging poll numbers.

In a similar situation later on, President George H. W. Bush went from 90 percent approval ratings after the 1991 Gulf War to an ignominious loss in 1992, mostly for violating his "Read my lips: No new taxes" pledge. The American electorate does not like to pay higher taxes, and it generally punishes tax increasers.

Before moving on to the great bull market of the 1980s and 1990s—what Ron Miller calls "el Toro Grande"—we need to look at something else that happened on February 10, 1966, the day the Dow touched 1000, intra-day, for the second straight day. Something happened that day that reflected deep problems in the American economy: Ralph Nader, speaking before a Senate committee, testified that the U.S. car industry was socially irresponsible. Not only were our cars "unsafe at any speed," but they were inefficient and poorly made, he said. Although wrong in some specific claims, he was right in the general sense that U.S. cars were poorly made and were unable to compete globally. The dollar was also artificially high, limiting America's ability to compete globally. Then came the German and Japanese competition in autos and electronics. In a reverse Marshall Plan, our former enemies invaded America with cheap but well-made goods. America was not competitive in the global marketplace until the 1980s.

The bear market continued for 16 and a half years, from February 1966 to August 1982, a time of terrible economic fundamentals: Unemployment reached double digits, and so did inflation. The Prime Rate reached 21 percent. From 1973 to 1982, the economy declined in 11 of 40 quarters, and in 8 of 12 quarters from 1979 to 1982. Fed Chairman Paul Volcker spent three years (1979–1982) choking off the money supply to kill inflation. But in August 1982, he stopped the punishment and began refueling the economy.

The 1982-1999 Bull Market Was Fueled by Tax Cuts and Volcker's War on Inflation

In August 1982, Volcker began easing the Discount Rate. The first cut was a full point, from 12 to 11 percent. That caused the market to stop falling on August 12, at 777 on the Dow. In all, the Fed lowered the Discount Rate five more times in the second half of 1982, down to 8.5 percent. Short-term (90-day) T-bills declined from 13.3 to 7.8 percent in the third quarter of 1982, and banks lowered their Prime Rate from 21 to 13 percent. The Fed was determined to flood the market with liquidity since we were entering a deflation.

The market turned up dramatically on Friday, August 13, 1982, but the economy kept heading south for four more months. The economic indicators released at the time of the market bottom in August 1982 were extremely downbeat. There was no apparent reason for the stock market to recover, at least not yet:

- Industrial production fell for the 12th time in 13 months.
- Retail sales were down 0.9 percent.
- Raw materials production was down for the 16th straight month.
- Durable goods orders were down 4 percent.

South of the border, matters were far worse in Latin America:

- The Mexican stock market was down 80 percent since the first of the year.
- Inflation rates reached triple digits in Argentina and Brazil. Debtor nations could not repay their loans.

But Volcker's medicine worked: Inflation was down below 4 percent and would remain that way for most of the next 27 years. His rapid reduction of the Discount Rate was the only ray of hope, but it was enough for most investors. The Dow quickly reached a new record of 1059 on October 21 (+36% in 10 weeks), and it was up another 20 percent to 1287 a year later. The market was off to the races, for more than 17 years.

And then, there was a repeat of the 1947 formula—an increase in free trade worldwide. On November 28, 1982, representatives from 88 nations gathered in Geneva to find ways for eradicating protectionist trade barriers. Once again, they did the right thing, removing barriers to trade and global markets took off.

Free trade is one of the major causes of the 1982–1999 bull market, just like it was in 1949–1966, and so was a more balanced and restrained monetary policy at the Fed. In addition, the Kemp-Roth tax cuts and supply-side economics also contributed to the 1980s bull market recovery. But the main cause was new Fed Chairman Paul Volcker's successful war on inflation and his timely course-change in August 1982.

The stock market enjoyed its most dramatic bull market of the 20th century, rising 15-fold from Dow 777 to Dow 11,724 in 17 and a half years, despite dramatic corrections along the way in 1987, 1990, and 1998.

The Record-Setting Bear Market of 2000–2009

The past year and the past decade have been the worst year and decade in modern market history. That may seem hard to believe at first, but Ibbotson Associates has kept track of overall market performance since 1926. In that 83-year period, which obviously includes the 1929 crash and 1930s depression, there have been only two 10- year periods when stocks have declined. One was 1929 to 1938, and the other was in the next decade from 1930 to 1939, and those declines were microscopic—down 0.89 and 0.05 percent, annualized, respectively, adjusted for inflation.

In the last month of 2008, however, we made history. In the decade from 1999 to 2008, we saw a new record decline of 1.4 percent per year, or roughly 4 percent per year after taking inflation into account. In real terms, that means that a basket of stocks in early 2009 had one-third less buying power than in 1999. (See Table 4.1.)

When it comes to monthly accounting periods, the situation in early 2009 was even darker than in the 1930s. The 10-year (120-month) period ending February 28, 2009, produced the worst real loss of all of the 880 historical 120-month periods calculated since 1926. Stocks declined 5.8 percent per year in real terms for the 120 months ending February 28, 2009, according to Ibbotson. That's a 45 percent

Table 4.1   2007–2009: The Fastest 50 Percent Decline in Market History

Bear Market	Decline (& Days)
1906–07	–49% in 665 days
1929–32	–89% in 1,039 days[1]
1937–38	–49% in 386 days
1973–74	–45% in 694 days
2000–02	–38% in 999 days
2002–	–55% in 514 days

[1] Beginning with a 49 percent drop in 49 trading days in late 1929.

Table 4.2   Five Worst Market Decades Since 1926

Ending Month	Total Real Loss
February 2009	–45.0%
March 2009	–42.0%
January 2009	–39.5%
September 1974	–36.5%
December 2008	32.1%

Source: Ibbotson Associates.

real decline in 10 years. In nominal terms, the Dow fell from 10,000 at the end of March 1999 to under 7000 in 2009.

As of March 31, 2009, four of the five worst 10-year net real losses were in the previous four months. (See Table 4.2.)

From peak to trough, the S&P 500 fell 57.7 percent in less than 17 months, from October 11, 2007, to March 6, 2009. The Dow and NASDAQ fell about 55 percent. As you math buffs know, a 55 percent decline requires gains of 122 percent to reach the former peak. That's more than 8 years at 10 percent per year—a long time to wait, so it's fair to ask: Will we have to wait 17 to 20 years before reaching the lofty market highs first set in early 2000?

The public still looks at the Dow for a handle on where the market stands. And the public still stumbles at round numbers. Here's an example: In 1966, the Dow first touched 1000, then fell back. In 1972, the Dow first closed above 1000. Ten years later, it finally had its final close below 1000. How long will we have to wait to see the final close below 10,000? Will it be 10 years, 16 years, or longer? The jury is still out. The answer is in our hands—in particular, our voting-lever hand—but first: What caused the crash?

What Caused the Mega-Crash of 2008? Fed Panic, Credit Fantasies, and "Guns and Butter II"

The stock market was certainly due for a big consolidation by 2000, especially the high-tech bubble sector, but a few policy decisions in the late 1990s made the crash worse than it should have been, and those measures also sowed the seeds for the later market crash of 2007–2009—which may not be over yet.

In 1999, the big scare was the advent of Y2K, and the supposed explosion of global commerce when all our computers shut down. This caused the Fed to expand liquidity way too fast in late 1999 (and then rake in that money too rapidly in early 2000), adding to the tech bubble and making its "pop" bigger.

In addition, the Gramm-Leach-Bliley Financial Services Modernization Act (passed overwhelmingly by a Republican Congress) was signed by Democratic President Clinton on November 12, 1999, right before the stock market's peak. Although the bill is named for three Republicans (Texas Senator Phil Gramm, Iowa Representative Jim Leach, and Virginia Representative Tom Bliley), it passed the House 362–57 and breezed through the Senate 90–8. Both parties overwhelmingly supported this deregulation package.

This 1999 Act repealed parts of the Glass-Steagall Act of 1934, opening up competition among banks, securities companies, and insurance companies. For instance, this law made it possible for Citibank to merge with Travelers, and for banks to acquire brokers. Lobbyists from big banks like Citigroup played a big part in drafting and passing the legislation. This law allowed banks like Citigroup to underwrite and trade today's controversial loans: mortgage-backed securities, collateralized debt obligations (CDOs), and structured investment vehicles (SIVs), names which have become infamous by now.

As a footnote to that Act, the Commodities and Futures Modernization Act was passed by the same Congress and was signed into law by lame-duck President Bill Clinton on December 21, 2000. This law allowed products offered by banking institutions to escape regulation as futures contracts. It was later called the "Enron loophole," since it allowed Enron to market unregulated energy trades. These and other laws, passed by a disinterested lame-duck Congress and president, had serious repercussions later on.

The market decline of 2007–2009 was also caused by massive government spending (Guns and Butter II) under President George W. Bush and a mostly Republican Congress. Trying to fight two wars while also trying to solve a variety of social ills—and never vetoing a bill—Bush's administration was a reflection of the same kind of hubris that destroyed Johnson's first Guns-and-Butter efforts back in the late 1960s.

The biggest cause, however, was easy money for housing speculation, courtesy of the Fed and Congress. First, Congress and President

Clinton tried to make home-owning near-universal, regardless of credit risk. Then, the Federal Reserve pushed interest rates too low after 9/11—down to 1 percent or below for nearly two years, encouraging too many Americans to buy too many homes and other major big-ticket items on easy credit. Later in the first decade of the new century, when interest rates inevitably rose, and house prices stopped soaring, the inevitable "morning after" made the market crash worse than it should have been.

Housing: America's Most Speculative Asset Class?

Even in the best of times, housing is our most speculative investment, due to high margins. But when our benevolent government encouraged widespread no-money-down loans, they encouraged total "naked" speculative buying in real estate by mom-and-pop Main Street families. In normal times—say the 1980s—if you put 10 percent down on a house, you knew it would eventually pay off for you after a decade or two.

The same is true of stocks, but if you had invested in stocks on 90 percent borrowed money, you would have been labeled as a speculator. Why don't we call 10 percent down "speculation"? Because we intend to live in our house for a long time: We don't trade houses on a stock market. But even the most conservative homeowner, putting 10 percent down, is speculating that the 90 percent of borrowed money will eventually pay off.

This new no-money-down world encouraged speculation: In 1995, just 5 percent of mortgages were backed by non-owner-occupied investors. But by 2005, 15 percent of mortgage loans were backed by absentee owners. Speculation in real estate had tripled. Speculation drove up home prices, which made most homes less affordable, which made Congress call for more mortgage subsidies. It was a vicious circle of speculation.

It all began with the noblest of intentions, in 1977, with the Community Reinvestment Act (CRA)—passed by a 66 percent Democratic Party Congress and signed by President Jimmy Carter. The purpose of this law was noble: to end racial discrimination in housing (called *redlining*). Like Affirmative Action, this law did not mandate racial quotas, but the clear inference was that a specific racial percentage, reflecting the population of the neighborhood, was the safest way to prove compliance, so banks adopted quotas.

The CRA did not become a problem until President Bill Clinton expanded its mandate. In early 1993, right after taking office, President Clinton ordered new regulations to beef up Carter's 1977 CRA law. He wanted the bill to increase access to mortgage credit for inner-city and distressed rural regions. The bill passed in 1994, before the Republican Congress could offer resistance in 1995. The new rules went into effect on January 31, 1995, requiring detailed numerical assessments to get a satisfactory CRA rating, breaking down all home-loan data by neighborhood, income group, and race, allowing community groups that marketed loans to targeted groups to collect a fee from the banks. As a result, the number of CRA mortgage loans grew by 39 percent between 1993 and 1998, while all other loans increased by only 17 percent.

This was a bonanza for community activists. The Senate Banking Committee estimated that as of 2000, as a result of CRA, community activist groups had received $9.5 billion in services to midwife these loans. Groups benefiting from this gravy train include ACORN Housing, which netted $760 million. The net result was a tsunami of new homeowners. From 1994 to 2004, homeownership rates rose from 64 to 69 percent. The yearly breakdown for minority loans from 1994 to 2004 shows that overall homeownership rose by 8 percent, while Hispanic or Latino homeownership rose over 20 percent, Asian-American rates rose by 17.2 percent, African-American rates rose by 13.6 percent, and Native American homeownership grew by 12.6 percent.*

One large and looming failure dominates the landscape of the current credit crisis: the role of the quasi-government bodies Freddie Mac and Fannie Mae. In 2005, Alan Greenspan warned Congress about the need to stop the growth of bad loans by increasing regulation for Freddie Mac and Fannie Mae. John McCain was one of three co-sponsors of a bill to do just that. The bill never came up for a vote because it was blocked by Democrats, on a strict party-line voting bloc, due in part to cash contributions from Fannie and Freddie. The three biggest beneficiaries of Freddie and Fannie's

---

*See: http://en.wikipedia.org/wiki/Homeownership_in_the_United_States.

support turned out to be the two leading Democrats in the 2008 presidential run: Senators Barack Obama and Hillary Clinton.*

In the end, this reform bill requiring tighter regulation of Fannie and Freddie was defeated by Democrats. This reform may not have avoided the current crisis, but it would have stopped the runaway housing bubble from growing further in 2005 and 2006 before blowing up in 2007 and 2008.

Conclusion: The Next Move Is Up to the Fed, Congress, and Voters (Like You and Me)

The bottom line of this history lesson is that specific financial blunders in 1930, 1965, and 1999 led to long and painful market declines, while the more enlightened policies in 1948 and 1982 led to dramatic market surges. What will be the government's next big mistake—or enlightened breakthrough? On the downside, it is possible that a "cap-and-trade" bill could become the Smoot-Hawley market-killer of this decade, pushing this already-long (10-year) bear market into its historical pattern of 17 years' duration.

Most recently, the Fed has fueled the economy with unprecedented liquidity—doubling the monetary base in the fourth quarter of 2008—while keeping interest rates super-low. That kept some "zombie banks" afloat, but it is also a dangerous cocktail of easy money, portending a weak dollar and potential inflation.

The future is not carved in stone. The decisions that President Obama, Congress, and the Fed make in the next year will determine whether we have 7 to 10 more bad years or can look back to March 6–9, 2009, as a major market bottom. Voters have the final word: The midterm elections of 2010 may rescue our portfolios. Recent history shows that the market soars and federal spending is restrained when one party controls the White House and the other controls Congress. Ironically, political "gridlock" may be our best hope.

---

*See http://www.bloomberg.com/apps/news?pid=newsarchive&sid=aSKSoiNbnQY0.

CHAPTER 5

Investing and Hedging Strategies for a Topsy-Turvy Financial World

H. Ronald Miller, CFP

If you can take good care of the present, the future will take care of itself, since the future is a time series of the present!

In the decade ending in 2009, we witnessed two major bear stock markets, two volatile rebounds, and an almost-total collapse of the global financial system. The U.S. and Western Europe, in particular, are dealing with the consequences of globalization and unbridled increases in individual and national debt. Over this past decade, the S&P 500 stock index actually lost 9.46 percent of its total return value, not including the loss of purchasing power due to inflation. It is one of the worst 10-year absolute stock market periods, along with the decade ending in 2008, since the Great Depression era. According to the CPI, the loss of purchasing power of the U.S. dollar over this past decade was 22.06 percent. That is a total loss of stock market purchasing power of 31.5 percent over a decade, even after the sharp rebound in 2009. These are truly difficult times and a topsy-turvy financial world for the investors to contemplate.

There are basically two types of investors. The first type is those who are young, let's say 45 or younger, and are saving money periodically in IRAs, 401(k)s, or other retirement-type accounts. This type of investing is a form of dollar cost averaging with a long-term viewpoint. These investors don't necessarily need to micromanage their investments in the early accumulation stage. In fact, the perfect circumstance would be for the stock market to do nothing for 20 or more years so that a lot of money could have been invested in shares of stocks or mutual funds at low prices. Then, they become the second type of investor (described in the next paragraph) and catch a secular bull market for the ride to a happy retirement with a nicely growing nest egg. However, in my experience, the chances of those perfect circumstances coming together are not very probable.

The other type of investor is typically older, and has accumulated a nest egg that represents a relatively larger amount of money. This investor needs to be more proactive in the risk management of these funds so that they don't substantially disappear in down markets. It is very hard to take big losses and recover in a timely fashion. The closer you are to needing these funds for retirement or other uses, the greater the need for proactive risk management. Bear markets typically go down in about one-third the time that it took for the bull market phase to go up. Investment performance should be measured over the total up and down legs of the full market cycle.

This chapter is primarily directed at the older investor with a nest egg who doesn't want to lose much of it and have to start over, or be relegated to lower-potential return-guaranteed investments. They would prefer an investment approach that allows them to continue to participate in growth opportunities when they occur, but with a risk management philosophy to help protect the downside potential. This preferred action is *not* a "buy-and-hold and hope for the best" approach with little attention to the prevailing investment environment or stock market direction.

Risk management and the protection of investment capital are very important considerations. My more than 40 years of financial market experience confirms the belief that, in most cases, market price action will usually precede changes in reported business and financial information for individual companies, industry sectors, and the economy in general. Therefore, the use of technical market analysis, which focuses on actual price action, is the most important ingredient in this portfolio risk management process. The basis of this tactical asset-allocation process is focused timing of the equity or fixed-income exposure to specific business sectors and/or management styles in response to favorable or adverse price trends. This is accomplished through the use of various hedging strategies and/or simply through raising cash. These portfolio risk management tactics will be discussed in more detail in later sections of this chapter.

We cannot take the conventional long-term viewpoint that time in the market will eventually bail you out of bad investments. That may or may not be true in any time horizon. Noted economist and investor John Maynard Keynes had a famous quote: "The stock market can remain irrational longer than we can remain solvent." Where is the logic in trusting your future to fate and hoping it will always work out? It is preferable to be proactive with focused timing and hedging strategies; these can be effective risk management tools that offer the opportunity of achieving risk management goals during volatile financial market trends. Do not follow the belief that you must be fully invested at all times and that it is not possible to be an effective risk manager.

There are three types of individuals involved in the financial and business world, and for that matter, life in general: There are optimists (the glass is half full), pessimists (the glass is half empty), and pragmatic realists (not focused on whether the glass is half full or half empty, but just on which way the liquid is flowing). I consider myself in the last category. Without a doubt, the nation is fortunate that there is a vast majority of optimists; otherwise, we would have remained an underdeveloped and poor country. It is also good that a few pessimists are around to help keep the optimists' feet on the ground or in check. The pragmatic realists are left to see the world as it is and to try to solve problems on a real-time basis.

Subsections of this chapter are as follows:

- Wall Street "Myths"
- "Investment Eras" Are Important Influences on Market Behavior
- Flexible Portfolio Method versus Modern Portfolio Theory
- Strategic Asset Allocations for the Times
- Equity Income Investing—the Preferred Core Holding
- Hedging Tactics for Portfolio Risk Management
- Simple or Complex Technical Analysis—Your Choice
- America's New Role in the Shrinking World

Wall Street "Myths"

The financial markets have been around for a long time. They have always been somewhat unpredictable and often volatile. However, over time, certain myths arise that take on the aura of "Wall Street wisdom." In reality, the myths may be useful for a while, but blind belief in this wisdom can be dangerous to your financial health. Following is a list of some myths that I have observed or discovered over the years and why I believe they are just that—*myths*. (*Note:* I have italicized the explanation of each exposed myth.)

Buying and Holding a Diversified Portfolio Is the Best Investment Strategy

This investment philosophy emanates from the famous "Portfolio Selection" article by Harry Markowitz published in 1952 in the *Journal of Finance.* It has become Wall Street's favorite portfolio management philosophy, known as *modern portfolio theory* (MPT) and the *efficient frontier hypothesis* (EFH). Simply put, these investment theories say that it is not possible to beat the market in the long term, so just stay broadly diversified and fully invested. The goal of MPT and EFH is to create optimal portfolios, offering the maximum possible expected return for a given level of risk without being concerned with the market direction at any particular point in time. You can see a detailed discussion at www.investopedia.com.

MPT is a comprehensive but primarily static portfolio management approach that works best in a bull market. In cyclical and secular bear markets it can be capital-destructive, as many investors have learned over the past decade (2000–2010) and in previous periods like 1966 through 1982. Our experience is that there is a better proactive risk management approach, which I call the flexible portfolio method (FPM), *that can work in both bull and bear markets. No investment approach will work perfectly, always getting you out at the exact top and in at the exact bottom. But it is possible to use risk management tools to effectively vary your market exposure in tune with market trends. This will be discussed in more detail in later sections.*

Dividends Don't Matter—Go for Growth

During the go-go years of the 1980s and 1990s, it became popular to buy growth stocks in preference to dividend-paying stocks. The rationale was that companies that reinvested profits rather than paying dividends made better use of the cash flow in expanding their businesses or buying other businesses. In addition, taxpaying investors would have to pay ordinary income taxes on the dividends most of the time as opposed to the potential for the lower long-term capital gain taxes in stocks.

However, these can be weak arguments, especially for retirement and charitable accounts since taxes aren't paid until distributions are taken, or never in the case of charitable foundations and other tax-exempt institutions. According to Standard & Poor's research, since 1926, dividends have contributed to approximately one-third of total return for the S&P 500 index while capital appreciations have contributed two-thirds. In fact, dividends are like a bird in the hand rather than two birds in the bush during volatile times. In addition, if you need income from your investments, dividends not only provide income, but they normally offer a rising stream of cash flow as dividends are increased, a feature not found with fixed-income investments. I believe an equity income strategy should be a part of any strategic investment allocation. Nine alternative equity income sectors are discussed in a later section.

Diversification Alone Provides Safety

The typical approach to portfolio diversification is to diversify across different asset classes, including some noncorrelated asset classes. A non-correlated asset class is one that usually goes up when another asset class goes down or vice versa. Within an asset class like stocks, you diversify among different styles and sectors, both domestic and international. Historically, there was typically a small correlation, say between domestic and international stocks, or gold mining and banking, and so forth. The basic MPT approach attempts to accomplish this diversification by including commodity assets with industrial equity assets and fixed-income assets in a strategic asset allocation investment program. The goal is to dampen adverse portfolio volatility.

Globalization has substantially reduced the availability of non-correlating asset classes. During a bear market in today's topsy-turvy world, when the stock market is going down, almost all stocks, domestic and international, are going down, some more or less than others but still in the same direction. When interest rates are rising or falling, they do so in a similar fashion over most bond sectors, whether domestically or globally. That is, the general trend direction of investments has become more correlated as a result of globalization. Being fully invested in a diversified portfolio no longer provides the safety investors are seeking. Using hedging strategies, and raising or deploying cash in line with the market direction, are two ways to effectively provide proactive risk management. This topic will be discussed in later sections.

Fundamental Security Analysis Can Always Be Trusted

In general, Wall Street has embraced security analysis as its primary methodology for stock picking. In the bond world, rating agencies analyze the creditworthiness of a company's or government entity's ability to make good on fixed-income payments. This process involves the study of a company's financial statements, cash flow, products and/or services, marketing strategy, management style, experience, and strength. Data sources include balance sheets, income statements, research and development reports, and anything that the company makes public, as well as trade publications that analyze and report on the industry in question and the competitive position of a company and its future outlook.

The basic theme of this analysis is: What is this company really worth now and in the future, or, How creditworthy is a bond for bond buyers? The classic reference for this activity is *Security Analysis*, by Benjamin Graham and David Dodd (McGraw Hill, 2004). In a broader context, macroeconomic issues pertaining to fiscal and monetary government policy also become a part of this valuation process.

Security analysis reports can be useful tools in determining areas for investment opportunities, but they should be read with a skeptical eye. They may not be very useful in determining when to buy or especially when to sell in a timely fashion.

The shortfall of security analysis is that the data are not always accurate or honest. They are subject to manipulation and can also be influenced by the biases of the analyst, and they normally represent dated (old) information. The Enron, WorldCom, and American International Group debacles illustrate these shortcomings, but the history of the stock market is full of many more examples. The recent book The Sellout *(HarperCollins, 2009) by Charles Gasparino is interesting commentary on some of the Wall Street shenanigans over several decades. However, a company's stock price is generally telegraphing what is happening in the company long before security analysis reports provide the reason for the price action. The introduction of SEC Rule*

FD in August 2000 addressed the unfair practice of security analysts getting company information privately before it was publicly announced. This essentially eliminated the previous advantage security analysts had in advising their clients of important company information prior to its public disclosure. Ultimately, price is the final arbiter of value.

Technical Analysis Doesn't Work

Technical analysis of the price action of securities has been around for several hundred years. For example, the Japanese *candlestick* technical analysis technique originated in the 1700s with the trading of rice futures (go to www.investopedia.com for an explanation of this technical system). The use of bar and point-and-figure charts depicting the price action of stocks became popular in the early 1900s for the analysis of stocks traded in the United States. However, financial analysts who focus on technical analysis techniques have often not been fully appreciated by Wall Street elitists.

The lack of respect for technical analysts, in some quarters, likely stems from the fact that you can be good at technical analysis without attending a prestigious business school. You just need to have an understanding of human nature and the workings of the "nonefficient" marketplace. It also shows that you don't really need fundamental security analysis to be successful in the stock market. Gee, and I spent all that time getting an MBA with a major in Finance. Even Jim Cramer, of TV's *Mad Money*, an avid proponent of fundamental security analysis, sometimes goes to the charts to try to explain what is happening when all else fails. The emergence of "behavioral economics," which challenges the authenticity of the efficient market hypothesis, lends credence to the concepts underlying technical analysis. Actually, I believe that many security analysts are closet technical analysts at heart.

Technical analysis doesn't always provide perfect guidance, but neither does fundamental security analysis or astrology or throwing darts. Nevertheless, it does provide a systematic portfolio management process for timely risk management and opportunity discovery. It provides an edge for improving the chances for success in investment endeavors. Technical Analysis of Stock Trends by Robert D. Edwards and John Magee (St. Lucie Press, 2001) is the classic text. However, there are many books on various aspects of technical analysis. There is more on technical analysis techniques for portfolio risk management in later sections.

Table 5.1   Missing Best or Worst Days

Days Out of Market	Missing Best Days	Missing Worst Days
0	14.2%	14.2%
10	9.9% (–4.3%)	20.9% (+6.7%)
20	7.4% (–6.8%)	24.9% (+9.9%)
40	2.3% (–11.9%)	29.2% (+15.0%)

There Are No Successful Market Timers

There are two arguments used to promote this myth. One involves the notion that if you miss *x* number of the best days in the market, your return goes down. One study, done by Smith Barney Quantitative Research for the period August 1982 to October 1995, when the S&P 500 averaged an annualized compounded return of 14.2 percent (excluding dividends), provided the data shown in Table 5.1.

Table 5.1 indicates that if you missed the 40 best days in the S&P 500 index, your annual return dropped from 14.2 to only 2.3 percent. Therefore, just stay fully invested and take what the market gives, which for that period of 13-plus years was a 14.2 percent annual average. Obviously, if someone could guarantee 14 percent perpetually, that would be worth considering. However, Missing Worst Days was also in the report. Let's look at these data in more detail, for the rest of the story, as the late radio great Paul Harvey would have said. The italicized numbers are my addition. Wall Street likes to remind us that by missing 40 of the best days, your annual return dropped by 11.9 percent. Therefore, that doesn't look like a very wise thing to do.

However, by missing 40 of the worst days, the average annual return jumped by 15.0 to 29.2 percent. Now, nobody can actually pick the 40 best days to be in the market or the 40 worst days to be out of the market. But the complete analysis of these data shows that the bias is to avoid the worst days— that is, a gain of 15.0 percent versus a loss of 11.9 percent in annual return. Consequently, this argument doesn't support the idea that market timing doesn't work. Yes, market timing is not easy and it does require close attention to what the markets are doing, but it does provide the potential for better results.

I recently found an archived article in the May 2005 issue of the Journal of Financial Planning, *by Paul J. Gire, CFP, entitled, "Missing the Ten Best." This was a more extensive study of this Wall Street myth that confirmed my basic conclusions. His data covered the period from January 1984 to December 1998 for the S&P 500. He found that the best and worst days often occurred in close proximity to each other. Since it is a mathematical fact that avoiding big down days is better than missing the big up days (e.g., down 50% takes a 100% rise to get even), the appropriate bias is to avoid the worst days. Note, both of these studies were done during a great bull market, not during the post-2000 period, when there have been a substantial number of down days in the 2000–2003 and 2007–2009 bear markets.*

The other argument for not being proactive in the risk management of your portfolio relies on the human emotions of greed and fear. Studies by mutual fund companies show that the inflow of investment dollars is normally the greatest at market tops and the outflow is normally the greatest at market bottoms. Using some math to determine the loss in total investment capital from outflows at market bottoms, the conclusion is that the investing public, in general, is underperforming the market compared to what a buy and hold through ups and downs yields.

I don't dispute this argument on how the general investment public acts, but the conclusion is flawed because it assumes that no one can overcome the human emotions of greed and fear, which cause bad decision making. It is not easy to do, but with systematic hedging tools and strategies and emotional discipline it is very possible to accomplish. Many professional investors (hedge funds, trading groups at major financial institutions, and investment advisors) have successful track records aided by risk management strategies. You do not have to pick exact tops or bottoms to be successful at risk management. You just have to try to stay reasonably in tune with what the market is doing. Keep in mind that technical analysis is only so-so in predicting the future, but is very astute at defining the present. More on the technical tools and strategies of risk management in later sections.

Equity Investing Requires a Long-Term Time Horizon

The Wall Street wisdom is that if you don't have a 10- or 20-year time horizon for your equity investing, you need to scale back equity investing. This is based on the premise that you have to allow plenty of time to recoup the losses occurring in bear markets. An old-fashioned rule of thumb has been to subtract your age from 100 to indicate how much to allocate to equity investing. The reality is that most Americans who have substantial nest eggs are over the age of 50. Most Wall Street advice ignores the needs of this age group, which has most of the private investment capital, by insisting on a buy-and-hold market participation. With systematic and effective portfolio risk management you can participate in the stock market with much shorter time horizons.

The key is just not taking the big loss, because it ain't easy getting even! You don't have to be a perfect market timer. That person probably doesn't exist. The mistake Wall Street makes in underestimating the benefit of managing exposure, or tactical asset allocation, *is in believing that you have to be perfect to be effective. As pointed out in a later discussion, market tops and bottoms are part of a process that typically unfolds over several weeks or months. There is normally plenty of time to deploy risk management tactics if you pay attention to market action. Whatever your age, if you have a good investment nest egg, risk management makes sense. The alternative to the MPT approach that we advocate is discussed in a later section, "Flexible Portfolio Method versus Modern Portfolio Theory."*

Bonds are Always "Safe" Investments

There are three types of risk for bond portfolios: rising interest rates, deteriorating credit rating, and loss of purchasing power at maturity due to inflation. I assume that everyone realizes that rising interest rates means declining bond prices and vice versa. The longer the time to maturity, the greater the volatility in bond prices. Laddered bond portfolios (e.g., laddered maturities of two to eight years) are designed to moderate the risk of interest rate changes. When bonds come due, the tactic is to reinvest at the longest maturity of your ladder and continue this process over time. In effect, the laddered bond portfolio averages the change in interest rates over time. In this strategy, you don't sell bonds until they mature. It is a conservative way to have a low-maintenance personal bond portfolio.

However, *credit risk* has become a greater concern in recent years. This is especially true as bond rating services came under reliability considerations during the credit debacle of 2007–2009. In my opinion, the failed concept of securitization of subprime mortgages and other lower quality credit-type securities into AAA-rated securities is one of the biggest mistakes in financial engineering of all time. Anyone with common sense would have challenged the underlying assumptions behind this concept if they were aware of how it was concocted. Fed Chairman Alan Greenspan testified to Congress on October 23, 2008, to the effect that the models behind securitization of mortgages were flawed because they used the data from the bull market of housing price appreciation of the 1980s and 1990s to justify the pricing of the risk premium for this type of financial instrument. The assumption was that the good times would never end for housing appreciation.

Even Treasury bonds have a risk factor in that the value of the dollar can erode over time, leaving you with less purchasing power even though you receive the same invested dollars back at maturity. Auction rate securities *is another example of a flawed concept that fell apart in difficult times. This idea was that long-term bonds could be traded as short-term bonds because investors would flock to this short-term, higher interest rate because the regular market auctions allowing liquidity were thought to be a stable market. The lesson learned in the fiasco of the credit crisis is that if you base your model on a positive historical period of financial results, you are setting yourself up for failure. In addition, bond funds typically don't have a maturity date as they continually roll over bond positions, so they are especially sensitive to interest rate trends. I believe all types of bonds can be reasonable trading instruments, but to think of them as safe investments is a big gamble.*

"Investment Eras" Are Important Influences on Market Behavior

> The problem with being an early contrarian is that the blood in the streets is often your own!

We use the term *investment era* to refer to periods of time when domestic and global conditions and influences have produced specific investment climates that have had a direct bearing on the general direction of equity prices over lengthy time periods. These conditions and influences include such things as war and peace, government fiscal and monetary philosophy, domestic and global politics and leaders, inventions, discoveries, and so on. That is the Big Picture! (See Figure 5.1.)

Twentieth-century investment eras have correlated quite well with the general trend of inflation, disinflation, or deflation and consequently long-term interest rates. High inflationary periods have produced volatile price trends but relatively stagnant stock market growth over an extended period of time. Look at the Dow Jones Industrial Average (DJIA) and the Consumer Price Index (CPI) on a semilogarithmic chart for investment era time spans, as shown in Figure 5.1. The period from 1915 to 1949 included two world wars,

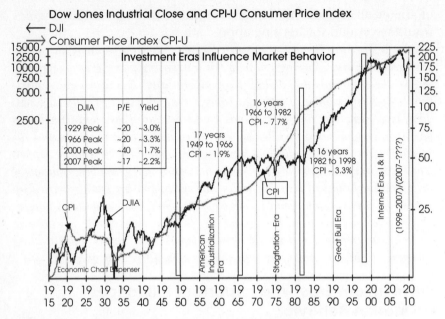

Figure 5.1 title and chart labels:

Dow Jones Industrial Close and CPI-U Consumer Price Index

← DJI
→ Consumer Price Index CPI-U

Investment Eras Influence Market Behavior

DJIA	P/E	Yield
1929 Peak	~20	~3.0%
1966 Peak	~20	~3.3%
2000 Peak	~40	~1.7%
2007 Peak	~17	~2.2%

17 years 1949 to 1966 CPI ~ 1.9%

16 years 1966 to 1982 CPI ~ 7.7%

16 years 1982 to 1998 CPI ~ 3.3%

CPI

DJIA

Economic Chart Dispenser

American Industrialization Era

Stagflation Era

Great Bull Era

Internet Eras I & II

(1998–2007)/(2007–????)

Figure 5.1   Investment Eras Influence Market Behavior

two deflations, the Roaring Twenties, a stock market crash, and the Great Depression. Obviously, these were very volatile times for America. However, I want to focus on the post–World War II investment eras defined by the vertical bars on the chart in Figure 5.1 at the inflection points in the CPI and DJIA beginning in 1949.

Generally, financial assets underperform tangible assets in an inflationary environment. Disinflation periods with low-to-moderate inflation produce major stock market advances and economic expansions. However, absolute deflation, such as that in the early 1930s, produces economic woes and both financial and tangible asset price collapses.

Inflation, disinflation, or deflation trends don't happen in a vacuum, but are the result of varied global and domestic conditions and influences, and often specific events with historical significance. An understanding of these Big Picture factors in the context of the current investment era can help you in interpreting market action and consequently in your choice of investment strategies.

I believe that we are now in the fifth investment era in the post–World War II period. According to my view, "Internet Era II—Global

Intercapitalization" took hold in the spring of 2007 with the establishment of China's Sovereign Wealth Fund (SWF). Its stated objective was to start diversifying China's massive U.S. dollar reserve holdings. SWFs have been around for decades. But the realization that these large international pools of investment capital could have far-reaching implications began, in my judgment, only when China's national oil company attempted to buy the U.S. oil company Unocal in 2005. The awareness escalated further when the United Arab Emirates proposed a working contract to take over management of key U.S. seaports in 2006. By the spring of 2007, it had become clear to almost everyone, and a concern to many, that these SWFs were now a major and growing force in the global investment arena.

Historical Perspective

The investment eras since World War II, in my opinion, can be broadly categorized as follows:

- 1949 to 1966: American Industrialization Era (17 years)
- 1966 to 1982: Stagflation Era (16 years)
- 1982 to 1998: Great Bull Era (16 years)
- 1998 to 2007: Internet Era I—Globalization (9 years)
- 2007 to ????: Internet Era II—Global Intercapitalization (in progress)

The American Industrialization Era.   I did not have any personal experience in the stock markets during most of this era. However, it is fair to say that in the post–World War II period, America was the dominant producer and financer to a world that was in the process of rebuilding after massive destruction from the war. Many American industrial companies went into their long-term growth mode to become American icons. In essence, America was the China of that day, at least from a manufacturing viewpoint.

Note the vertical bar in Figure 5.1 at 1949 and the change in the slope of the CPI line. The inflation rate from 1932 to 1949 had averaged 3.3 percent. From 1949 to 1966, the CPI moderated to an average rate of 1.9 percent and interest rates remained low. This spurred a major bull market that lasted until 1966. During this period, American workers enjoyed a substantial improvement in their standard of living, especially when compared to the rest of the world. The pent-up demand from the war years for consumer goods powered industrial growth. Production of war goods switched to consumer goods. It was an unprecedented positive period for America's middle classes. A typical factory worker's income alone could raise a family in moderate middle-class comfort. Credit was something to be *avoided*. Most stores had "layaway plans." You saw something you wanted to buy and the store would lay it away for you. You saved until you could pay for it before receiving it. However, over the past few decades, most Americans buy on credit and worry about paying for it later.

In 1962, I received a Master of Science degree in Aeronautical Engineering and began a career in Aerospace research on the West Coast. I was hardly aware that there was a stock market. In the fall of 1963, my family was living in Orange County, California, and I was working in El Segundo near the LA airport, and in a carpool driving 35 miles each way. The stock market had had a sharp selloff during the Cuban missile crisis in the fall of 1962. A bull market reemerged when that crisis was over that year. Coming home in the carpool commute, during 1963 to 1966, listing to the news, I started realizing that there was a stock market. Each day, the radio report for the Dow Jones Industrial Average said it was up 2, up 7, up 5; it seemed that there were no down days. That caught my attention and that was the beginning of my lifelong passion for solving the challenges of the stock market. In 1971, I received an MBA with a major in Finance and entered the investment business full time after being an active investor since 1965.

The Stagflation Era.   This investment era was characterized by rising inflation, rising interest rates, and a stagnant economy. The escalation of the Vietnam War and the War on Poverty, initiated by President Johnson in 1965, resulted in fiscal stimulus that proved to be very inflationary. The assassination of President Kennedy is an example of a specific event that changes the course of history (i.e., Johnson's policies on war and the role of government were most likely different from what Kennedy's would have been). In general, the government's fiscal and monetary policies were reactive and behind the economic curve most of the time and often tied to the presidential cycle. This resulted in large volatility in the real economy with big quarter-to-quarter changes in the GDP fairly common. The individual was the dominant investor but was not well informed compared to today. The trend in a company's stock price often unfolded over weeks and months as good or bad news took a while to be fully disseminated and acted on. In the Internet Era, it now takes only seconds.

The institutional investor was insignificant in terms of the capital controlled during much of the Stagflation Era. It was tough to make money during this period unless you were an adept trader. The long-term secular growth trend for equities was essentially flat but with a lot of volatility. Interest rates soared as a result of escalating inflation. The cyclical bear market of 1973–1974 was a disaster. The popular *nifty-50 stocks* (the *one-decision* stocks as they were called then—buy-and-hold forever) dropped on average about 85 percent from their 1973 highs before that bear market low was made in the fall of 1974. However, the market continued to have a broad trading range but with no secular growth for many more years. In 1979, a *BusinessWeek* cover story even expounded on the death of equities as a viable investment alternative.

The most successful investment strategies during the Stagflation Era were intermediate-term trading, convertible bond hedging, inflation hedges like oil and gas reserves, precious metals, real estate, and call option writing and put hedging strategies (*listed call options* were introduced in April 1973 and *put options* were introduced in June 1976). Buy-and-hold was not a successful approach during this era.

The Great Bull Era.   A series of events took place during the 1970s that were the precursors for the emergence of the dramatic great bull market that began in August 1982. Of course, the winding down of the Vietnam War removed one of the major drivers of inflation. In 1974, ERISA legislation was passed, which promoted and regulated retirement plans (IRAs, 401(k)s, etc.) and required personal accountability on the part of business owners and corporate officers for the performance of retirement plans. This provided the rationale for the rapid growth of retirement plan assets placed with institutional money managers during the Great Bull Era.

In May 1975, the fixed commission practice that had been a cornerstone of Wall Street since its beginning was abolished. This gave birth to discount brokers and the cost effectiveness of active trading by individuals and institutional investors (mutual funds and/or investment advisors). In 1978, Paul Volcker became chairman of the Federal Reserve. He implemented a successful plan to break the back of inflation through an engineered recession with tighter monetary policy. He abandoned the policy of catering to the four-year presidential cycle (resulting business cycle) that had dominated economic policy for many decades. In 1981, newly elected President Reagan promoted lower income taxes and a supply-side economic policy that helped revitalize economic innovation and growth.

These precursor conditions enabled the Great Bull Era to take hold in August 1982. When the Great Bull Era began, the Dow Jones Industrial Average was near 777. The P/E on the S&P 500 was around 8 and interest rates on government bonds were in the mid-teens. After the recession of 1981–1982, the economy began a prolonged uptrend as the technology and telecommunications revolution became the driving business force. The institutional investor became the dominant player as various retirement plans grew by leaps and bounds. Individual investors turned a large portion of their investment dollars over to professional money managers.

As before in history, the disinflation cycle drove interest rates lower, which helped expand the P/E multiple at which stocks would trade. This shifted the flow of capital from inflation hedges back to the stock and bond markets. The cost of trading declined and the flow of information and capital around the world increased greatly through satellite telecommunications. The fall of the Berlin Wall in 1989 allowed the establishment of capitalism and free markets in previously communist countries, whose added low cost production extended the disinflation cycle. It was an unprecedented favorable period for financial assets. "Buy every dip and stay fully invested" was the battle cry of Wall Street. Although portfolio risk management continued to provide a lower risk approach to equity investing, the Great Bull Era of declining interest rates, lower inflation, and strong economic growth with an identifiable driver (such as the technology revolution) is the type of investment era in which buy and hold can also produce good results. A key for investment success is recognizing when the investing era is changing and adapting accordingly.

Internet Era I: Globalization.   I believe the expansion of the Internet to all walks of life and business enterprises ushered in a new investment era. Individual investors once again became major players through the active direction of their retirement plan assets to specific mutual funds and investment advisors. As this new era began, the benefits of the long disinflation cycle had pretty much been expended and inflation pressures in certain areas began an upward trend. Although the CPI has remained somewhat docile as a result of cheap consumer imports, most domestic services, health-care, real estate, and other consumer areas not subject to foreign imports felt strong inflationary pressures. The excess creation of monetary liquidity and easy credit was a contributing factor to this more-specific stealth inflation.

Interest rates declined to relatively low levels not seen since the Great Depression, so that their further positive impact on P/E expansions going forward seemed muted compared to the P/E multiple expansion during the Great Bull Era. We saw earnings growth rates receding somewhat as a result of global production overcapacity and competitive pricing pressures via the Internet. Should interest rates begin a cyclical rise, a further compression of P/E multiples from historical highs would ensue. Although many "old economy" stock groups topped out in the 1998 period, the technology- and Internet-related companies created an investment bubble (related closely to the capital expenditure needed to upgrade computer technology for Y2K) that carried the major indexes (DJIA, S&P500, NASDAQ, etc.) to manic highs by early 2000.

This equity valuation bubble then continued a process of deflating as Internet Era I continued its sideways machinations. For example, the Dow Jones Industrial Average (DJIA) on March 31, 1998, stood at 8800. Prior to 2007, the high occurred on January 1, 2000 at 11,723. The closing low was 7286 on October 9, 2002. The point is that as of March 31, 2007, the DJIA stood at 12,254, only 40.4 percent above the level when Internet Era I began on March 31, 1998.

That is about a 3.8 percent compounded annual rate of return, excluding dividends, over that nine-year period. The S&P 500 compounded annual return over the same nine years was only about 2.5 percent. In other words, a buy-and-hold equity strategy during Internet Era I did not produce satisfactory returns. More importantly, the decline from the stock market top in early 2000 was not kind to the nest eggs of investors nearing or in their retirement years.

Based on the Stagflation Era's (1966–1982) typical DJIA trading range between 700 and 1000 for most of those 16 years, we anticipated that the DJIA would range most of the time between 8,000 and 12,000 during the Internet Era I, with 10,000 being the center of gravity, so to speak. Up until the end of 2006, our original forecast of a 12,000 upper limit had stood for over six years.

Nevertheless, the global economic, social, financial, and military environment that contributed to Internet Era I had not changed, in my opinion.

Internet Era II: Global Intercapitalization.   I am pegging the birth of this new investment era at March 31, 2007, for tracking purposes. Most of the conditions experienced in Internet Era I as described previously are still present. However, I believe a more descriptive name for the second phase of globalization that we are now experiencing is *Global Intercapitalization.* Internet Era I, from March 31, 1998 to March 31, 2007 (nine years), provided for the transfer of knowledge, technology, and capital to developing economies worldwide along with the establishment of freer markets for global commerce.

Two substantial circumstances are defining this new era. First, there is the substantial growth of investment capital and production capability. This has resulted in new economic power in the hands of foreign individuals and governments, both of which are benefiting from America's consumer mentality and our living beyond our means. Although foreign ownership of U.S. companies has been growing for decades, it has been a stealth phenomenon, sort of beneath America's public radar. This is changing and becoming much more visible as American industrial icons are being picked off one by one.

I believe that a number of these larger international emerging economies have now reached a critical capital mass and are now starting to flex their investment capital muscles. The number of foreign players with big U.S. dollars to spend is likely to increase even more over time. The massive pools of global capital, especially in what are called *sovereign wealth funds* (SWFs), that are controlled indirectly or directly by country governments or dictators are entering a new phase. Most of this abundance of capital is a result of the growth of international economies that benefited the most from America's appetite for energy and consumer goods. These pools of capital now have a lot of money (U.S. dollars) to spend and they are inclined to diversify these reserves into real assets and global businesses as the U.S. dollar continues its long-term loss of purchasing power. Holding U.S. debt is no longer an attractive long-term investment, as many foreigners are now realizing.

Much is being written about the influence of SWFs on global commerce and investment trends. A report by Morgan Stanley in the spring of 2007 estimated that the capital in SWFs would reach

$2.5 trillion in 2007 and could grow to over $17 trillion over the next 10 years. In comparison, the value of all stocks listed on U.S. exchanges, including the NASDAQ OTC market, at the peak in 2007 was around $15.6 trillion. It dropped to a low around $7 trillion in March 2009. By the end of 2009, it had rebounded to around $11.5 trillion. Obviously, SWFs were impacted by the bear market, so the accumulated values have likely been affected accordingly. A good gauge of the total value of the U.S. equity markets is the Total Stock Market Index (formerly Wilshire 5000 Index) times 1 billion, as reported by the *Wall Street Journal.*

More recently, the buying spree of China's SWF was the feature article in the October 26, 2009, issue of *Fortune* magazine. However, China is not the only foreign buyer of global assets. I found it amusing that India's Tata Motors bought Jaguar and Land Rover from Ford in 2008. At one time, these two auto companies were the automotive jewels of England, which ruled India for two centuries, ending in 1947. I don't know whether Tata Motors thinks it can make money with these two former English auto icons, but it definitely makes a statement about how the global economic power framework is changing. I don't doubt that Ratan N. Tata, chairman of Tata Sons and Tata Motors, had a big smile on his face as this deal was signed.

SWFs and foreign companies are in the process of buying natural resources and producing assets on a global scale of unprecedented magnitude in order to diversify their excess of U.S. dollar currency reserves into real assets and global businesses. The list is very long of American enterprises being transferred to foreign hands. I believe the 2009 purchase of Anheuser-Busch, an American icon, by InBev, a global company with European and Brazilian heritage and based in Belgium, was a telling event. The tables have been turned on the United States, which historically was the major buyer of foreign assets.

In essence, the SWFs are becoming big endowments that surpass most U.S. university endowments and charitable foundations in size. These country SWFs know that a day may come when their exports of energy and cheap goods will diminish. They want to own global natural resources to support their internal growth needs as well as owning producing assets around the world as a diversified source of additional revenue. That is, they apparently don't want to rely solely on their various internal tax revenues to support their governmental programs.

The second condition or driving force of the present investment era is the fragile condition of the global financial system as a result of both government and private bungling of historic proportions, to put it in printable terms. This fragile financial system resulted from excessive financial leverage by both private and governmental global entities combined with a basic lack of common sense on the part of key decision makers, especially with regard to easy credit terms and monetary policy.

As is often the historical case, actions by governments and/or exogenous events contribute to unfavorable future outcomes and unintended consequences. I will point out two conditions that I believe were instrumental in bringing about the 2008/2009 credit crisis: The repeal of the Glass-Steagall Act and the passing of the Financial Services Modernization Act (FSMA) in 1999 (which facilitated the growth of "too-big-to-fail" financial institutions), and the 2004 Consolidated Supervised Entities program of the Securities and Exchange Commission (which allowed investment banks, not included in the FSMA, to voluntarily submit to SEC regulatory oversight) eventually led to financial industry conditions that nearly destroyed the global financial system.

The Glass-Steagall Act was established by Congress in 1933 to separate *commercial* banking activities from *investment* banking activities. The idea behind this government action was to assure that the commercial banking sector would stick to attracting checking and savings accounts. They would redeploy these deposits into retail and business loans, but not be involved in the perceivably riskier investment banking activities of broker/dealers, stock market investments, and other speculations with these customer deposits. In addition, the capital reserve requirements of banks had been substantially watered down over the past couple of decades. After the recent credit crisis, these capital reserve requirements are once again being strengthened. Unfortunately, the lessons of history have to be learned all over again about every 70 to 80 years, or a typical expected lifetime of memories.

The 2004 Consolidated Supervised Entities (CSE) program established by the Securities and Exchange Commission is not as well known but had a profound influence on the recent credit crisis. Fortunately, it was ended on September 26, 2008. Unfortunately, the damage was already done, like closing the barn door after the horses have escaped. In short, five key investment banks (Goldman

Sachs, Morgan Stanley, Merrill Lynch, Lehman Brothers, and Bear Stearns) went to Washington and lobbied the SEC to allow them to continue the amount of leverage they employed in their business activities. The SEC agreed and the regulatory limit for them was raised to as high as 40 to 1, with the condition that the bank's leverage would be monitored and supervised so that things wouldn't get out of hand. We know how that went, and where Bear, Lehman, and Merrill went.

Unbelievably, Alan Greenspan, in testimony to Congress on October 23, 2008, said, "Those of us who have looked to the self-interest of lending institutions to protect shareholder equity—myself especially—are in a state of shocked disbelief." His being shocked that Wall Street, Congress, and quasi-government-backed agencies like Fannie Mae and Freddie Mac would do risky things with other people's money is an unmitigated lapse of common sense.

I believe that Internet Era II has both bullish and not-so-bullish aspects to it with regard to the American consumer and investor. Nevertheless, I think that it will be a very interesting era from many perspectives. Unfortunately, this will most likely be at the expense of the American middle-class standard of living for a generation or more. Like Internet Era I before it, there will likely be numerous cyclical bull and bear market swings of 30 to 40 percent or more in the DJIA. Other major averages with greater volatility will obviously have larger percentage moves in either direction. I expect continuous rotation between the more favorable portfolio management styles and industrial sectors. It is probable that the secular growth trend for most U.S. equities could be somewhat better than what occurred during Internet Era I, once the global financial system is put on sounder footings. However, the U.S. equity markets will still likely lag the stock market returns of international emerging economies benefiting the most from globalization.

Basically, what the United States has been experiencing since the technology-led stock market peak in 2000 for major indices has been a contraction of P/E multiples and a regression to the mean in valuation metrics. This contraction is not dissimilar from the process following the 1973 peak in valuations, which saw the contraction of P/E ratios even as earnings continued to increase for much of the rest of that decade. This regression to the mean for U.S. equity valuations, based on actual reported trailing 12-month earnings, not projected future earnings, still has further to go, in my opinion.

Table 5.2   Internet Eras I and II: Buy-and-Hold Performance Results

	3/31/98 Value	12/31/09 Value	Total Gain	11.75 Yr. Annualized %	11.75 Yr. High
Dow Jones Industrial Average	8800	10428	18.5%	1.46%	14165
S&P 500 Index	1102	1115	1.18%	0.10%	1565
S&P 400 MidCap Index	369	727	97.0%	5.94%	926
Russell 2000 Small Cap Index	481	625	29.9%	2.25%	852
NASDAQ Composite Index	1836	2269	23.6%	1.82%	5049
Goldman Sachs Commodity Index	167	525	214%	10.2%	890
XAU Gold Mining Index	82	168	105%	6.3%	206
Gold Bullion	308	1097	256%	11.4%	1220

The Internet Era I—Globalization and Internet Era II—Global Intercapitalization subpar performances of key market indexes and sectors are compared to Natural Resources and Gold in Table 5.2.

The best-performing major stock index style in Table 5.2 is the S&P 400 Midcap Index. Its annualized return since March 31, 1998, has been 5.94 percent. The high for this index occurred on July 13, 2007 at a level of 926. So, even after being up 35 percent in 2009, it is still 21.5 percent below its 2007 peak. These annualized performances since March 31, 1998, easily favor the Natural Resources and Precious Metals sectors. These results confirm the investment outlook and portfolio management focus that we have espoused since the beginning of the new millennium. Nevertheless, most styles and sectors, both domestic and international, will offer opportunities at times; but investment time horizons, for investors seeking proactive risk management of their investment nest egg, should be measured in weeks and months, not years and decades. In my judgment, there remains a real risk of global financial market turmoil.

No one knows what the future holds with certainty. But the cost of the war on terrorism in blood and treasure and the squeeze on middle-class America resulting from globalization points to an extended period of cyclical stock and bond market volatility swings. I expect rather modest secular growth trends in most broad stock market measures. The emerging economies of the world that are benefiting the most from globalization will likely continue to provide strong, albeit volatile, investment opportunities.

Therefore, short- to intermediate-term trading strategies, both bullish and bearish, will be in vogue. Proactive risk management strategies will be paramount in terms of protecting capital during adverse market trends. We believe that securities that can produce a rising stream of cash income are very attractive to the Baby Boomers, who are nearing or already in retirement. We also remain positive on the secular trend for energy, defense, and natural resources–related sectors as globalization empowers a new massive cadre of worldwide consumers.

Flexible Portfolio Method versus Modern Portfolio Theory

It pays to listen to the market, not humans, for the best advice!

The idea of proactive risk management through tactical asset allocation has been mentioned several times already. What does this mean? Figure 5.2 is a simple way to visualize it. Classical MPT is often discussed with a chart similar to this one. The vertical axis is the Potential Rate of Return and the horizontal axis is the Potential Risk being accepted by the investor. The risk is normally

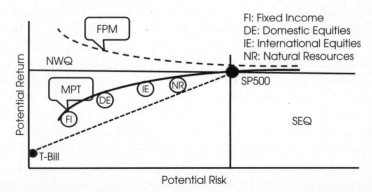

Figure 5.2   Flexible Portfolio Method versus Modern Portfolio Theory

thought of as the volatility in quarterly returns. That is, the greater the volatility in quarterly returns the greater the risk that investors are accepting since they may need their funds at some point when the market is down. If the quarterly up-and-down changes are large, the chance of loss is greater than if the quarterly up-and-down changes are very small.

The simple idea is that you can invest in Treasury bills and have a small return and essentially no risk other than the potential loss of purchasing power of the U.S. dollar. Or you can invest in, say, the S&P 500 and accept that average return and the volatility (risk) of the S&P 500. You can vary your ratio of return to risk by varying the ratio of T-bills to the S&P 500 index held in the portfolio, as represented by the dashed line connecting the T-bill and S&P 500 dots on the chart.

In reality, the investment process is made up of many different investment classes such as fixed income, domestic equities, international equities, and natural resources as well as different strategies, styles, and sectors within each class of investment. For example, *domestic equities* may include *strategies* such as option writing, convertible bond hedging, or dividend capture; *styles* such as large-cap growth, small-cap value, or mid-cap blend; *sectors* such as technology, financial services, or utilities; and *natural resources* such as energy, real estate, agricultural commodities, or managed futures. There are many more choices, but you get the picture. The variance of styles and sectors among all classes is extensive. The circles on the chart represent key investment classes. If all strategies, styles, and sectors were shown, there would be a solid wall of circles, so only a few are shown on the chart for clarity. I like to call these circles *balloons*.

The famous article "Portfolio Selection" by Harry Markowitz, published in the *Journal of Finance* in 1952, basically says that there is some combination of all of the investment classes, styles, and sectors that, via an analysis of historical data, would provide a better expected return for the same risk than the dashed line connecting the Treasury bill dot to the S&P 500 dot on the chart. This is the essence of MPT.

Linear regression–type analysis of historical data provides this combination of investments that make up what is called the Efficient Frontier curve of MPT, as noted in Figure 5.2. Think of each of the balloons as a cloud of gas representing all of the investors (mutual funds, managed accounts, etc.) in a particular class, style, or sector. The leading edge of each of these balloons represents the best performing of these investors from a return and risk viewpoint. The idea is that you should invest in the entities that are the best in what they do and diversify over various classes, styles, and sectors including noncorrelated investments to reduce market volatility resulting from changing market trends.

The assumption of MPT is that the market is efficient (the efficient market hypothesis), so it is not possible to outperform the market with market timing. In theory, you can do better by investing in a diversified portfolio that is composed of the best-performing styles and sectors based on historical data. A philosophical condition of MPT is that these various investment relationships change very slowly over time and that the non-correlating components also change very slowly. The foundation principle is that return and risk have a static relationship, defined as "the greater the return, the greater the risk." That is why the MPT curve is upward sloping to the right of Figure 5.2

Flexible Portfolio Method

In the real world, the financial markets are *not* efficient. The behavior of investors is not consistent, even given the same set of information. Investors differ in how they respond to fear and greed pressures. Consequently, the balloons representing the various strategies, styles, and sectors are not static but float up and down and to the left and to the right in terms of return and risk in response to various investment eras and market environments. This is especially true for the full market cycle of a bull phase and a bear phase. Few if any market professionals believe in the efficient market hypothesis, so I will leave its defense to the academic community.

The FPM tries to focus on balloons that are floating up and to the left, and reduce exposure to balloons floating to the right and losing altitude—that is, to place full market cycle performance in what is called the North-West Quadrant (NWQ), with better performance and less risk as shown on the return-versus-risk chart in Figure 5.2. Portfolio managers try to avoid performance that would fall into the South-East Quadrant (SEQ), with greater risk and lesser return. The FPM is a dynamic approach to tactical asset allocation as opposed to the more static MPT approach. A key ingredient of FPM is the use of hedging strategies and/or raising cash during adverse market trends to reduce the net exposure to the market. This requires paying attention to what the market is doing. This is an added dimension to portfolio management that I believe is best accomplished through technical analysis of market action.

Successfully done, the FPM offers the opportunity to achieve greater returns with less risk for full market cycles. This is depicted by the downward-sloping-to-the-right curve for FPM on the return-versus-risk chart in the figure. You don't have to be perfect in the risk management process to produce better results. An added benefit of the FPM is that if you have been proactive and reduced exposure closer to the beginning of adverse market trends, you are less likely to panic near bottoms and sell out rather than starting to buy back into the market. Psychology plays a part in successful portfolio management and any edge you can generate helps the bottom line.

There are relatively simple tactics that investors can employ to be proactive in the defense of their investments, as well as more sophisticated tactics that require more dedication. Hedging tactics will be discussed later in the chapter.

Strategic Asset Allocations for the Times—Prepare for Boom, Bust, or Muddling Through

Think of the stock market as a carousel, not as a train leaving the station—You can get on or off the horses anytime you want!

We are living in volatile and dangerous times. During the fall of 2008 and early 2009, the global financial system almost collapsed completely. No one knows for sure what conditions would be like today if that had happened, but I think it is fair to say that it would not be nice. The question is, how do you prepare for volatile times in your investments? Burying your head in the sand and hoping for the best is not a very satisfactory choice.

Putting all of your investment capital into T-bills may not be a safe idea, either. Hyperinflation could wreak havoc on your purchasing power. Staying fully invested in the stock market could destroy your net worth in a secular bear market. My answer is that you want to have a flexible strategic asset allocation plan. Inflation, disinflation, and deflation are major drivers of an investment era, as discussed earlier in this chapter. The matrix shown in Table 5.3

Table 5.3 Economic State Asset Category—Strategic Asset Allocation Matrix

	Depression & Deflation	Recession & Disinflation	Low Growth & Low Inflation	Low Growth & High Inflation	High Growth & High Inflation	Depression & Hyperinflation
Precious Metals B/M	15/0	10/0	5/5	5/10	5/10	15/10
Natural Resources R/E	−5/−10	−5/−5	0/10	10/15	10/15	15/10
Foreign Equities	−10	−5	15	20	25	−10
Domestic Equities	−10	−5	10	10	10	−5
Equity Income	10	15	35	25	15	15
Fixed Income G/C	25/0	35/0	10/5	0/5	−5/−5	−10/−5
Global Currencies	15	20	5	0	0	−5

Note: This Strategic Asset Allocation Matrix is an indication of how a strategic asset allocation for an investor could vary based on the economic environment as described in the column headings. These allocation percentages are subject to change. There are no assurances that any specific strategic asset allocation will be successful. B/M = Bullion/ Mining Companies; R/E = Real commodities/Equities of commodity producers; G/C = Government/Corporate, which could refer to U.S. or foreign bonds. A minus sign means a targeted net bearish allocation.

is an effort to define strategic asset allocations geared to the global conditions that may be occurring. It requires you to look around and see what is happening and act accordingly. It is at least a starting point.

I believe that portfolio management is a two-pronged approach that includes both a strategic and a tactical asset allocation viewpoint. A tactical asset-allocation risk management process would be layered on top of the strategic allocation. For example, in the "Low Growth & Low Inflation" scenario in Table 5.3, each of the asset categories would vary around the targeted allocation based on technical analysis of current trends. You may have allocated 15 percent of your total investment assets to foreign equities, but this position could be 100 percent or less invested, with the ability to move to a modest net bearish position at times for aggressive investors. Similarly, in a "Recession & Disinflation" scenario you might have only a 5 percent allocation to foreign equities, but this position could be net bullish or bearish based on the current market trend.

The key is to have a flexible strategic asset-allocation strategy that can shift investment focus according to the economic environment in a timely fashion. This includes the ability to hedge a specific investment portfolio with bear funds and increased cash allocations while responding to changes in secular economic trends affecting the strategic asset allocations.

The first step in the FPM is to determine what is the prevailing investment environment and design a strategic asset-allocation overview that tries to benefit from the prevailing economic environment in concert with the investor's goals and risk tolerance. I call this process the "InDe-flation Watch." That is, are we *inflating* or *deflating* prices, and what is the direction of economic activity?

My current viewpoint (as of 2010) is that we are attempting to transition from a "Recession & Disinflation" environment for most of 2008 and 2009 to a "Low Growth & Low Inflation" environment, as shown in the Strategic Asset Allocation Matrix (Table 5.3). I believe that there are still many hurdles to overcome for this transition to be accomplished and that there are no assurances that it will be a successful one. However, the positive stock market action during the past three quarters of 2009 acted as though the transition was progressing. As noted by many economists and economic pundits, unemployment is very likely to be a troublesome condition for quite a while, even as GDP growth has shown improvement in the second half of 2009. Although I have reasoned doubts that a new secular bull market has begun and that somehow the economy will improve substantially in the foreseeable future, I never rule out any possibility.

The risk of much higher inflation as a result of substantial U.S. dollar weakness, not from consumer demand from economic growth, is a real possibility. It is just hard to predict when it may happen and how severe it may be. The Treasury and the Federal Reserve are well aware of this risk. The big question is whether they can make the right decisions at the right time to avoid this possibility. Until proven otherwise, the Internet Eras continue to act a lot like the Stagflation Era of 1966 to 1982. Our approach is to do our best to stay in tune with what is happening, not what we think or hope will happen. Volatility in financial markets is very likely to be a chronic condition for the foreseeable future and beyond.

Equity Income Investing—the Preferred Core Holding

Cash flow is real, capital gains are a vision!

There is another aspect to the strategic asset process that has to be addressed. That is the needs of investors for income from their investment nest egg. My belief is that the income needs should be met by actual cash flow from dividends and interest, not from hoped-for capital gains. The pressure to rely on capital gains to provide current income can lead to poor judgments in the portfolio management process. That is, the fear factor is enhanced, especially when the market is in a downtrend. Cash flow can come from dividend-paying securities or interest from fixed-income securities. We are biased toward equity income securities that produce dividends but also realize that some fixed income can be in the mix. In this regard I am partial to high-yield bond funds, but only with a risk management approach.

$10,000 Bond Investment	$10,000 Equity Income Investment
Annual interest of 5% = $500 3% average annual inflation Total interest cash flow = $5,000 at 10-year maturity 　　$10,000 bond has inflation-adjusted 　　purchasing power of $6,878 　　$5,000 cash flow has inflation- 　　adjusted value of $4,243 　　　　••••• **Total funds at 10 years = $15,000** **Total purchasing power value = $11,121**	Current annual dividend of 5% = $500 3% annual earnings & dividend growth Total dividend cash flow = $6,720 at end of 10 years & P/E remained constant 　　Equity has grown to $13,439 with 　　inflation-adjusted value of $10,000 　　$6,720 cash flow has inflation- 　　adjusted value of　　$5,000 　　　　••••• **Total funds at 10 years = $20,159** **Total purchasing power value = $15,000**

Figure 5.3   Advantage of Equity Dividends

Hypothetical Example of Why Dividends Trump Interest Most of the Time

Figure 5.3 is an illustration of the advantage of dividend income over bond income. Importantly, dividends offer the potential to increase in magnitude as companies raise the dividend payout over time in concert with growing earnings in an inflationary environment. If you anticipate a long-term deflation environment, then fixed income would normally be the better choice. My belief is that a long-term inflation bias is the odds-on bet as that has been the dominant economic environment for most of the past 100 years.

In determining the strategic asset allocation to equity income–producing assets, I normally use 7 percent as a rule of thumb. If you need annual income of $70,000 from your investment nest egg to supplement other income, then divide $70,000 by 7 percent (70,000/.07 = $1,000,000). Historically, the equity income cash flow rate has been in excess of 7 percent in my experience, but it is a variable, so use a number that you think may be more appropriate for the times under consideration.

So, what are your cash flow paying choices? I believe there are nine different income sectors that can provide ideas for the construction of equity income portfolios. The broad sectors are listed in Table 5.4. A brief discussion of each of these broad income sectors follows.

Energy and Natural Resources Transportation.   There are three major components of this income and growth sector. The first is

Table 5.4 Nine Income Sectors

Energy & Natural Resources Transportation	Business Development Finance Companies	Telecommunications—Regular & Hybrid Securities
Energy & Natural Resources Production	Miscellaneous Income Securities	Specialty Income Strategies
Energy & Natural Resources Utilities	Bond Fund Trading Strategies	Real Estate Investment Trust

pipelines that carry crude oil or natural gas from the production fields to refiners and pipelines that carry refined petroleum products and natural gas to end users. I believe the first pipeline to be organized as a master limited partnership (MLP) was Buckeye Partners, LP, which was a spinoff from the Penn Central Company in December 1986. I personally invested along with clients in this initial public offering, which was the beginning of a long-term favorable investment experience with this industry.

The second component of this sector is shipping companies that use large tankers to carry crude oil or refined petroleum products from countries that produce oil to countries that need this energy. The third component, and a more recent addition for investors to consider, are dry bulk shippers that carry natural resources such as grains and minerals from countries that produce these commodities to countries that need these commodities. A primary example is China's import of natural resources in dry bulk ships and then their export of products in large container ships to developed countries that like their cheaper manufactured products.

Pipelines are relatively stable businesses, whereas shipping can be very volatile. It is very hard to build pipelines on land, so the supply is more constrained. However, there is plenty of room on the oceans to handle as many ships as companies want to build. Consequently, the earnings and dividends from shippers are more volatile, but very attractive at times. You can own MLPs directly, which offers some current tax advantages but requires you report the financial results on a K-1 report, or own closed-end funds that own MLPs and pay a qualifying dividend.

Energy and Natural Resources Production. A popular income and growth component of this sector is energy royalty trusts, both in the United States and Canada. Basically, these royalty trusts buy producing oil and gas fields and/or drill in developed oil and gas fields to obtain energy that is then sold into the market. A relatively large portion of net income is distributed to unit holders. The advantage of this type of investment is the relatively high yields and exposure to the price of energy as an inflation hedge. Of course, this can be a double-edged sword. Canadian tax law changes for their royalty trusts, scheduled to begin in 2011, is a factor to be considered in making this investment. Many royalty trusts are expected to convert to corporations, so their cash flow distributions are likely to be affected. However, if energy prices rise, this impact could be moderated. Another investment consideration for this sector is companies that produce other types of natural resources, such as minerals, that may be paying good dividends.

Energy and Natural Resource Utilities. This sector of equity income dividends is better known by the investing public. It includes electrical, natural gas, propane, and water companies. As the demand for retirement income has grown with the Baby Boomers entering retirement age, this sector has been a favorite target and was bid up in the years prior to the 2007 market peak with a resulting drop in dividend yields typically into the 2 to 4 percent range. I refrained from investing in securities in this sector, which have a yield of much less than 6 percent, for our equity income portfolios. However, at the end of 2009, many electric utility yields, for example, were back into the 4 to 6 percent range and were more attractive once again. Propane distributers normally offer higher dividend yields, but can also have more volatility in their stock market price.

Miscellaneous Income Securities. This includes anything that doesn't fall into one of the other income sectors—consumer goods and services companies that may have better growth outlooks but with dividends in the 2 to 4 percent range. These companies are usually most attractive when there has been a major stock market decline that has kicked up their dividend yield. Think Dow Jones Industrial Average–type stocks. A few of these might be sprinkled into an equity income portfolio.

Business Development Finance Companies. This sector became popular in the 1980s and helped facilitate the financing of small-to-midsize companies benefiting from the Great Bull Era. These companies primarily provide financing that commercial banks have shied away from. The business development companies (BDCs) were able to generate income and growth because they structured debt with various types of profit or equity participation. Sometimes this included securities such as warrants that were later cashed in when the borrowing companies had public offerings. At the bottom line, the BDCs were normally able to pay relatively high yields and maintain their growth in earnings from cashing in, at appropriate times, the profit incentives earned on the loans they made.

However, the current credit crisis has played havoc with these companies and most have eliminated their dividends and lost essentially all or a big portion of their stock market value. This is a good example of why buy-and-hold can be a risky investment approach. If and when an economic recovery takes hold on a solid footing and the credit crunch dissipates, this sector may once again provide income and growth. For now, I would consider this sector a speculation. BDCs involved with the energy and natural resources industries have fared somewhat better.

Bond Fund Trading Strategies. I prefer bond funds for income and growth opportunities rather than individual bonds. Bond funds typically do not have a fixed maturity, so they can be more sensitive to interest rate changes than an individual bond. This can be an advantage since volatility can provide more trading opportunities. In addition, bond funds either are traded on an exchange or are open-ended mutual funds that can be easily bought or sold. You don't have to find a buyer for your individual bond. Interestingly, bond funds generally have smoother price time series that are especially amenable to technical analysis.

The domestic high-yield corporate bond funds in particular often provide high income and attractive trading opportunities. However, there are a number of other bond sectors that also provide interesting opportunities from time to time. For example, there are investment-grade international bonds, both hedged to the U.S. dollar and not hedged to the U.S. dollar; international emerging-market bonds that offer a somewhat more conservative way to invest in the emerging markets than related equities; investment-grade domestic bonds; and U.S. Treasury and agency bonds. There are now bear bond funds that are designed to rise in price when interest rates rise. They can be used to hedge interest rate risk in both bond and equity income portfolios.

Telecommunications—Regular and Hybrid Securities.   The breakup of AT&T in 1982 was promoted on the basis that breaking up this monopoly would result in lower telephone rates and more innovation. The innovation part was true, but monthly phone bills back then were typically in the $10 to $30 range. Now, just about every family member has a cell phone with an Internet connection. You can communicate in real time from almost anywhere in the world, but the monthly telecommunications bill often competes in being the highest utility expense for the household. Interestingly, some of the original AT&T pieces are back together again. (Isn't it exciting how history plays out at times?) Nevertheless, this is still an attractive sector for equity income investing. Major telecom companies have had their ups and downs over the years, and currently are substantially down from their 2007 peaks and now offer dividends in the 5 to 6 percent range.

However, the telecom subsector that we have favored in recent years has been the rural telecoms. The Research Insight Corporation has a web site that provides a detailed report on the rural telecom industry, which had its beginning when Congress passed the 1996 Telecom Act with explicit language that telecom service in rural areas be comparable to what was available in urban areas, including access to advanced telecommunications and information services. This Act sparked a new industry for rural America. Obtain a telecom license, raise capital, and start a telecom company. This is not much different from the startup small-bank concept that has been a very popular investment concept for communities all over America. The basic idea is to grow the business to the point where it will be gobbled up by a bigger fish, which in turn is eventually gobbled up by an even bigger fish, and so on. Each buyout often provides early investors another multiple on their original capital. This is a great investment concept unless it is overdone or there is an economic collapse such as what has recently happened in the banking industry.

Let's get back to rural telecom investments. Many of these rural telecom companies raised cash with a hybrid-type security (sometimes called *income deposit securities*) that is part debt and part equity. The cash flow that these securities distribute is part interest and part dividend and is reported to the IRS on a 1099 form. The advantage of this hybrid security is that the interest rate is deductable from corporate revenues and therefore the size of the cash distribution can be increased relative to just cash flow from dividends alone, which are after corporate tax distributions. I believe it also helps in raising capital because the investors get a higher cash flow and also participation in the potential growth of the company. The dividends for these rural telecom companies are currently in the 8 to 10 percent range. Of course, dividend yields are a function of the actual cash distribution as well as what you pay for the security. There is always the risk that dividends can be cut or eliminated in poor economic times for any equity investment sector, so they are normally considered riskier than bonds on a company's financial balance sheet.

Specialty Equity Income Strategies.   These strategies are a blend of the "old with some new wrinkles" and the "new with some old wrinkles" approaches to equity income investing. The old-with-new-wrinkles approach involves call option writing. *Listed* call option writing dates back to April 1973, although over-the-counter option writing existed for many years prior to 1973. Classically this involves selling call options on individual stocks, which gives the buyer of the call option the right to buy the underlying stock at a certain price for a certain period of time. The seller of the call option takes in the call premium as potential income and realizes that he may have to sell the underlying stock to the call buyer. In reality, only a small percentage of options are ever actually exercised as both buyers and sellers tend to close out their in-the-money options prior to expiration, while options that are out-of-the-money just expire with no value.

A relatively new wrinkle has come on the scene in recent years where closed-end mutual funds focus on a particular stock market index, say the NASDAQ 100 index. They use various evaluation tools to try to pick maybe 50 or 70 of what they think are the best choices out of the 100 to choose from. There are other funds that model other indices, both domestic and international. Their goal is to outperform the underlying index. In addition, they will write call options on the indexes, not the individual stocks. They may sell only enough call options to cover a portion of the portfolio holdings. The idea is to get some of the upside potential of the underlying index while also producing dividend income from call option premiums at a higher rate than would be otherwise available. The investor still has the risk of equity investing. Also, be aware that closed-end funds can trade at a premium or discount to their net asset value (NAV). Typically, you want to avoid funds that are at a big premium to their NAV.

The new-with-some-old-wrinkles approach involves a concept called *dividend capture*. The idea is to buy stocks that pay good dividends, but capture more than the normal number of dividends, typically four in the case of quarterly dividends. The *tax efficient* version tries to follow the rules for generating *qualifying* dividends so that they are subject only to the current qualifying income tax rate of 15 percent. However, at the end of 2010, this rate will be raised unless new or revised federal tax law is passed. The bottom line is that this strategy is constrained to about six time periods a year because the dividend-paying stock has to be held for 61 days in a window 60 days either side of the ex-dividend date to qualify for the better tax treatment.

If taxes are not a consideration, as in tax-exempt accounts, then the other style of dividend capture, which doesn't worry about holding stocks for 61 days, is the better choice. The idea is to turn the portfolio over as often as is effective in grabbing dividends. However, keep in mind that you are not really making money unless the stock that paid the dividend recovers the ex-dividend markdown in price equal to the dividend paid out to shareholders before it is sold. This strategy typically looks at both domestic and international stocks. In fact, many international stocks pay dividends only once or twice a year. This is tailor made for this strategy. If the once-a-year dividend is, say, 4 percent and you have to capture it only once, rather than 1 percent four times a year, that is a much more efficient process and allows for potentially more capture opportunities and more income.

Real Estate Investment Trust.   Real estate investment trusts (REITs) have been a very popular income and growth investment vehicle for many decades. However, the recent credit crisis has had a major negative impact on this sector and it is still a concern. Housing and commercial real estate still have a long way to go in coming out of this bear market as I write this chapter. There are selected areas in high-quality mortgage-related REITs that have fared better, but caution is in order when looking at this sector until there is a light at the end of tunnel for a real estate recovery.

Table 5.5   Asset Class and Sector Allocations

	Income Bias %	Growth Bias %
Gold (Mining Equities/Bullion)	0/5	5/5
International Equities	10	30
Energy/Defense/Resources	5	15
Domestic Growth Equities	5	10
Equity Income Securities	70	30
Cash Reserves	5	5

Final Comment on Equity Income Investing.   These income sectors can be very volatile in bear market environments. They are popular with the *carry trade* investors who borrow money at low interest rates and invest in these sectors. However, the carry trade investors may have to reverse their positions quickly in negative credit environments. Therefore, have a risk management approach in place to help protect your capital in this event.

How much you have in income-related securities depends on what are your income needs from your investment nest egg. If you want only one type of strategy, this is what I would recommend. Table 5.5 shows how a strategic asset allocation might look depending on your income needs. For growth, I am biased toward international investing—especially the emerging markets of the world whose economies are benefiting the most from globalization.

Hedging Tactics for Portfolio Risk Management

If you lose a lot of money, it ain't easy getting even!

Never before in the history of the stock market have there been as many tools to protect capital as there are now, in my judgment. In addition, the cost of transactions is essentially a nonconsideration with very low trading expenses or fee-based accounts where no transaction commissions are charged. The following comments are a discussion of some portfolio risk management strategies that I have used over the years.

I manage many accounts of various sizes and with various investment strategies. I generally use the approach shown in Figure 5.4,

BULLISH POSTURE		MODERATE DEFENSE		FULL DEFENSE	
CORE HOLDINGS	70%	CORE HOLDINGS	70%	CORE HOLDINGS	70%
Various Securities		*Various Securities*		*Various Securities*	
SWING HOLDINGS	25%	SWING HOLDINGS	0%	SWING HOLDINGS	0%
ETFs and/or Stocks		*ETFs and/or Stocks*		*ETFs and/or Stocks*	
INVERSE HOLDINGS	0%	INVERSE HOLDINGS	0%	INVERSE HOLDINGS	25%
ETFs or Regular Funds		*ETFs or Regular Funds*		*ETFs or Regular Funds*	
MARKET EXPOSURE	95%	MARKET EXPOSURE	70%	MARKET EXPOSURE	20/45%
CASH	5%	CASH	30%	CASH	5%
				CASH	30%

Figure 5.4   My Typical Risk Management Approach

which works very well for this type of multi-account circumstance. It should work just as well for individuals managing their own account.

Figure 5.4 shows three panels: Bullish Posture, Moderate Defense, and Full Defense. The Core holdings are made up of the holdings that represent the strategy of this portfolio. They could be individual securities or various types of mutual funds representing this portfolio strategy. The intention is to hold these securities unless there is a good reason to sell and replace with a better choice. The Swing holdings are made up of liquid securities such as *exchange-traded funds* (ETFs) or other holdings that are not considered a part of the Core allocation. They may be in the same sector or style as the Core holdings or just index market exposure. The Inverse holdings are comprised of open-ended mutual funds or ETFs that are bear index funds that go up when the market goes down. I normally hold a small amount of cash in a portfolio in order to avoid over-expenditures in the trading process, which can involve various simultaneous transactions.

When your analysis of the market indicates that risk is increasing, you can move to a moderately defensive posture by starting to remove your Swing holdings. This does not have to be an all-or-nothing process. I usually tend to increase or reduce market exposure in several steps. If all of the Swing holdings had been removed, market exposure would have been reduced to 70 percent as indicated on the middle chart. If you are responding to a more bearish trend, then the Swing positions can begin to hold bear-type inverse funds. Nonleveraged bear funds could be the first response. If the 25 percent cash raised is reinvested in bear funds, then the net market exposure would be reduced from 70 percent to 45 percent. A full defensive posture could be achieved by using two-to-one leveraged bear funds. In this event, the net market exposure would be reduced to only 20 percent.

Remember, the risk management philosophy is to get an edge on the market; you don't have to be perfect in picking tops or bottoms. Swing positions can be actively traded. If the Swing positions are just a few holdings, like maybe two or three ETFs, it is possible to go from 95 percent invested to 20 percent invested with just a few trades, if leveraged inverse ETFs are used, while the Core holdings are untouched. By reducing the Core holdings to say 60 percent and having a 30 percent Swing holding, it is possible to go to a zero market exposure just as easily and still hold the 60 percent Core positions. That is a powerful risk management capability. Although the Inverse bear hedges may not be a perfect match for the Core holdings, they can still be effective in the risk management process. The key is to try *not* to have the big loss, because it ain't easy getting even!

Put options on ETFs that track key market indexes can be purchased to hedge a portfolio. This protects the downside but doesn't restrict the upside potential. The cost of the put is like the cost of an insurance premium. Of course, put options on an individual security rather than indices can be used to hedge a specific holding. Continuing to buy puts to hedge a portfolio is expensive if maintained over long periods of time.

A variation of hedging with options is the *synthetic short*, which is another hedging tactic that can be effective in the risk management process. A synthetic short is created when an at-the-money put option is purchased on a specific stock or index and at the same time a call option is sold on the same security. If the put-and-call combination are not on a security held in the account, this transaction must be done in a margin-type account with assets to cover the naked call position. However, little money is actually spent as the price of the put is usually close to the price of the call. If the option prices are out-of-the-money, this is also called a *collar*, with some range of security price movement between the put and call strike prices before one or the other option would be in-the-money. This is a rather sophisticated strategy that you need to research more before attempting to execute.

Volatility drag is something that affects all portfolio performance and it is especially something to be aware of when using leveraged inverse index funds to hedge. Let's take a portfolio of $100,000 and see how volatility drag works without any hedging when the market goes up and down 10 percent for five consecutive cycles. Table 5.6 shows three examples: no hedge, one-to-one non-leveraged full hedge, and two-to-one leveraged full hedge. The portfolio value at the end of each 10 percent move for the three examples is shown in Table 5.6.

This a highly hypothetical example, but it is an indication that shows the negative impact of volatility on portfolio performance. In the No Hedge example, after five complete cycles of plus and minus 10 percent, the $100,000 portfolio would have lost 4.9 percent. The portfolio with a one-to-one bear hedge ($100,000 long positions and $100,000 in an inverse bear fund) would have lost 4.9 percent in each holding or 4.9 percent of $200,000. The total portfolio loss in the two-to-one fully hedged $150,000 portfolio would be $4,900 on the long position plus $9,230 on the $50,000 leveraged bear fund for a total of $14,130 or 9.42 percent ($14,130/$150,000) of the total portfolio.

The key to the leveraged hedging is to rebalance the total position when there has been a significant move in one direction. For example, the same five up and down price swings of 10 percent with rebalancing each swing results in a zero loss from volatility. However, rebalancing, like most hedging activity, is helpful but not a precise remedy in practice.

Obviously, stocks and indexes don't go up and down exactly the same amount consistently. In a smooth advance or decline, volatility drag has much less of an impact. Also, in a rising market the bear hedge is declining in value, so that unless the position is rebalanced to cover the increased value of the long position, you have less hedge. However, in a declining market, the hedge is increasing in value, so it is more important to rebalance in my judgment, unless you desire to become increasingly net short.

Finally, just reducing market exposure and increasing cash in the portfolio is a simple and effective way to exercise risk management. In the topsy-turvy world of today, staying fully invested on the long side, regardless of market environment, can be financially unhealthy, especially if you want to protect your nest egg.

Table 5.6 Volatility Drag Illustration

No Hedge	+10%	-10%	+10%	-10%	+10%	-10%	+10%	-10%	+10%	-10%	Net Loss
$100,000	$110,000	$99,000	$108,900	$98,010	$107,811	$97,030	$106,733	$96,060	$105,666	$95,099	-4.9%
1×1 Hedge $100,000	90,000	99,000	89,100	90,010	88,210	97,030	87,330	96,060	86,450	95,100	-4.9%
2×1 Hedge $50,000	$ 40,000	$48,000	$ 38,400	$46,080	$ 36,860	$44,240	$ 35,390	$42,470	$ 33,970	$40,770	-18.46%

Simple or Complex Technical Analysis—Your Choice

The trend is your friend, unless it is about to reverse direction!

Technical analysis of stock and bond trends is not as difficult as you might think—especially if you want to protect your nest egg in cyclical to secular bear markets and ride through a short- to intermediate-term bear market. I will discuss some relative aspects of the simple approach, and finish up with the more complex approach that I have used since 1996. Robert Prechter, a noted and respected technical analyst and a strong advocate of the Elliott Wave analysis theory, brings additional perspective to the realm of technical market analysis in a later chapter of the book.

As discussed earlier in the "Myths" section of this chapter, there is no one perfect way to participate in the very serious concept of investing through technical analysis methods. If technical analysis piques your interest, then browse through the Traders Library web site and see the many books listed on technical analysis. In particular, I found William Jiler's *How Charts Can Help You in the Stock Market* to be a good basic presentation in a relatively thin book. Obviously, my goal is not to teach and inform you in one section of a chapter of all the aspects of technical analysis, but a few hints from my experiences can be helpful.

The beauty of technical analysis is that there are just five pieces of raw data that are real and precise, not biased or subjective. They are the *open, high, low,* and *closing* prices, along with the *volume* of trading for the time frame on which you are focused—minutes, days, weeks, months, and so on. These five pieces of information, presented in a time series, make up the database of all technical analysis systems. However, there are countless ways this information is massaged and formulated.

There are also only five basic methodologies that make up the framework for technical analysis. They are *trend lines, moving averages, oscillators, divergences,* and *patterns.* Trend lines and moving averages are self-explanatory. Oscillators are usually shorter-term moving averages that are not a continuous accumulation series—for example, the plot of only 10 days' moving average where each new day is added, and the oldest day from the series is removed from the total. These oscillators are useful in identifying oversold or over-bought market action based on historical trends in a specific data set. Divergences are typically used to identify changes in the rate-of-change in the relationship between two sets of data. Patterns range from classical price patterns, such as head-and-shoulders, ascending or descending triangles, and so on, to the Japanese candlestick concept, which shows the open, high, low, and close more visually over one to three successive time periods. The formation of candlestick patterns can be an indication of a pending change in direction.

I believe that "price is the final arbitrator of value" at any particular moment in time. That is, a buyer and a seller agree that for the transaction to take place they are willing to pay or receive, respectively, the agreed-upon amount. That is not the same as saying that the current price is the accurate reflection of future value, whether that is one minute, one day, or one year later, or whatever the timeframe.

Basic Low-Maintenance Risk Management

Unless you want to spend a lot of time in the market, it is best to keep relatively few mutual funds (open-ended, closed-end, or ETFs) that cover key areas and watch their 50-day moving average (or a moving average that best defines the lows during the bull phase over several previous intermediate-term price cycles). If the price of the fund in question is above the 50 day moving average (dma), you should be long. If the mutual fund (MF) price drops below the 50 dma, then sell the Swing position allocation. However, it normally is best to wait to see whether the price stays below 50 dma. Normally, it is best to see three days below before taking action. If the price quickly begins moving back toward the 50 dma, then wait to sell until the low price in the first three days is penetrated to the downside again. If it isn't and the price moves back above the 50 dma, then the original sell signal is negated until the price drops below the 50 dma again. Often, the 50 dma is penetrated for a few days and then the price continues the upward trend. This approach will help reduce whipsaws.

If the 50 dma turns down, then a more defensive posture is advisable. You may even want to be fully hedged or out of the market as long as the price is below a declining 50 dma. This won't necessarily get you out at tops and in at bottoms, but it should help in keeping you from taking the big loss in cyclical and secular bear markets. Actions on price moves above a declining 50 dma are often deceptive and quickly fail, so use your Swing allocation to reenter the market only until the 50 dma is once again rising. Keep in mind that this doesn't have to be an all-or-nothing process. For example, if the 200-day moving average is trending up, you may want to have a Swing position of only 30 to 50 percent. Don't worry about whipsaws where you may be buying back into your Swing position at prices above where you sold. That is just part of the risk management process. A free web site, www.stockcharts.com, provides access to technical charts with various technical indicators, including moving averages, for any security symbol you plug into their SharpCharts workbench.

Of course, you can place your assets with investment advisors who offer a risk management approach to investing. There are also numerous investment newsletters that offer advice and recommendations on portfolio management. Several of the ones we have subscribed to over the years have contributed chapters of this book discussing various aspects of investing.

The Five-Indicator Method

This is a real-time approach that I have used for many years that can also be applied without sophisticated computer programs. It doesn't require back-testing of a multiple-variable model. It tells you what is currently happening a little more quickly than the basic approach just discussed, so you can produce more timely buy and sell decisions. If you use daily data, you get more noise in your analysis and potentially more whipsaws. If you use weekly data, you usually get fewer and better intermediate-term signals. For most investors, I believe weekly data is the better choice. For this analysis, you want to use securities that also provide trading volume data—for example, ETFs rather than open-ended mutual funds that don't provide volume data.

The five indicators to analyze are the *price above or below a chosen moving average,* the *trend of the moving average, Granville's On-Balance Volume (OBV), Appel's Moving Average Convergence Divergence (MACD),* and *Wilder's Relative Strength (RSI).* These are well-known technical indicators that can be plotted on the charts provided at www.stockcharts.com.

Explanations of each can be found at www.investopedia.com. Each provides a particular technical metric indicating the direction or strength of the move for the security being analyzed.

I have my own proprietary method of weighting and evaluating the contribution of each of these five indicators to yield a buy or sell signal. You would have to develop your own methodology, but the point is that these five indicators give you enough technical information to make timely and informed risk management decisions. Basically, if three or more of these five metrics are positive, that could be a buy indicator; if three or more are negative, that could be a sell indicator. The number of days or weeks in the chosen moving average determines the cyclical time frame that you are interested in following. That is, the longer the length of time being considered, the less sensitive the analysis is likely to be to short-term volatility.

Complex Technical Analysis Approach to Risk Management

I have used a technical analysis software program called the OMNI Trader, developed by Nirvana Systems in Austin, Texas, since 1996 for the study of a broad range of financial market styles and sectors. In essence, this is a technical analysis toolbox that includes most of the technical tools and systems that have been developed by many different market players since time began. You can use one technical tool or system or use all of them and weight them differently. Users have to develop the analysis approach that they want to incorporate in their technical analysis of financial markets. It is a very sophisticated toolbox, and requires substantial time to tune to your investment style.

I follow thousands of mutual funds and individual financial securities daily with this program. The mutual funds are organized into specific styles and sectors, typically with 10 funds representing each style or sector. For example, there are 10 biotech funds, 10 banking funds, 10 energy funds, and so on. Altogether, 54 styles and sectors are followed. Each mutual fund receives a green light or a red light based on this technical analysis. If 60 percent or more of the funds in a style or sector have a green light, that style or sector could be attractive for investment allocation; if 60 percent or more have a red light, that would be an indicator for defensive action in that style or sector. My experience is that the validity of signals is improved with this majority-rule approach. It is sort of like polling results—the greater the number of data samples, the greater the accuracy of the results.

This chapter is not about discussing which styles or sectors currently have specific red or green lights. This could change the day after it is written. However, we have focused primarily on equity income securities, energy and natural resources sectors, and international investing during the two Internet eras we have previous discussed. This focus is not likely to change anytime soon. There have been two major bear markets since the beginning of 2000. There will likely be more as the nation works through the economic problems and excess in the marketplace.

America's New Role in the Shrinking World

The financial markets will act in such a way to fool the greatest number of intelligent participants at the most critical times!

As you can gather from previous comments in this chapter, global communications made possible through satellites and fiber-optic undersea cables, coupled with wireless signals and the magic of the Internet, are changing the world in profound ways. Now, for the first time in history, even the smallest, most remote habitations on the planet can have instant access to knowledge, technology, and capital. My three- and five-year-old great granddaughters have access to Mom's iPhone to play educational games. They maneuver it like they were born with it in their hands. I once saw an ad with the picture of an Asian worker in what looked like a rice paddy, pedaling a stationary bicycle to energize a battery hooked to an IBM laptop computer, presumably writing software code. I can travel most places in the world and connect to the Internet and conduct my portfolio management activities, in real time. It is amazing what has happened over just the past 100 years of human endeavor compared to the previous 10,000 years.

In the late 1960s, I was working as an aerospace scientist, and I told my dad, an Oklahoma farm boy in his youth and then a successful small business owner of a saddle and horse tack company, that shortly America was going to put a man on the moon. He looked at me as though my education had warped my mind and said, "That's impossible," and went back to tending his business. Today, I see technology about which, only a few years ago, I would have said, "That's impossible." I went through engineering school with only a slide-rule to do all the calculations required. The only place you are likely to see a slide-rule today is in a museum.

The Internet is the genie that has been let out of the bottle. Short of global nuclear war, or being hit by a giant asteroid that destroys humankind, this genie is not going back into the bottle. It means that America's post–World War II period—a generation or two of global dominance with essentially a monopoly on manufacturing, technology, and innovation—is waning. This is partly because America has become somewhat complacent, but mostly because the Internet doesn't allow monopolies on knowledge, technology, or innovation to exist for very long for anyone, anywhere, anymore. Thomas Friedman discussed this phenomena in his book, *The Flat World: A Brief History of the Twenty-first Century* (Farrar Straus and Giroux, 2005). However, I think of it as the "Shrinking World," where nowhere is very far away, especially with Google Earth at your fingertips and e-mail or fax to transmit documents of all sizes, shapes, and content.

The fall of the Berlin Wall in 1989 was a cultural spark that awakened the suppressed peoples of the world. The Internet has provided the means for their rapid ascendency to full participation in the global economies, and for now, they are willing to work hard for lower pay and standard of living than Americans have become accustomed to. That discrepancy will pass in time, but it could take a generation or more for equalization to occur. America is in the transition period of adjustment from being *the* superstar on the world scene to sharing that role with other emerging stars. This transition is inevitable, regardless of America's leadership. It is an evolutionary process, in my judgment. America's strength is a well-honed culture of individual freedom enhanced by a strong work ethic and innovative thinking that will continue to serve us well in a multi-star world.

Think of the class demographics from the post–World War II era up until around 1990, with America in the shape of a grapefruit, represented by the big dark circle, and the rest of the world in a pear shape, represented by the dashed lines in Figure 5.5. America had a small rich class at the top and a small poor class at the bottom and a massive middle class in between. Almost everyone

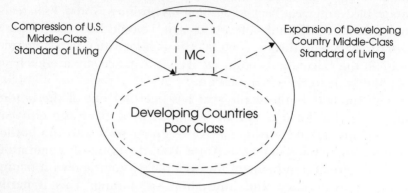

U.S. Class Demographics Post–World War II to 1990s

Compression of U.S.
Middle-Class
Standard of Living

MC

Expansion of Developing
Country Middle-Class
Standard of Living

Developing Countries
Poor Class

**Figure 5.5   Compression of America's Middle Classes
Is a Multigenerational Process Facilitated by Globalization
and the Internet**

could think of themselves as middle class of some sort: lower-middle
class, middle class, or upper-middle class. The dashed lines show
that most of the world had a very small rich class, and a small middle
class, made up primarily of technocrats such as attorneys, doctors,
merchants, engineers, and connected bureaucrats. The rest of the
population made up the poor class. Think of India, China, and
Eastern Europe, in particular, but many other nations also had the
pear-shaped demographic.

The Shrinking World environment is compressing America's
middle class so that it can no longer sustain a very high relative standard of living as a result of globalization and the Internet. At the
same time, the developing countries benefiting from globalization
and America's appetite for cheap consumer goods and energy are
expanding their middle class and elevating workers out of their poor
class. The PIMCO principals, Bill Gross and Mohammed El-Erian,
have labeled the economic ramifications of this environment for
America the "new normal." In reality, a lot of the new-normal aspects
such as lower secular economic and investment growth coupled with
higher underemployment have been in progress for many years,
during much of Internet Eras I and II.

The main culprit is the massive global debt that has been created
in an effort to keep consumers happy and living above their means.
Higher inflation, higher taxes, and plenty of defaults are the likely
and obvious outcome. Global defaults are already in progress. Higher

inflation and taxes are not far behind, in my judgment. It is going to take a lot of time to work through this global mess. The bipolar financial market trends are likely to persist far into the future.

The compression of America's middle classes has been in progress since the early 1970s. However, it has been masked by a couple of factors. From the 1950s through the early 1970s, a middle-class income from one family worker was usually sufficient to raise a family. The inflation of the 1970s reduced the purchasing power of this income as wage increases failed to keep up with the real inflation rate. So, two family members' incomes became the norm for Middle America to maintain the family's relatively high standard of living. This sufficed through the Great Bull Era of America's economic prosperity, 1982–1998.

Let's first explore the CPI adjustment in wages a little more to illustrate how modification in this index in itself has squeezed Americans, especially the middle class. When I left the aerospace industry in 1971, my annual salary was $16,500, which provided a good middle-class standard of living at the time. According to People History (www.peoplehistory.com), the 1971 average annual income was $10,500 and the average cost of a new home was $25,250. According to the Bureau of Labor Statistics (BLS), the CPI-adjusted salary of $16,500 now would have to be $87,453 or 5.3 times greater. An engineering placement professional told me that figure was in the ballpark of what engineers with a decade of experience can command, and maybe up to $130,000 (7.9 times) with an advanced degree, outstanding resume, and project management experience. You can go to www.Salary.com for a more extensive analysis of engineering salaries as a function of industry, location, education, and experience.

However, the CPI calculation methodology has undergone substantial changes in how it is computed relative to 1971. All of the CPI computation changes have helped to hold down the effect of actual inflation for the BLS-computed CPI, and consequently the cost-of-living adjustments for industry salaries and government entitlement programs. The Shadow Government Statistics (SGS) web site (www.shadowstats.com) chronicles these changes and computes an alternative CPI based on how the CPI was calculated in the 1970s. A comparable salary with the same purchasing power today, according to the SGS computation, would be $266,265 (16.1 times).

Even if you average together the BLS and SGS computations of the CPI, you come up with $176,859 (10.7 times) to have the same purchasing power. So, even $130,000 (7.9 times) today is still a substantial 26 percent loss of purchasing power and corresponding squeeze on a middle- to upper-middle-class standard of living. Although this is just anecdotal evidence, the prices of many common items I buy today are often 8 to 12 times or more higher than what I remember them to be in the early 1970s.

Since Internet Era I began in 1998, the outsourcing of jobs has increased and offshore manufacturing has also increased rapidly, to the further detriment of America's working middle class. The Internet Era also put downward pressure on the increase of middle-class incomes of the employed. To make up the difference, various forms of credit filled the gap. The rise in home prices allowed equity lines of credit to provide a personal ATM for homeowners. Of course, we know what the low interest rates and easy credit consequences have been. It has taken an unprecedented increase in government debt and involvement in private businesses to avoid a possible total collapse of the global financial system.

The easy credit and low interest rates promoted over the past decade or so by the Federal Reserve, Congress, and the Treasury have been an attempt to keep America's middle class happy even though the reality of globalization is that their relatively high standard of living is unsustainable in the real world of real incomes. For over a decade, America's grapefruit demographic has been becoming a little more pear shaped, and the developing countries' pear shape has been becoming more grapefruit-like. This global standard of living equalization process will probably take another generation or more to complete. Maybe the final world demographic will look more like an egg shape. Nevertheless, in free societies there will always be stratified demographics based on talent, work ethic, and contribution; that is the historic norm.

With regard to the present, the further attempts to increase public debt by orders of magnitude in order to provide increased entitlements is an unwise policy for the future of America, in my judgment. We have to learn to live within our means as a nation. Paying via the "magic wand" of being able to create the world's reserve currency with little constraint, as well as borrow substantial amounts from foreign investors to fund our excess spending, may not always remain an easy road for America to travel.

We need to focus on generating a robust jobs environment rather than entitlements. There is an economic concept called *comparative advantage* that basically contends that it is better to let someone else produce a product or service at a lower cost than you can, so that you can move up the food chain of productive employment to a higher standard of living. This has worked well historically as more-advanced nations could let less-developed nations with lower wages and technology capability take that role. However, this economic philosophy has taken a toll on the manufacturing workers of America over recent decades as various manufacturing workers and a growing number of information technology workers can attest.

The problem with the comparative advantage theory developed by David Ricardo in his 1817 book, *On the Principles of Political Economy and Taxation*, as discussed by economist Paul Craig Roberts ("Statement to the U.S.–China Economic and Security Review Commission," Washington, DC, December 25, 2003), is that in today's globalization- and Internet-driven mobility of knowledge, technology, and capital to all corners of the world, the theory may have limited applicability, when essentially everyone has the potential to move up that food chain of productivity. Even the high-technology-type jobs in America are now being outsourced. If your highest-technology jobs in engineering, finance, and science are subject to outsourcing, you are left with only hands-on local jobs. Trading high-paying jobs for low-paying jobs is not what "comparative advantage" was supposed to accomplish. It is not surprising that vocational training for hands-on jobs is making a comeback.

It seems that some outside-the-box economic thinking is needed that can show nations how to be self-perpetuating with less emphasis on import or export trade and a better balance of employment opportunities for their middle classes. The comparative-advantage approach seems to be running out of steam as a result of the Internet and globalization. Maybe American industry (foreign or domestic owned) needs to primarily make goods and provide services for Americans, Chinese industry (foreign or domestic owned) needs to primarily make goods and provide services for Chinese, Brazilian industry (foreign or domestic owned) needs to primarily make goods and provide services for Brazilians, and so on. The goal would be to grow domestic demand in line with domestic production with international trade at the margin and in relatively equal amounts between nations. Imposed protectionism is not likely to be the right answer.

A new economic model for a Shrinking World needs to evolve naturally, in my opinion. I would expect a simplified national tax policy that includes some form of national sales tax in order to incorporate the underground economy, as well as all Americans, into the national tax system. There should be less focus on income taxation as a part of a new economic model—maybe a single lower income tax rate for personal incomes above three times the median income, but no deductions for any expenses or charitable contributions. If an individual wants to live in a million-dollar home, there is no reason other Americans should help subsidize the expenditure by allowing interest to be deducted from income.

Corporate income taxes should be totally eliminated and replaced with a small revenue tax with no deductions for corporate expenses. If a corporate executive wants a Gulfstream aircraft, or a gleaming new office building, why should other American taxpayers help to subsidize the purchase? The national tax system with regard to corporations should be based on revenues, not profits. What a company spends would be between company management and the shareholders. These are just a few ideas that could greatly simplify the tax system. Others could be explored, but the current system is out of touch with today's realities, in my judgment.

America has primarily been trading its paper dollars for internationally produced goods and services as indicated by the enormous balance of trade deficit that has grown for decades. It will not be easy to break this cycle of foreign dependency to maintain our standard of living. It is more likely to be a forced withdrawal than a freely chosen course of action by America.

This nation was built on manufacturing; it can be revitalized through the reestablishment of all levels of manufacturing. Service jobs alone cannot support a vibrant middle class. Substantially lowering or eliminating the corporate income tax, which is one of the highest in the world, could attract more manufacturing back to the United States and help create good jobs faster and better than any other approach, in my judgment. When foreign companies can move production to America, such as some automakers and smaller manufacturers have been doing, and be profitable, there is a future for manufacturing in America, albeit at a lower cost of production than what supported the standard of living that middle-class Americans enjoyed for a couple of generations in the post–World War II era.

What does all of this have to do with investing? It puts into perspective the investment era environment that must be considered when choosing investment strategies. Although adversity is a mainstay of human endeavors, equity markets seem to endure and continue to provide investment opportunities. The ownership of assets often changes hands; some investors are successful and others are not. There are good times and bad. That is the nature of the free marketplace.

I believe that there is an enhanced need for flexibility and risk management in this particular investment era because the dynamics of the marketplace can now move at close to the speed of light and enormous amounts of capital can move at the push of a button. Jobs creation and the overhang of massive unfunded liabilities are serious problems to be solved. This means that volatility and very modest secular growth will remain for the foreseeable future, in my judgment.

However, the leverage in investment activity will be more constrained as a result of the recent credit debacle, and that is a positive. Existing financial market regulation will be more energetically enforced and needed regulatory improvement adopted, and that is a positive. To think that greed is a self-regulating aspect of human nature is nonsense, especially when it primarily involves risking other people's money.

Nevertheless, a big risk on the horizon that I foresee is the potential of the U.S. dollar being replaced as the world's reserve currency. This would take away America's magic wand, and this could change the nature of America's role in the Shrinking World overnight, with unpredictable consequences for the future of Americans. We need to get our national economic and financial house in order soon to avoid this potential outcome.

The comments and opinions presented in this chapter are solely those of Ron Miller and do not represent the positions or opinions of Morgan Keegan & Co., Inc. on any of the topics discussed. Data, computations, and analysis contained in this chapter are believed to be accurate and from reliable sources but their accuracy cannot be guaranteed. Additional information about Ron Miller and his current market commentary and the Investment Planning & Management Group services can be found on their web site (www.ipmg.mkadvisor.com).

CHAPTER

Conquer the Crash,
Condensed*

Robert Prechter

My first book, *Elliott Wave Principle*, which I wrote with A. J. Frost, was very bullish. It came out in November 1978, with the Dow at 790. Today the outlook is much different. Now is not the time to take financial risks. It's time to batten the hatches so you can emerge safe from the storm.

A Myth Exposed

How many times over the past decade have you heard glowing reports about the "New Economy"? Economists proclaim that economic growth in the new Information Age has been "unprecedented" in its vibrancy, resilience, and scope. Rhetoric is cheap. Evidence is something else.

What would you say if you discovered that *we have not had anything near a New Economy*, that all that talk is a lie?

Figure 6.1 summarizes a shocking fact: The economic expansion during wave V, which lasted from 1974 to 2000, was demonstrably weaker than that during the preceding rising phase, wave III, which

---

* The following material is excerpted from *Conquer the Crash* (John Wiley & Sons, 2002), by Robert Prechter, written three years before real estate prices peaked and the credit crisis began. Its content is still applicable today.

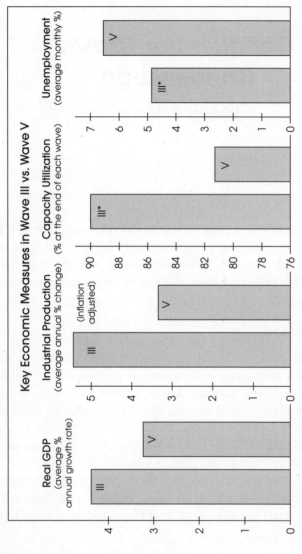

Figure 6.1 Economic Expansion Phases

Source: © 2002 Elliott Wave International; data courtesy of Federal Reserve Board.

lasted from 1942 to 1966. This tremendous bull market in stocks in wave V is the great "boom" that people feel in their bones. The economic vigor of wave V, the one that has received so much radiant press, failed to measure up to that of wave III by every meaningful comparison.

So you see, *it has not been a New Economy after all* but rather a comparatively lackluster one.

Economic Deterioration During the Final Decade of Wave V

The economic expansion waned not only on a long-term basis but also on a near-term basis, *within* wave V. For example, average annual corporate profit growth fell from *10.8* percent in the first 15 years of the bull market (1975 through 1989) to *8.8* percent in the 1990s. From the stock market's low in September/October 1998 through the third quarter of 2000 (the peak of economic performance for that period), profit growth averaged only *4.6* percent, revealing further slowing as wave V crested.

Portent of Reversal?

Collectively, these statistics reveal that economic growth in the United States has been slowing *at multiple degrees of scale.* The persistent deceleration in the U.S. economy is vitally important because, in my opinion, it portends a major reversal from economic expansion to economic contraction.

Similarly to today, the economy of the 1920s failed to keep pace with the advance in stock prices *and* underperformed the prior expansion. The aftermath was the Great Depression.

Depressions and the Stock Market

If you study Figure 6.2, you will see that the largest stock-market collapses appear *not* after lengthy periods of market deterioration indicating a slow process of long-term change but quite suddenly after long periods of rising stock prices and economic expansion. The abrupt change from increasing optimism to increasing pessimism initiates the economic contraction. If you are guessing that maybe one of the hints of reversal is a slowing economy in the face of such advances, you're right.

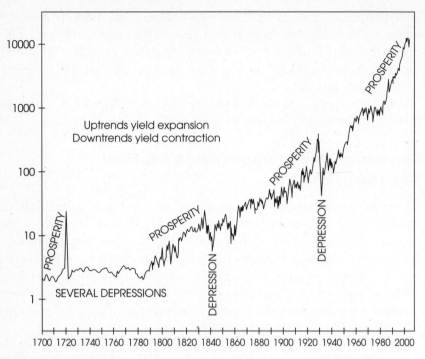

Figure 6.2   Economic Results of Major Mood Trends—British, Then American Stock Price Record, 1700–2002

Source: © 2002 Elliott Wave International.

What Are the Signs of a Topping Stock Market?

Simply stated, under a market model called the Wave Principle a stock market uptrend ends when five waves of a specific construction are complete. The larger the degree of those five waves, the larger will be the ensuing partial retracement of their progress.

To help overcome difficulty in real-world application, I recorded certain traits that waves seem always to display. Figure 6.3 illustrates some of these traits.

Figure 6.4 displays my interpretation of the stock market's wave position today.

The latter half of the past 60 years has seen deterioration both in the breadth of stock participation in the market's advance and, as already shown, in the long-term rate of economic progress. The degree of slowing—covering decades—confirms that the advance since 1974 is a *fifth wave*, which supports the wave labeling of Figure 6.4.

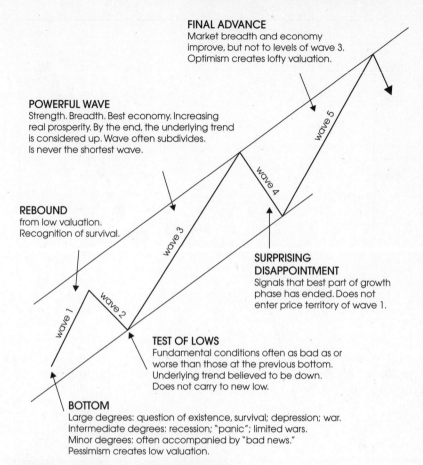

FINAL ADVANCE
Market breadth and economy
improve, but not to levels of wave 3.
Optimism creates lofty valuation.

POWERFUL WAVE
Strength. Breadth. Best economy. Increasing
real prosperity. By the end, the underlying trend
is considered up. Wave often subdivides.
Is never the shortest wave.

REBOUND
from low valuation.
Recognition of survival.

**SURPRISING
DISAPPOINTMENT**
Signals that best part of growth
phase has ended. Does not
enter price territory of wave 1.

TEST OF LOWS
Fundamental conditions often as bad as or
worse than those at the previous bottom.
Underlying trend believed to be down.
Does not carry to new low.

BOTTOM
Large degrees: question of existence, survival; depression; war.
Intermediate degrees: recession; "panic"; limited wars.
Minor degrees: often accompanied by "bad news."
Pessimism creates low valuation.

Figure 6.3   Elliott Wave Characteristics
Source: © 1980/2002 Elliott Wave International.

Historically High Stock Market Valuation

Figure 6.5 says that fifth waves produce "lofty valuation" for stocks.
In 2000, the Dow's dividend yield did something that it had never
done before. It reached a low of 1.5 percent. A larger index of
industrial stocks, the Standard & Poor's 400 Industrials, yielded
only 1 percent. This is historically high valuation.

Figure 6.6 displays the P/E ratio for the S&P 500 Composite
index from the mid-1920s to the present. The P/E ratio at the
end of December 2001 was 46, the highest *ever.* P/E ratios for
the S&P 500 have ranged from around 7 at bear market bottoms

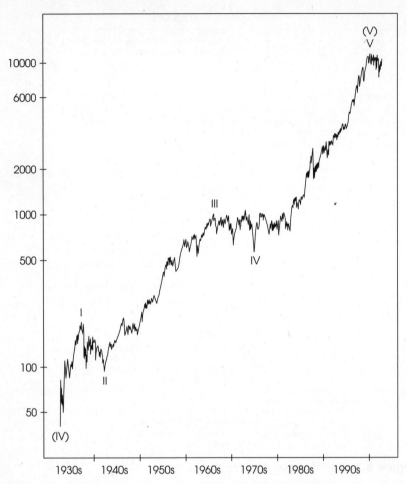

Figure 6.4   Supercycle Wave (V) DJIA Monthly Log Scale
Source: © 2002 Elliott Wave International.

to the low-to-mid 20s at bull market tops. So the S&P's P/E ratio today is twice what it is at a typical bull-market top and *six to seven times* what it is at a typical bear-market bottom. In other words, the S&P would have to fall about 85 percent to get its P/E to normal bottom levels, *and that's if earnings fall no further.* Earnings *will* fall in a bear market that size, so today's P/E ratios portend the same stock price debacle that is implied by the slowing in the economy, the stock market's wave structure, and the low dividend payout.

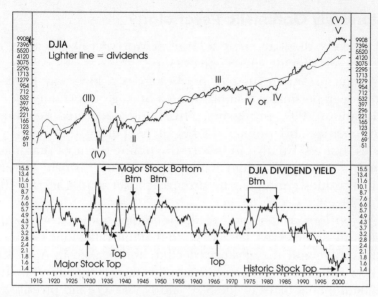

Figure 6.5 Stock Market versus Dividend Yield

Source: © 2002 Elliott Wave International; data courtesy of Ned Davis Research.

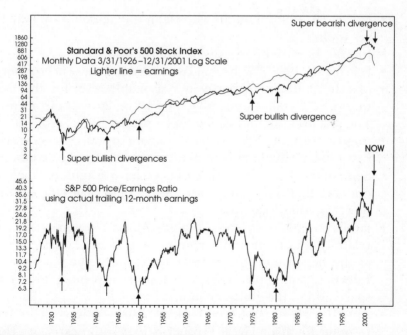

Figure 6.6 Major Trend Confirmation—Signals from P/E Ratio

Source: © 2002 Elliott Wave International; background chart courtesy of Ned Davis Research.

Historically Optimistic Psychology

Bull markets, they say, climb a "Wall of Worry." I like to add, "and bear markets slide down a Slope of Hope."

As you are about to see, psychology is a long way from the shared deep pessimism that produces a buying opportunity.

In about 1997, professors, PhDs, and decorated economists at universities and think-tanks began peppering the media with articles that essentially put before the public the idea that macro-economic science has lent its sanction to the historic extremes in stock values generated by the great asset mania of the 1980s and 1990s.

As you look at the dates of the following quotes from some of these professorial essays, keep in mind that the Value Line Geometric stock average and the advance/decline line peaked in April 1998, the Dow and S&P in gold and commodity terms topped in July 1999, and the nominal highs in the S&P and NASDAQ (and probably the Dow as well) took place in the first quarter of 2000. Here is what the experts have told us:

- March 30, 1998: "Pundits who claim the market is overvalued are foolish."
- July 30, 1998: "This expansion will run forever."
- February 3, 1999: "We have at last arrived in a new-era economy."
- March 19, 1999: "A perfectly reasonable level for the Dow would be 36,000—tomorrow, not 10 or 20 years from now. The risk premium is headed for its proper level: zero."
- August 30, 1999: "The recent dramatic upswing represents a rosy estimate about growth in future profits for the economy."
- September 18, 1999: "Researchers have found compelling evidence that conventional accounting understates the earning power of today's companies."
- January 1, 2000: "In much the way Albert Einstein's theory of relativity transformed the time-space grid of classical physics at the beginning of the twentieth century, the Einsteins of Internet communications are now transforming the time-space grid of the global economy."
- April 18, 2000: "Don't be fooled. Historical forces continue to point toward a Great Prosperity that could carry the Dow Jones Industrial Average to 35,000 by the end of the decade and 100,000 by 2020."

If this one-sided outpouring of scholarly judgment proves to be anything other than a manifestation of the prevailing optimistic mass psychology that crystallized after 7 decades of mostly rising stock prices and 2½ decades of dramatically rising stock prices, I will be mightily surprised.

In the aggregate, money managers are always most invested in stocks at tops and least invested at bottoms. Figure 6.7 shows how pension funds and insurance companies increased their percentage of stock holdings from 7 percent of total assets in 1952 to 53 percent on New Year's Day, 2000. Figure 6.8 shows the percentage of cash

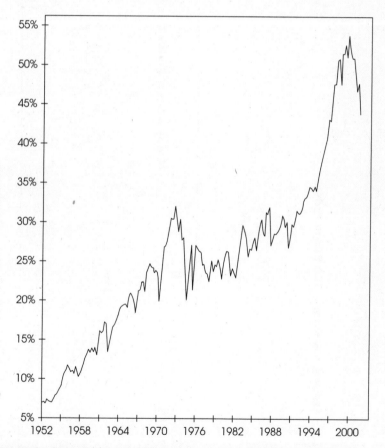

Figure 6.7 **Pension Fund and Insurance Co. Equity Assets as a Percent of Total Financial Assets**

Source: © 2002 Elliott Wave International; data courtesy of Federal Reserve Board.

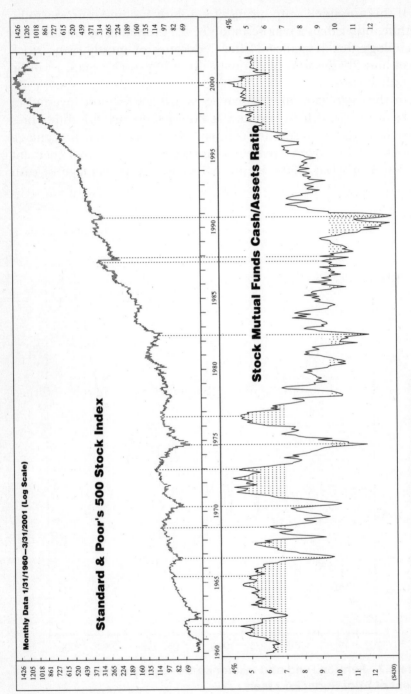

Figure 6.8   An Indicator of Professional Psychology

Source: Investment Company Institute; chart courtesy of Ned Davis Research.

that stock mutual funds hold in their portfolios. Again, they usually hold lots of cash at bottoms and little at tops. Needless to say, it would benefit their clients if they did the opposite. Needless to say, it can be no different.

The Next Psychological Trend

When the stock market turns back down, academics, economists, advisors, money managers, and media commentators will begin to turn bearish. Bad news will begin pouring out of the newspapers as a consequence of the emerging negative-mood trend. The more the market falls, the higher the number of bears will become, because enough time will go by that the trends not only of the present but also of the recent past will be down. The largest number of bears, public and professional, will be at the bottom.

How Far Will the Market Fall?

A mania is always followed by a collapse so severe that it brings values to *below* where they were when the mania began. This has been true of every mania, from the Tulip mania of the 1630s to the South Sea Bubble of the 1720s to the "Roaring" stock boom of the 1920s. The apparent reason for this outcome is that so many ordinary people entrust their fortunes to the mania that its reversal brings widespread financial distress, which feeds on itself to force an immense liquidation of investment media.

Therefore, the Dow should fall to below the starting point of its mania. That level is 777, the August 1982 low.

When Does Deflation Occur?

Deflation requires a precondition: a major societal buildup in the extension of credit (and its flip side, the assumption of debt). Austrian economists Ludwig von Mises and Friedrich Hayek warned of the consequences of credit expansion, as have a handful of other economists, who today are mostly ignored.

What Triggers the Change to Deflation

Near the end of a major expansion, few creditors expect default, which is why they lend freely to weak borrowers. Few borrowers expect their fortunes to change, which is why they borrow freely.

A trend of credit expansion has two components: the general *willingness* to lend and borrow and the general *ability* of borrowers to pay interest and principal. These components depend respectively upon (1) the trend of people's confidence, that is, whether both creditors and debtors *think* that debtors will be able to pay; and (2) the trend of production, which makes it either easier or harder *in actuality* for debtors to pay. So as long as confidence and production increase, the supply of credit tends to expand. The expansion of credit ends when the desire or ability to sustain the trend can no longer be maintained. As confidence and production decrease, the supply of credit contracts.

The psychological aspect of deflation and depression cannot be overstated. When the social mood trend changes from optimism to pessimism, creditors, debtors, producers, and consumers change their primary orientation from *expansion* to *conservation*. As creditors become more conservative, they slow their lending. As debtors and potential debtors become more conservative, they borrow less or not at all. As producers become more conservative, they reduce expansion plans. As consumers become more conservative, they save more and spend less. These behaviors reduce the "velocity" of money, that is, the speed with which it circulates to make purchases, thus putting downside pressure on prices. These forces reverse the former trend.

The structural aspect of deflation and depression is also crucial. The ability of the financial system to sustain increasing levels of credit rests upon a vibrant economy. At some point, a rising debt level requires so much energy to sustain—in terms of meeting interest payments, monitoring credit ratings, chasing delinquent borrowers, and writing off bad loans—that it slows overall economic performance. A high-debt situation becomes unsustainable when the rate of economic growth falls beneath the prevailing rate of interest on money owed and creditors refuse to underwrite the interest payments with more credit.

When the burden becomes too great for the economy to support and the trend reverses, reductions in lending, spending, and production cause debtors to earn less money with which to pay off their debts, so defaults rise. Default and fear of default exacerbate the new trend in psychology, which in turn causes creditors to reduce lending further. A downward "spiral" begins, feeding on pessimism just as the previous boom fed on optimism. The resulting cascade of debt liquidation is a deflationary crash. Debts are retired by paying them off, "restructuring," or default. In the first case, no value is lost; in the second, some value; in the third, all value. In desperately trying to raise cash to pay off loans, borrowers bring all kinds of assets to market, including stocks, bonds, commodities, and real estate, causing their prices to plummet. The process ends only after the supply of credit falls to a level at which it is collateralized acceptably to the surviving creditors.

Why Deflationary Crashes and Depressions Go Together

A deflationary crash is characterized in part by a persistent, sustained, deep, general decline in people's desire and ability to lend and borrow. A depression is characterized in part by a persistent, sustained, deep, general decline in production. Since a decline in production reduces debtors' means to repay and service debt, a depression supports deflation. Since a decline in credit reduces new investment in economic activity, deflation supports depression. Because both credit and production support prices for investment assets, their prices fall in a deflationary depression. As asset prices fall, people lose wealth, which reduces their ability to offer credit, service debt, and support production. This mix of forces is self-reinforcing.

The United States has experienced two major deflationary depressions, which lasted from 1835 to 1842 and from 1929 to 1932, respectively. Each one followed a period of substantial credit expansion. Credit expansion schemes have always ended in bust. The credit expansion scheme fostered by worldwide central banking is the greatest ever. The bust, however long it takes, will be commensurate. If my outlook is correct, the deflationary crash that lies ahead will be even bigger than the two largest such episodes of the past 200 years.

Can the Fed Stop Deflation?

Seventy years of nearly continuous inflation have made most people utterly confident of its permanence. If the majority of economists have any monetary fear at all, it is fear of inflation, which is the opposite of deflation.

Countless people say that deflation is impossible because the Federal Reserve Bank can just *print money* to stave off deflation. If the Fed's main jobs were simply establishing new checking accounts and grinding out banknotes, that's what it might do. But in terms of *volume*, that has not been the Fed's primary function, which for 89 years has been in fact to foster the *expansion of credit*. Printed fiat currency depends almost entirely upon the whims of the issuer, but credit is another matter entirely.

A defensive credit market can scuttle the Fed's efforts to get lenders and borrowers to agree to transact at all, much less at some desired target rate. If people and corporations are unwilling to borrow or unable to finance debt, and if banks and investors are disinclined to lend, central banks cannot force them to do so. During deflation, they cannot even *induce* them to do so with a zero interest rate.

Thus, regardless of assertions to the contrary, the Fed's purported "control" of borrowing, lending, and interest rates ultimately depends upon an accommodating market psychology and cannot be set by decree. So ultimately, the Fed does not control either interest rates or the total supply of credit; the market does.

In contrast to the assumptions of conventional macroeconomic models, people are not machines. They get emotional. People become depressed, fearful, cautious, and angry during depressions; that's essentially what causes them. A change in the population's mental state from a desire to expand to a desire to conserve is key to understanding why central bank machinations cannot avert deflation.

With these thoughts in mind, let's return to the idea that the Fed could just print banknotes to stave off bank failures. One can imagine a scenario in which the Fed, beginning soon after the onset of deflation, trades banknotes for portfolios of bad loans, replacing a sea of bad debt with an equal ocean of banknotes, thus smoothly monetizing all defaults in the system without a ripple of protest, reaction, or deflation. There are two problems with this scenario. One is that the Fed is a bank, and it would have no desire to go broke buying up worthless portfolios, debasing its own reserves to nothing. Only a government mandate triggered by crisis could compel such an action, which would come only *after* deflation had ravaged the system. Even in 1933, when the Fed agreed to monetize some banks' loans, it offered cash in exchange for only the very best loans in the banks' portfolios, not the precarious ones. Second, the smooth reflation scenario is an ivory-tower concoction that sounds plausible only by omitting human beings from it. While the Fed could embark on an aggressive plan to liquefy the banking system with cash in response to a developing credit crisis, that action itself ironically could serve to aggravate deflation, not relieve it. In a defensive emotional environment, evidence that the Fed or the government had decided to adopt a deliberate policy of inflating the currency could give bondholders an excuse, justified or not, to panic. It could be taken as evidence that the crisis is worse than they thought, which would make them fear defaults among weak borrowers, or that hyperinflation lay ahead, which could make them fear the depreciation of all dollar-denominated debt. Nervous holders of suspect debt that was near expiration could simply decline to exercise their option to repurchase it once the current holding term ran out. Fearful holders of suspect long-term debt far from expiration could dump their notes and bonds on the market, making prices collapse. If this were to happen, the net result of an attempt at inflating would be a system-wide reduction in the purchasing power of dollar-denominated debt, in other words, a drop in the dollar value of total credit extended, which is deflation.

The problems that the Fed faces are due to the fact that the world is not so much awash in money as it is awash in *credit.* Because today the amount of outstanding credit dwarfs the quantity of money, debt investors, who always have the option to sell bonds in large quantities, are in the driver's seat with respect to interest rates, currency values, and the total quantity of credit, which means that they, not the Fed, are now in charge of the prospects for inflation and deflation. The Fed has become a slave to trends that it has already fostered for 70 years, to events that have already transpired. For the Fed, the mass of credit that it has nursed into the world is like having raised King Kong from babyhood as a pet. He might behave, but only if you can figure out what he wants and keep him satisfied.

Endgame

The lack of solutions to the deflation problem is due to the fact that the problem results from prior excesses. Like the discomfort of drug addiction withdrawal, the discomfort of credit addiction withdrawal cannot be avoided. The time to have thought about avoiding a system-wide deflation was years ago. Now it's too late.

It does not matter how it happens; in the right psychological environment, *deflation will win*, at least initially. People today, raised in the benign, expansive environment of persistent advance from 1932, love to quote the conventional wisdom, "Don't fight the Fed." Now that the environment is about to change, I think that the cry of the truly wise should be, "Don't fight the *waves*."

Currency Hyperinflation

While I can discern no obvious forces that would counteract deflation, *after* deflation is another matter. At the bottom, when there is little credit left to destroy, currency inflation, perhaps even hyperinflation, could well come into play. In fact, I think this outcome has a fairly high probability in the next Kondratieff cycle.

Making Preparations and Taking Action

The ultimate effect of deflation is to reduce the supply of money and credit. Your goal is to make sure that it doesn't reduce the supply of *your* money and credit. The ultimate effect of depression is financial ruin. Your goal is to make sure that it doesn't ruin *you*.

Many investment advisors speak as if making money by investing is easy. It's not. What's easy is *losing* money, which is exactly what most investors do. They might make money for a while, but they lose eventually. Just keeping what you have over a lifetime of investing can be an achievement. That's what this book is designed to help you do, in perhaps the single most difficult financial environment that exists.

In a crash and depression, we will see stocks going down 90 percent and more, mutual funds collapsing, massive layoffs, high unemployment, corporate and municipal bankruptcies, bank and insurance company failures, and ultimately financial and political crises. The average person, who has no inkling of the risks in the financial system, will be shocked that such things could happen, despite the fact that they have happened repeatedly throughout history.

Being unprepared will leave you vulnerable to a major disruption in your life. Being prepared will allow you to make exceptional profits both in the crash and in the ensuing recovery. For now, you should focus on making sure that you do not become a zombie-eyed victim of the depression. Then, at the bottom, you can buy the home, office building, or business facility of your dreams for 10 cents or less per dollar of its peak value.

Countless advisors have touted "stocks only," "gold only," "diversification," a "balanced portfolio," and other end-all solutions to the problem of attending to your investments. These approaches are usually delusions. As I try to make clear in the following pages, no investment strategy will provide stability *forever*. You will have to be nimble enough to see major trends coming and make changes accordingly. What follows is a good guide, I think, but it is only a guide.

The main goal of investing in a crash environment is *safety*. When deflation looms, almost every investment category becomes associated with immense risks. Most investors have no idea of these risks and will think you are a fool for taking precautions.

Few people have the foggiest idea how to prepare their investments for a deflationary crash and depression, so the techniques are almost like secrets today. Here are a few steps that will make your finances secure despite almost anything that such an environment can throw at them.

Don't:
- Don't own stocks.
- Don't invest in real estate.
- Don't buy commodities.
- Don't invest in collectibles.
- Don't trust standard rating services.
- Don't presume that government agencies will protect your finances.
- Don't buy goods you don't need just because they are a bargain. They will probably get cheaper.

Do:
- Open accounts at two or three of the safest banks in the world.
- Invest in short-term money market instruments issued by the soundest governments.
- Own some physical gold, silver, and platinum.
- Have some cash on hand.
- If you are so inclined, speculate conservatively in anticipation of a declining stock market.
- Sell any collectibles that you own for investment purposes.
- If it is right for your circumstances, sell your business.
- Make a list of things you want to buy at much lower prices when they go on "liquidation sale."

For detailed instructions on how to protect yourself and profit from deflation and depression, please see Part Two of Robert Prechter's book, Conquer the Crash. *The brand new Second Edition includes updated contact information on safe banks, insurance companies, gold dealers, money managers, and Treasury-only money market funds. The book is available from all major online booksellers. For financial market commentary, visit elliottwave.com.*

CHAPTER 7

The Gone Fishin' Portfolio*

Alexander Green

I'd like to share with you my single best idea for investors seeking long-term capital appreciation.

It's an investment system that allows you to increase your returns, reduce your risk, do an end-run around mountainous Wall Street fees, and keep the taxman at bay, too. It's called the Gone Fishin' Portfolio. And it comes as close as anything I've seen to guaranteeing long-term investment success.

The strategy itself is battle tested. It's built on the most advanced—and realistic—theories of money management. And it works, beating the S&P 500 every year—with far less risk than being fully invested in stocks—for well over a decade.

Moreover, in the pages ahead, I'm going to do something almost unheard of. I'm going to show you—very specifically—where to put your money. And then I'm going to show you how to run it year after year. Once you've set up your portfolio as I suggest, managing it will take less than 20 minutes a year.

The Gone Fishin' Portfolio is based on an entirely realistic premise—that, to a great extent, the future is unknowable. So don't expect me to draw on my gift of prophecy and tell you what's going

---

*Portions of this chapter are excerpted from *The Gone Fishin' Portfolio: Get Wise, Get Wealthy . . . and Get On with Your Life* (John Wiley & Sons, 2008), by Alexander Green.

to happen to the economy, interest rates, the dollar, or world stock markets. (No one is more surprised than me how market action unfolds each year.) Nor will we ignore the investment clouds or pretend we have a system that has eliminated them. Instead, we're going to use uncertainty, make it our friend. In short, we're going to capitalize on it.

Yet we're also going to keep risk strictly limited. When it comes to running your money, there are plenty of potential pitfalls out there. In my experience, however, investors who wind up in retirement with an investment portfolio that won't support their chosen lifestyle have almost always fallen prey to one of four basic mistakes:

1. They were too conservative, so their portfolio didn't grow enough to generate the income necessary to meet their spending requirements.
2. They were too aggressive, so a significant percentage of their portfolio went up in flames along the way.
3. They tried—and failed—to time the market. (Confident they would be in for market rallies and out for market corrections, they ended up doing just the opposite much of the time.)
4. They delegated poorly, turning their financial affairs over to someone who didn't get the job done properly.

If your nest egg is lying in pieces late in life, you generally don't have the opportunity—or the time—to build another one. The consequences, both personal and financial, can be devastating.

Planning your financial future is a momentous responsibility. And while the Gone Fishin' Portfolio has a light-hearted name, it enables you to handle your serious money—the money you need to live on in retirement—in a serious way.

There are, of course, few guarantees in the world of investing. In fact, once you get beyond the risk-free world of Treasuries and certificates of deposit, there are virtually none. However, the Gone Fishin' Portfolio eliminates a number of major investment risks. And it will allow you to spend your time as you please. While others struggle to manage their money effectively, you'll be able to relax . . . play golf . . . go fishin' . . . travel the world . . . spend more time with your kids or grandkids . . . or just swing on a hammock in the shade with a glass of ice-cold lemonade. Because your investments will be on autopilot.

This is not just a strategy for today's markets, incidentally. The Gone Fishin' Portfolio is designed to prosper—and generate peace of mind—through all market environments. And it works. Investors who have put their money to work this way have enjoyed years of market-beating returns while taking less risk than being fully invested in stocks.

So let's get started.

The Unvarnished Truth About Your Money

The philosophy behind the Gone Fishin' Portfolio goes all the way back to 327 B.C., when perhaps the world's first great book was written: Plato's *Apology*.

According to Plato, the oracle at Delphi had pronounced Socrates the wisest man in Athens. No one was more astonished—or more disbelieving—than Socrates himself. He immediately set out to disprove the oracle by finding a wiser man.

He started by examining a politician with a reputation for great wisdom, and the ego to go with it. Not only was the old gentleman unable to validate his beliefs, but he resented Socrates' challenge to his authority. "So I left him," says Socrates,

> saying to myself, as I went away: Well, although I do not suppose that either of us knows anything really beautiful and good, I am better off than he is, for he knows nothing, and thinks that he knows; I neither know nor think that I know. In this latter particular, then, I seem to have slightly the advantage of him. Then I went to another who had still higher pretensions to wisdom, and my conclusion was exactly the same. Whereupon I made another enemy of him, and of many others besides him.

In the end, Socrates discovers that he is indeed the wisest man in Athens. Not because of how much he knows, but because he is the only one who understands how much he doesn't know.

Nowhere is this lesson in humility more valuable than in the world of investing. It comes as a surprise to many investors, but even the most experienced economists and analysts can't tell you how fast the economy is likely to grow, whether interest rates will rise or fall, or where the dollar is headed.

Each year, *The Wall Street Journal* polls 55 of the nation's leading economists to see what lies ahead for the economy, interest rates, the dollar, and other economic variables. Most of them are way off.

It's gotten to the point where even the *Journal*'s staff is in on the joke. Reporter Jesse Eisinger recently wrote, "Pity the poor Wall Street economist. Big staffs, sophisticated models, reams of historical data, degrees from schools known by merely the name of the biggest benefactor, and still they forecast about as well as groundhogs."

The world's greatest investors have always known this. For example, legendary fund manager Peter Lynch says, "If you spend 13 minutes per year trying to predict the economy, you have wasted 10 minutes."

Investment success begins with a strong dose of humility. Not just about your own knowledge but, just as importantly, the knowledge of various "experts." Consider yourself finally on the right track the day you say to yourself, "Since no one can tell me with any certainty what the economy or the stock market is going to do next year, how should I run my portfolio?"

Some would call this a confession of ignorance. In reality, it is the beginning of investment wisdom. In the financial markets, uncertainty will forever be your inseparable companion.

And that's okay. Successful money management is about the intelligent management of risk. You can't avoid risk or eliminate risk. You have to take it by the horns and deal with it.

Every investment choice entails risk. Even if you keep all your money in cash—not a terribly good idea, incidentally—you are taking the sizable risk that your purchasing power fails to keep pace with inflation.

However, history shows that over the long run you are well compensated for withstanding the vicissitudes of the financial markets. If, on the other hand, you seek stability in your investments first and foremost, your returns are guaranteed to be low. Investments in money market funds and certificates of deposit return very little after taxes and inflation. Over the past 80 years, T-bills have returned an average of only 3.8 percent per year. And sometimes cash returns are considerably worse. In 2009, for example, the average money market yield in the United States was approximately one-tenth of 1 percent.

Stocks, on the other hand, have given superior long-term returns. (Just not always in the short term.) Yet many investors are frightened of them. The market seems like a giant casino to them. But, over the long term, nothing could be further from the truth.

Stocks are not simply slips of paper with corporate names on them. A share of stock is a fractional interest in a business. When results are measured over long periods, nothing has rewarded investors better than owning a business—or a portfolio of businesses. That's why I call common stocks "the greatest wealth-creating machine of all time."

"What about the looming bear market?" some may ask. "Shouldn't we wait until the coast is clear?" Unfortunately, no one ever signals the "all-clear" in the stock market. At any given time, there are always factors out there that dim the outlook for stocks. And this has been true in spades, lately.

If you try to figure out when to be in the market and when to be out, you are engaged in market timing. This has a seductive allure. After all, when you look backward it's glaringly obvious when you should have been in the market and when you should have been out. Look forward, however, and it gets a whole lot tougher. All you see is a blank slate.

Market timers often concede their timing won't be perfect, but even missing some of the decline is better than enduring the whole thing, right? Wrong. To successfully time the market requires you to buy low, sell high, and then buy low again (while covering all spreads, trading costs, and capital gains taxes). Fail and you'll get left behind while the equity train rumbles on.

As Vanguard founder John Bogle once remarked, "I don't know anyone who's ever gotten market timing right. I don't even know anyone who knows anyone who's gotten it right."

And you don't have to outguess the market. Despite dramatic setbacks from time to time, over the long haul common stocks have historically beaten everything else through expansion, recession, inflation, deflation, and war. Waiting until the backdrop feels "safe" has not been a good method of achieving high future returns.

Of course, the market can always go lower than you think it will—and for longer than you think it will—before a major uptrend appears. For this reason, investors—as opposed to short-term traders—should not have money invested in stocks that they will need in less than five years. And even long-term investors should diversify beyond the stock market.

The Road to Financial Freedom

Harry Truman claimed that there is nothing new in the world but the history you don't know. And history clearly demonstrates that common stocks should provide the foundation of any portfolio designed to maximize total returns. So the next question is which stocks should you own? With the Gone Fishin' Portfolio the answer is simple: all of them. We're going to capture the performance of every major publicly traded company around the world.

And the easiest way to do this is through mutual funds. There are several advantages:

- *Diversification.* The risk of owning a portfolio of stocks is less than the risk of holding any one of the individual stocks.
- *Professional management.* Whether you own an index fund or an actively managed fund, there is a professional manager overseeing the portfolio.
- *Low minimums.* It takes a lot of capital to replicate the world's stock and bond indexes without using mutual funds.
- *Liquidity.* Mutual fund companies will allow you to redeem (sell) all or part of your shares on any day the market is open for trading.
- *Automatic reinvestment.* You can arrange for all your fund's dividends and capital gains to be automatically reinvested in the fund—or directed to other funds—without charge.
- *Convenience.* You can buy and redeem most fund shares online, by phone, or by mail.
- *Simplified record keeping.* You will receive regular statements showing the value of your account and any activity. At the end of each year, you'll receive the tax-reporting information you need, too.
- *Customer service.* If you have a question, a problem, or need to make changes to your account, you can call your fund's toll-free customer service line and get the help you need at no additional cost.

There are essentially two types of mutual funds: actively managed funds and index funds. With indexing, the fund manager attempts to replicate the return of a particular benchmark, such as the S&P 500. Index fund managers do not buy stocks and bonds that are not included in the benchmark. Active managers, on the other hand, try to outperform the benchmark by selecting the best-performing stocks or trying to time the market.

For this strategy we're going to use primarily index funds. Some readers may question why we would settle for the performance of an index when we can use a fund manager who swings for the fences. After all, people like Peter Lynch and John Templeton became household names by beating the indexes soundly over time.

However, most investors don't realize just how exceptional these men were. Investing in actively managed funds is a mug's game. Why? Because the overwhelming majority of actively managed funds fail to beat their benchmarks.

In *The Little Book of Common Sense Investing*,* David Swensen, chief investment officer of the Yale University Endowment Fund, reports that, "A miniscule 4 percent of funds produce market-beating after-tax results with a scant 0.6 percent (annual) margin of gain. The 96 percent of funds that fail to meet or beat the Vanguard 500 Index Fund lose by a wealth-destroying margin of 4.8 percent per annum."

Of course, some financial advisors simply shrug and tell you, "Don't buy the average funds. Buy the stellar ones." But there's the rub. Studies show that a fund that beats the market one year is no more likely than its competitors to beat it the following year.

When the fund industry prints its famous disclaimer, "Past performance is no guarantee of future results," they aren't just whistling "Dixie." When it comes to analyzing the performance of top-performing funds, past is not prologue. No wonder over half of all institutional monies are invested using indexing strategies.

One of the best ways to create the Gone Fishin' Portfolio is using Vanguard funds, with the lowest fees in the industry. Why are costs here so low? The Vanguard Group has more than $1.1 trillion in assets under management. Such a large asset base allows the company to enjoy economies of scale that—combined with its unique ownership structure—allow it to maintain its position as the lowest cost fund family in the industry.

Plus, its structure is unique. The company is owned entirely by its individual funds, and, ultimately, the shareholders. The profits

---

* John Bogle, *The Little Book of Common Sense Investing* (John Wiley & Sons, 2007).

of the entire company are distributed back to the funds themselves, and thus to you the investor. That means no fund family is likely to seriously challenge Vanguard's low-cost leadership.

Vanguard fees are only one-fourth of the industry average. Here are the annual expenses charged by Vanguard compared to the average fund in each asset class, according to Morningstar:

Fund	Vanguard Fee	Average Fee*
Small Cap Index	0.23%	1.43%
Emerging Markets Index	0.42%	1.83%
European Stock Index	0.27%	1.69%
Short-Term Bond Index	0.21%	0.97%
REIT Index	0.21%	1.48%
Inflation Protected Securities Fund	0.20%	0.92%
Pacific Stock Index	0.27%	1.70%
Total Stock Market Index	0.19%	1.13%
High Yield Corporate Bond Fund	0.26%	1.24%
American Century Global Gold	0.67%	1.53%

*Fund class average from Morningstar

Your Single Most Important Investment Decision

Now let's get down to brass tacks. There are six factors that determine the long-term value of your investment portfolio.

1. How much you save
2. How long your investments compound
3. Your asset allocation
4. Those assets' annual return
5. How much you pay in annual expenses
6. How much you pay in taxes

That's it. Whether you're investing $10,000 or $10 million, these are the determinants of your portfolio's future value.

Note that of these six essential factors, only one is completely beyond your control. Which one? Regardless of your level of expertise, you cannot control your portfolio's investment returns.

Yet it's the one factor that most investors spend their time fretting about. What is the stock market going to do? When will my bonds bounce back? Will gold continue to rally? You might as well ask what the weather will be like six weeks from now. Nobody knows.

"Of course nobody knows," some investors reply. "But you have to guess." No, you don't. That's just my point. The Gone Fishin' Portfolio is designed to eliminate the perpetual guessing game about what lies ahead for the economy and the markets. Instead, you accept what you don't know and can't control and focus on those things you *do* know and *can* control. Specifically, saving, compounding, asset allocation, expenses, and taxes.

Of these five factors we can control, the most important is your asset allocation. There's plenty of evidence to support this claim.

In the 1980s, Gary Brinson, a noted money manager and financial analyst, published two sophisticated studies in *Financial Analysts Journal*, analyzing the returns of pension fund managers. They clearly demonstrated that—over the long term—asset allocation accounted for over 90 percent of the total return of a diversified investment portfolio. The rest was due to other factors, including security selection and market timing.

These results—which have been confirmed by many other studies—are startling. It means that your chosen asset allocation is likely to be 10 times as important as security selection and market timing combined.

The goal of asset allocation is to create a diversified portfolio with the highest possible return within an acceptable level of risk. You achieve this by combining non-correlated assets, like stocks, bonds, and real estate investment trusts. Academics call it building an "efficient portfolio."

Unfortunately, when I talk to investors about asset allocation, they are often dismissive. Many of them say, "oh, I understand asset allocation. That means you should diversify. I do that already."

But asset allocation is more than diversification. If you own an S&P 500 index fund, for example, you are indeed broadly diversified. (After all, you own a piece of 500 different companies.) But you aren't properly asset allocated, because the S&P 500 only gives you exposure to U.S. large-cap stocks.

Other investors tell me they don't have an asset allocation. But, of course, they do. Everyone does. Even if all your money is in

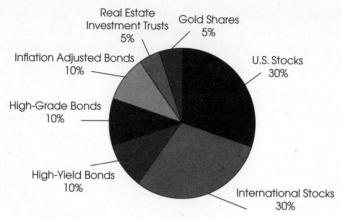

Figure 7.1   Asset Classes

Treasury bills, you have an asset allocation. It's not a particularly good one, however. It's 100 percent cash.

To determine your asset allocation, simply total up the value of all your liquid assets—stocks, bonds, mutual funds, and bank accounts—and then determine what percentage of your total portfolio is in stocks, bonds, and cash. Those percentages make up your basic asset allocation. (If you are uncertain which funds you own fall in which asset classes, contact the funds themselves. They'll be happy to tell you.)

The Gone Fishin' Portfolio takes things a step further. We have a basic asset allocation that is 70 percent stocks and 30 percent bonds. But we have a sub-allocation that is aggressive enough to boost your long-term returns and uncorrelated enough to reduce your risk.

Here are the asset classes we'll be using (see Figure 7.1):

1. *U.S. large-cap stocks.* Large-cap is short for *large capitalization.* (A company's market capitalization is calculated by multiplying the number of shares outstanding by the price per share.) Large-cap stocks are the biggest companies, typically ones with a market capitalization of $5 billion or more. Historically, they have returned an average of 11 percent per year. This category includes blue-chip household names like Intel, Coca-Cola, American Express, and General Electric.
2. *U.S. small-cap stocks.* Small-cap stocks are smaller companies, generally with a market capitalization that puts them in the bottom

20 percent of the New York Stock Exchange by size. Historically, they have returned 12 percent per year. These returns are slightly better than large-cap stocks, but the price of admission is higher volatility. During rocky periods in the market, small-cap stocks will make you feel like you've entered a bull-riding competition.

3. *European stocks.* Europe, of course, has both large and small companies, just like the United States. For the purposes of the Gone Fishin' Portfolio, we'll be using European large-caps.

4. *Pacific Rim stocks.* Here we'll be focusing on large-cap stocks, primarily in Japan, but also in Australia, Hong Kong, Singapore, and New Zealand.

5. *Emerging market stocks.* These are shares of the leading companies in developing markets, primarily in Latin America, Eastern Europe, and Asia.

6. *Precious metals mining stocks.* These are the world's largest gold mining companies. Many of them also produce silver, platinum, and industrial metals.

7. *Real estate investment trusts.* These are companies that trade like stocks but invest in commercial properties like shopping centers, hotels, apartment complexes, office parks, and warehouses. REITs qualify for preferential tax treatment by distributing more than 90 percent of their net cash flow each year.

8. *Short-term corporate bonds.* A corporate bond is a company's IOU, a debt security that represents a promise to repay a sum of money at a fixed interest rate over a certain period of time. Short-term bonds generally yield less than long-term bonds. (Although when the yield curve is inverted they may yield more.) Their shorter maturities make them less volatile than long-term bonds.

9. *High-yield bonds.* High-yield or "junk" bonds are corporate bonds that do not qualify for investment-grade ratings. These bonds pay higher rates of interest because the issuers are less creditworthy. Default rates are higher than on investment-grade bonds as well. (According to Moody's, the annual default for BB/Ba bonds is about 1.5%.)

10. *Inflation-adjusted Treasury bonds.* These are U.S. government bonds where the principal moves with inflation, as measured by the Consumer Price Index. The interest rate is

fixed, but if there's inflation (and you can bank on that), you earn that rate on a higher principal value, so your payments actually rise.

Each of these 10 asset classes has beaten inflation over the long haul. In any given year, of course, their returns will fluctuate and may occasionally be negative. However, it is reasonable to expect that the returns will be close to their long-term averages. Furthermore, by combining these assets together we can look forward to earning a handsome return without taking the risk of being fully invested in stocks.

As I mentioned before, these asset classes are not perfectly correlated. They don't necessarily move in the same direction at the same time. When some zig, others will zag. This actually smoothes out the bumps you'd otherwise see on your statements month to month—and year to year.

For instance, foreign stocks may be climbing when our domestic market is tanking. U.S. stocks and short-term corporate bonds are actually negatively correlated. That means these bonds are more likely to be rising if U.S. stocks are falling, and so on.

When you blend your portfolio among assets that give uncorrelated results, you take your first step toward what I call the "Holy Grail of Investing." Not because you'll generate eye-popping returns, although that may happen from time to time. The reason I call it the Holy Grail is because investing in a diversified portfolio of these assets will allow you to spend your time how you want, secure in the knowledge that you are using a sophisticated system that comes as close to guaranteeing long-term investment success as anything out there.

This is not just my opinion, by the way.

In 1990, the Nobel Prize in economics was awarded to Harry Markowitz, Merton Miller, and William Sharpe. They understood that financial markets are extremely efficient at pricing securities. (That means share prices reflect all material, public information about most companies, most of the time.) Markowitz's groundbreaking paper, "Portfolio Selection," published in the *Journal of Finance*, laid the groundwork for much of today's asset allocation strategies.

Although many of the concepts used by Dr. Markowitz are esoteric, he won the world's most prestigious award by showing investors how they can master uncertainty and, at the same time, generate excellent investment results.

Of course, Markowitz doesn't eliminate uncertainty, either. As I've said from the outset, no one can strip uncertainty from the investment process. What he did was develop a system that shows investors how to profit despite uncertainty.

Markowitz helped define and develop the *efficient frontier*, the point where you are generating the highest investment returns possible with the least amount of risk.

That's the Holy Grail: higher returns, less risk. Conventional wisdom says it's not possible. A Nobel Prize in economics—and decades of real-world experience—says it is.

The Gone Fishin' Portfolio Unveiled

There are two primary reasons we asset allocate. One is to increase returns. The other is to lessen the volatility of a pure stock portfolio. Remember, market volatility is not your biggest risk. Inflation is. Like a slow leak in your pool, it is gradually draining your purchasing power. You may not notice it in the short-term. But it's there in the long term, gnawing at the value of your portfolio like termites in an antebellum mansion.

If you shrink from risk and volatility and try to keep your money invested in Treasury bills, certificates of deposit, and other cash investments, inflation is likely to win. That means less purchasing power and a diminished standard of living.

Interest-generating investments are fine for setting aside an emergency fund or reaching short-term investment goals. But susceptibility to inflation makes them unsuitable for reaching your long-term investment goals.

By asset allocating properly, you can earn the returns you need without the hair-raising volatility of a 100 percent stock portfolio.

From personal experience, I know that many individual investors are unable to patiently ride out the inevitable downturns in the stock market. They become emotional. They get impatient. That's why it makes sense to diversify a portion of your investment portfolio into assets that are not highly correlated with stocks. For the Gone Fishin' Portfolio, those alternative investments are real estate investment trusts and three different types of bonds. These are assets that won't move in sync with the broad market.

Let's take a moment to examine them in a little closer detail.

A real estate investment trust (REIT) is a company that derives its revenue from the management of commercial property. Think of a REIT as a mutual fund made up of hotels, office parks, apartment buildings, shopping centers, or warehouses. Ordinarily, you may find commercial properties like these difficult investments to make, provided your last name isn't Trump or Rockefeller.

These trusts make it possible. A big part of our return will come in the form of dividends since REITs are required to pay out over 90 percent of their net income to shareholders each year to avoid paying corporate income taxes. These trusts have historically returned 8 percent a year, a little less than stocks. But they return more than bonds and don't move in unison with either stocks or bonds. So, again, they will reduce the overall volatility of your portfolio.

Now let's turn to bonds. When you purchase an individual bond, you're actually lending money to the issuer. When you do, you're promised a return on your investment that is the bond's yield to maturity and the return of the face value of the bond (usually $1,000) at a specified future date, known as the maturity date.

The maturity date may be as far off as 30 years or less than a year. In essence, a bond is simply an IOU, a promissory note that pays interest (usually every six months) until maturity.

Over the long haul, bonds don't generally return as much as stocks, although they have on occasion. (However, you'd have to go back to the period from 1831 through 1861 to find a 30-year period when the return on either short- or long-term bonds exceeded the return on equities.) The primary benefit of bonds is that they have a low correlation with stocks. So they have a stabilizing effect on your portfolio.

As I mentioned before, our Gone Fishin' Portfolio will use three types of bonds: short-term corporate bonds, high-yield bonds, and inflation-adjusted Treasuries.

Corporate bonds offer fixed interest payments over time. That payment does not vary with the profitability of the firm. We are using corporate bonds instead of Treasuries because they pay more. In fact, by buying high-grade, short-term corporate bonds you can essentially get the same returns as long-term government bonds without the volatility of long-term bonds. As long as we're using bonds to reduce the swings in our portfolio, why not choose the less volatile alternative?

High-yield bonds, also called non-investment-grade bonds, are also corporate bonds. These are bonds rated BBB- by the rating agency Standard & Poor's. They are issued by companies less credit-worthy than those that issue investment-grade bonds and are considered speculative. But don't let the name "junk bond" throw you. A diversified portfolio of these bonds, even after accounting for defaults, has returned more than either Treasuries or high-grade corporates. And while they do tend to be more highly correlated with the stock market than most bonds, they do not move in lock-step with equities, giving you some diversification advantage.

Inflation-adjusted Treasuries, more commonly referred to as TIPs, are the only bonds that guarantee you a return over and above infla-tion. TIPs pay interest every six months, just like a regular T-bond. But, unlike traditional bonds, your principal increases each year by the amount of inflation, as measured by the consumer price index (CPI). Semiannual interest payments also increase by the amount of inflation. The interest you receive is exempt from state and local (but not federal) income taxes. And like other Treasuries, your investment is backed by the full faith and credit of the U.S. government. TIPs are less volatile than traditional bonds. And they are great portfolio diversifiers because they tend to rise when traditional bonds—as well as stocks—are falling.

So we'll make good use of bond funds in our Gone Fishin' Portfolio. But we won't overdo it. As I said, stocks are the greatest wealth-creating machine of all time. So, our Gone Fishin' Portfolio will have greater exposure to stocks than bonds.

But we're taking human nature into account, as well. It takes nerves of steel—something lacking in most mortals—to place your liquid net worth in a 100 percent stock portfolio and ride out severe bear markets, especially as your portfolio grows in value. So we're going to balance our volatile stock holdings with investments that will reduce the volatility of the portfolio as a whole.

Although you could create the Gone Fishin' Portfolio with virtu-ally any fund family that offers each asset class, here is how you could implement the strategy using low-cost Vanguard mutual funds:

- *Invest 15 percent of your portfolio in the Vanguard Total Stock Market Index (VTSMX).* This fund will capture the return of U.S. large-cap stocks, as the fund's benchmark is the Dow Jones Wilshire 5000 Index, a stock index that includes all NYSE and AMEX stocks as well as the most active over-the-counter stocks. (This index is considerably broader than either the Dow Jones Industrial Average or the S&P 500.) The fund holds a blend of both growth and value stocks. Its expense ratio is 0.19 percent (compared to 1.12% for the average large-cap stock).

- *Invest 15 percent of your portfolio in the Vanguard Small Cap Index (NAESX).* This fund will capture the return of U.S. small-cap stocks. Its benchmark is the Russell 2000 Index, a stock index that measures the performance of the smallest 2,000 companies in the Russell 3000 Index of the 3,000 largest U.S. companies. Like the Vanguard Total Stock Market Index, it holds a blend of both growth and value stocks. The annual expense ratio is 0.23 percent (compared to 1.42% for the average small-cap fund).

Next, we move to international stocks, where our Asset Allocation Model suggests you have another 30 percent of your portfolio invested. Again, we're dividing our investment into separate parts—rather than investing in a single diversified international fund—because the movement of these different assets is often uncorrelated. (This lack of correlation will reward us when we make our annual adjustment to the portfolio, which I'll describe in just a moment.)

- *Invest 10 percent of your portfolio in the Vanguard European Stock Index Fund (VEURX).* This fund's benchmark is the MSCI Europe Index, an index that measures the performance of stocks in more than 15 developed European markets. It holds both growth and value stocks. The annual expense ratio is 0.27 percent (compared to 1.69% for the average European stock fund.)
- *Invest 10 percent of your portfolio in the Vanguard Pacific Stock Index Fund (VPACX).* This fund's benchmark is the MSCI Pacific Index, an index that tracks stocks from developed markets in Asia, Australia, and other parts of the Pacific Rim. It too holds both growth and value stocks. The annual expense ratio is 0.27 percent (compared to 1.69% for the average Japan and Asia stock fund).
- *Invest 10 percent of your portfolio in the Vanguard Emerging Markets Stock Index Fund (VEIEX).* This fund captures the return of major equity markets in Latin America, Eastern Europe, and

Southeast Asia. This fund's benchmark is the Select Emerging Markets Index. The fund assesses a 0.5 percent fee ($5 per $1,000 invested) on purchases. This is not a load. The fee is paid directly to the fund. The fund also assesses a 0.5 percent fee on redemptions. This fee, too, is paid directly to the fund and is not a load. The annual expense ratio is 0.42 percent (compared to 1.83% for the average diversified emerging market fund).

- *Invest 5 percent of your portfolio in the Vanguard Precious Metals and Mining Fund (VGPMX).* This fund's benchmark is the MSCI Gold Mines Index. The fund assesses a 1 percent fee ($10 per $1,000 invested) on sales of shares held less than one year. (Again, not a load. As a long-term shareholder you benefit from all the short-term traders who absorb this cost when they cash out of the fund in less than 12 months.) This fund closes to new investors from time to time.

Now let's turn to real estate investment trusts (REITs). As I mentioned earlier, these are trusts that allow investors to own an interest in commercial properties, including shopping centers, office parks, hotels, warehouses, industrial centers, and apartment complexes.

REITs offer several benefits over traditional real estate. They are highly liquid, trading on an exchange like a stock. They allow an investor to own a diversified portfolio of properties in a single investment. They also tend to pay sizable dividends, since the law requires them to pay out over 90 percent of their annual net cash flow to avoid corporate taxes. They also have a fairly low correlation with the stock market, making REITs a great portfolio diversifier.

- *Invest 5 percent of your portfolio in the Vanguard REIT Index Fund (VGSIX).* The fund is based on the MSCI U.S. REIT Index. The fund assesses a 1 percent fee on sales of shares held less than one year. The annual expense ratio is 0.21 percent (compared to 1.47% for the average REIT fund). (Here, too, Vanguard assesses a 1% fee on sales of shares held less than one year.)

Now let's move to the fixed-income side. We know that bonds return less than stocks over time. But they also provide balance and reduce risk in your portfolio. Our Asset Allocation Model suggests you have 10 percent of your portfolio in high-grade bonds,

10 percent in high-yield bonds, and 10 percent in inflation-adjusted Treasuries.

- *Invest 10 percent of your portfolio in the Vanguard Short-Term Investment Grade Fund (VFSTX).* The fund's benchmark is the Barclays U.S. 1- to 5-Year Credit Index. This is an index of corporate and international dollar-denominated bonds with maturities of 1 to 5 years. The annual expense ratio is 0.21 percent (compared to 96% for the average short-term bond fund).
- *Invest 10 percent of your portfolio in the Vanguard High-Yield Corporate Fund (VWEHX).* This fund's benchmark is the Barclays U.S. Corp High Yield Index. This index includes mainly intermediate-term corporate bonds with credit ratings at or below Ba1 (Moody's) or BB+ (Standard & Poor's). (Most of the fund's holdings are generally below investment grade.) The annual expense ratio is 0.26 percent (compared to 1.24% for the average high-yield bond fund.) The fund assesses a 1 percent fee on sales of shares held less than a year.
- *Invest 10 percent of your portfolio in the Vanguard Inflation-Protected Securities Fund (VIPSX).* The fund's benchmark is the Barclays U.S. Treasury Inflation Protected Index. The fund's holdings have an average duration of 6.1 years. The expense ratio is 0.2 percent (compared to 0.92% for the average inflation-protected bond fund).

Each of these funds has an initial investment minimum of $3,000 and a subsequent investment minimum of $100. (See Table 7.1.)

Table 7.1   Gone Fishin' Portfolio Annual Returns

Year	GFP	S&P 500
2003	32.7%	28.6%
2004	15.2%	10.8%
2005	11.9%	4.9%
2006	16.9%	15.8%
2007	10.7%	5.4%
2008	−31.7%	−37.0%
2009	34.3%	23.4%

Since there are 10 funds that make up our Gone Fishin' Portfolio, this means you will need a minimum of $30,000 to get started. (If you're a small investor and can't meet this minimum, don't despair. I'll propose an alternative that will allow you to use the Gone Fishin' strategy starting with smaller amounts.)

Once you've set your portfolio up this way, there is still a step you'll need to take, one that will take less than 20 minutes each year. It's called *rebalancing*, and it's a vitally important part of our strategy.

Here's why. As you're aware, every fund in the Gone Fishin' Portfolio represents a specific percentage of your total portfolio. But over time, those percentages will change significantly, depending on the performance of the financial markets. For instance, bonds may finish the year higher, and stocks may be lower. Inflation-adjusted Treasuries may have appreciated, and gold mining shares may have fallen, and so on.

The job of rebalancing is to bring your asset allocation back to your original target percentages. This prevents your being overinvested in any one area. Over the years, rebalancing will also deliver a significant performance boost. Why? Because it requires you to reduce the amount you have invested in outperforming asset classes and add to those that have underperformed. Since all assets move in cycles, rebalancing forces you to sell high and buy low.

There are essentially two ways to rebalance. You can add new money to those funds that have fallen below your target asset allocation. Or you can simply redeem part of those funds that have risen above your target percentages and add the proceeds to those that have declined below your target percentages. It's as simple as that.

When should you do this? You should do it approximately once a year. The exact date that you do it is not important. But there needs to be an interval of at least a year and a day between each time you set your portfolio and rebalance.

Why? First, you'll avoid paying short-term capital gains taxes by waiting at least a year and a day. (The long-term capital gains rate is a maximum of 15%. Short-term capital gains taxes, on the other hand, can be as high as 35%.) Second, you'll avoid paying the 1 percent redemption fee imposed on investments held less than a year in the Vanguard High Yield Bond Fund, Vanguard Real Estate Investment Trust Index Fund, and Vanguard Emerging Markets Index Fund.

Again, unless your investments are held entirely in a qualified retirement plan—like an IRA or 401(k)—where a fund redemption is not a taxable event, it's preferable to rebalance your portfolio by adding money to lagging funds.

Adding to those sectors that are down sounds simple enough. But I can tell you from working with hundreds of investors that most have a strong compulsion to add to those asset classes that are performing best, not those that are performing worst. Long-term investors need to fight this instinct and think like Ebenezer Scrooge instead. Forget what the hot assets are doing. You want to buy what's cheapest because of the long-term advantage it confers.

As investment great John Templeton has said, "To buy when others are despondently selling and to sell when others are avidly buying requires the greatest fortitude and pays the greatest reward."

Don't thwart the power of this strategy by succumbing to the temptation to buy more of your winning funds. Given enough time, each asset class will experience a down cycle. That's when you'll add to them—when they're cheap and out of favor, not when they're popular and expensive.

A perfect example is the recent bear market from October 2007 to March 2009. Those who stepped up and bought stocks as they were being trashed were handsomely rewarded as the market made a historic rally off the bottom.

The beauty of our rebalancing strategy is that it provides you with a clear discipline of when to sell and what to sell. Remember, it's impossible to predict which asset class will be the best or worst performing in any given year.

By adding to the lagging assets, you may occasionally feel like you're throwing good money after bad. Rest assured, you're not. Research from Ibbotson Associates conclusively demonstrates that the strategy of rebalancing reduces the level of portfolio risk in both market upturns and downturns. More importantly, Ibbotson found the reduction in risk is greater during market downturns.

In short, the Gone Fishin' Portfolio requires you to take only one action a year, rebalancing. But it is essential to maximizing your returns. (Studies show that annual rebalancing can enhance portfolio returns about 1 percent a year.) So do it. And keep doing it, year after year. It will both reduce your risk and increase your returns. Plus, it helps instill the discipline required for investment success.

The Proof Is In the Pudding

The proof of any investment system, of course, is the actual results it delivers over time. And here the Gone Fishin' Portfolio has shined, beating the S&P 500 every year since I created it seven years ago.

Figure 7.2 shows a summary of its year-by-year performance.

The numbers speak for themselves. Moreover, this strategy removes three layers of risk—active manager risk, individual security risk, and high expenses—that could potentially derail your retirement plans or cause you to fail to meet your investment objectives.

If you are unable to access Vanguard funds in your portfolio or can't meet their investment minimums, there is another alternative: *exchange-traded funds* (ETFs).

ETFs are essentially mutual funds that trade on an exchange, like a stock. Here's what exchange-traded funds offer:

1. Unlike ordinary mutual funds, which can be bought or redeemed only at the day's closing price, ETFs have an exchange listing and trade continuously throughout the day.
2. They are linked to an index rather than actively managed (although the index may use an active rather than a passive strategy).
3. ETFs are more tax efficient, too. You should experience little or no unexpected pass-through capital gains.

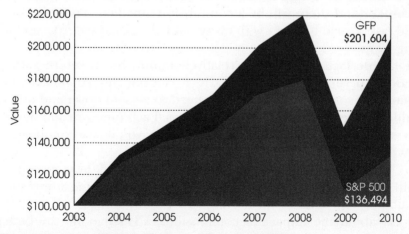

Figure 7.2   Gone Fishin' Portfolio versus S&P 500

However, there are drawbacks with ETFs to consider, too. For example, the market price and the net asset value of an ETF can diverge temporarily. You could wind up buying a fund at a premium to its net asset value or selling it at a discount.

Two things keep the net asset value and market price from straying too far apart, however. First, since the NAV is often quoted intra-day, traders who spot the discrepancy can immediately buy or sell ETF shares to exploit the difference. In this way, self-interested investors keep the market prices close to net asset values.

Clearly, ETFs have many benefits. And there is an ETF for every asset class in our Gone Fishin' Portfolio. For some investors, these ETFs could provide advantages over traditional Vanguard mutual funds. For others, the Vanguard funds (or some other no-load group) are the better choice.

The first thing to consider in evaluating whether ETFs are right for you is the cost ratio. I've already written about the paramount importance of running your portfolio like Ebenezer Scrooge. Using no-load index funds instead of actively managed funds can cut your average annual costs from 3 percent to around 1.5 percent. By using Vanguard funds, you can lower them to around 0.25 percent.

Using ETFs, however, you can halve even that amount to around 0.12 percent. Still, there are a few disadvantages to consider, too—brokerage commissions, for starters. Trading an ETF is like buying or selling a stock. The order must be placed through a broker and there will be a commission attached. There is also a bid/ask spread to cover with every publicly traded security, including ETFs.

These factors may seem relatively minor. But if you're adding money to your portfolio regularly, it can add up. At rebalancing time, too, some of your ETFs may need to be sold down and others added to, resulting in more transactions. Each time you add money to your portfolio or change its composition, you'll face commissions on the transactions.

No-load mutual fund companies like Vanguard, by comparison, will charge you nothing for transactions. Still, for those investing amounts too small to meet Vanguard's minimums or too large to worry about the impact of commissions, ETFs may be the better alternative.

Here's how you could construct the Gone Fishin' Portfolio using ETFs alone:

The Gone Fishin'ETF Portfolio

Index	Fund	Symbol	
MSCI® U.S. Broad Market Index	Vanguard Total Stock Market	VTI	15%
MSCI® U.S. Small Cap 1750 Index	Vanguard Small-Cap	VB	15%
Barclays Capital U.S. Treasury Inflation Protected Securities Index	iShares Barclays TIPs	TIP	10%
Amex Gold Miners Index	Market Vectors Gold Miners	GDX	5%
MSCI Emerging Markets Index	Vanguard Emerging Markets	VWO	10%
MSCI® U.S. REIT Index	Vanguard REIT	VNQ	5%
iBoxx $ Liquid High Yield Index	iShares iBoxx High Yield Corporate Bond	HYG	10%
Barclays Capital U.S. Aggregate Bond Index	Vanguard Total Bond Market	BND	10%
MSCI Pacific Index	Vanguard Pacific	VPL	10%
MSCI Europe Index	Vanguard European	VGK	10%

The total annual expense ratio for this ETF portfolio is only 0.21 percent. That's rock bottom.

So the choice is yours. You can create the Gone Fishin' Portfolio using mutual funds or ETFs. (The asset allocation is exactly the same.) Or you can create it using a combination. If the Vanguard Precious Metals and Mining Fund is closed to new investors—as it is now, for example—you can always buy the Market Vectors Gold Miners Fund and invest the rest in Vanguard funds.

The key to this strategy is to allocate properly, keep taxes and operating costs to a minimum, and rebalance regularly. It doesn't get much simpler than that.

With far less risk than being fully invested in stocks, the Gone Fishin' Portfolio has beaten the S&P 500 each year, gaining more than the market when it was up and declining less when it was down.

I've also back-tested the portfolio through the 2000–2002 bear market and even back to January 1, 1998. (We can't go back further than that because one investment in the portfolio—inflation-adjusted Treasuries—were only created by the U.S. government in 1997.)

The annual results can be verified easily and independently. The Gone Fishin' Portfolio has beaten the market, not just over the entire period but every year.

Is there any guarantee that this will continue to be the case in the future? Of course not—no strategy could guarantee that. Yet I know of no other investment system that offers a higher probability of long-term investment success.

To summarize the advantages of the Gone Fishin' Portfolio:

- It has beaten the market and over 90 percent of investment professionals each year for more than a decade, with only a fraction of the risk of being fully invested in stocks. (Even Warren Buffett has lagged its performance.)
- It allows you to do a complete end-run around Wall Street and its mountain of fees.
- It is based on the only investment strategy that won the Nobel Prize in Economics.
- Yet it is so simple to use, it allows you to manage your money in just 20 minutes a year. The rest of the time you are encouraged to travel, play golf—or just go fishin'.

Better still, this strategy completely eliminates your five biggest investment risks:

1. It eliminates the risk of being in or out of the stock market at the wrong time.
2. It keeps you from handling your money too conservatively, so you don't have to worry about shortfall risk.
3. You won't be too aggressive, so you don't have to worry about your portfolio self-destructing.
4. It doesn't require you to own individual stocks or bonds. So there is no possibility of company-specific disasters—like Enron, WorldCom, or Bear Stearns—causing your portfolio to crater.
5. It eliminates the risk of unwise delegation.

Despite its many advantages, the portfolio will not go up every year. During especially poor years for the stock market, it is likely to decline (although it has historically always fallen less than the S&P 500).

Of course, some investors complain that that's not good enough. They want a system that gives great returns in both good years and bad. Ironically, that's exactly what Bernie Madoff was promising.

So let's get real. As market commentator Richard Russell puts it, the winner in a bull market is he who makes the most; the winner in a bear market is he who loses the least. By that realistic standard, our returns have been more than satisfactory, and should be for many years to come.

For more complete information on this strategy—including various ways to tax-manage the portfolio—you may want to pick up a copy of my book, *The Gone Fishin' Portfolio: Get Wise, Get Wealthy . . . and Get On with Your Life* (Wiley, 2007).

And please remember that time, not money, is your most precious resource. It is perishable, irreplaceable, and, unlike money, cannot be saved.

The beauty of this investment system is that it allows you to redirect your time from worries about money to high-value activities, whether that's work you enjoy, time spent pursuing your favorite activities, or just relaxing with your friends and family.

In *The Pleasures of Life*, Sir John Lubbock writes, "All other good gifts depend on time for their value. What are friends, books, or health, the interest of travel or the delights of home, if we have not time for their enjoyment? Time is often said to be money, but it is more—it is life; and yet many who would cling desperately to life, think nothing of wasting time."

The Gone Fishin' Portfolio gives you a superb opportunity to grow your wealth. But it *guarantees* you more time to devote to the people and pastimes you love.

Perhaps that is what recommends it most.

CHAPTER 8

How You Can Profit from Chaostan*

Richard Maybury

An economic system is the result of its legal system.

My newsletter, *U.S. & World Early Warning Report for Investors (EWR)*, uses the two fundamental principles of the old English Common Law as the basis of its legal model. These principles can be expressed in 17 words: Do all you have agreed to do, and do not encroach on other persons or their property. These two laws are taught by all religions. They are "common" (Common Law) to all.

In the absence of these laws, the only possibilities are tyranny or chaos. Genuine liberty and free markets are not possible, because contracts and property rights are not protected.

Chaostan is the most important area that never developed legal systems based on these laws. *Chaostan* (pronounced "Chaos-tan") is the term I coined in 1992 for the land of the Great Chaos.

In other words, at bottom, there are only three possible political conditions—liberty, tyranny, and chaos. All political systems are variations of these three.

The inhabitants of Chaostan have no heritage or understanding of liberty (how many Americans still understand the system of liberty?), so, in Chaostan there are only two possibilities: tyranny or chaos.

---

* Portions of this chapter are excerpted from the *U.S. & World Early Warning Report* by Richard Maybury.

Washington has been removing the tyranny, throwing this third of the world into chaos, and making it into a factory for mass-producing new enemies.

The area from the Arctic Ocean to the Indian Ocean and Poland to the Pacific, plus North Africa, Chaostan contains thousands of nations, tribes, and ethnic groups who have hated and fought each other for centuries. Washington has long meddled in nearly every quarrel in Chaostan, and on 9/11 its enemies began extensive retaliation.

For centuries, Chaostan, and especially Russia, has had tyranny. Now the area is deeply into chaos. I think chaos is more frightening, so these hundreds of millions of people will soon be begging for a return to tyranny, as the Germans were in the 1930s. Chaostan is headed for a new plague of wars, and the wars will affect the global economy and our investments profoundly.

In my November 1997 *Early Warning Report*, I ran the article, "Our Frightening Heap of Profits." This explained that the mountain of investment gains we earned from the Chaostan model during the 1990s was certainly nice but it was not good news. It meant the model was correct and Chaostan was about to come unglued.

And, so it has. Russia has slid into fascism, wars have broken out in Iraq, Afghanistan, Pakistan, and many other places, the tension between Israel and Iran is growing, Sudan and Somalia are catastrophes, China is beset by uprisings, and so on.

Now we will watch the drama unfold further, and collect the even bigger profits that will pour down on us when the oncoming inflation and global monetary crisis are full roar.

I am 95 percent confident the Chaostan model is correct, so I have that much confidence that the next decade will bring mountainous profits in weapons stocks, security equipment stocks, and natural resources including gold, silver, platinum, and oil.

Geopolitical Threats (from the April 2009 *Early Warning Report*)

The October and November 2001 *EWR*s predicted that the war would wreck the economy: "The war will dominate the Federal Reserve's monetary policy, congressional fiscal policy, business and consumer confidence, business and consumer spending, money demand, velocity, and nearly every other important economic force."

That has clearly come to pass. At bottom, today's economic crisis is the result of the federal government inflating the supply of the world reserve currency, the U.S. dollar, to pay for the war.

Now, on February 12, the new director of national intelligence warned that the top threat facing the United States is international upheaval caused by the global economic turmoil.* I think he's right.

It's what happened in World War II. The Great Depression of the 1930s impoverished and radicalized populations until they were willing to follow Hitler and other lunatics into world war.

Is history truly repeating? Here's the story.

Riots, Strikes, and Large Demonstrations

Riots, strikes, and large demonstrations have broken out in Britain, Bulgaria, China, France, Germany, Greece, Iceland, Latvia, Lithuania, Russia, and even Switzerland.†

Here are, in my opinion, the biggest threats to American security, in order of importance, with #1 being the most serious.

1. Washington's Closed-Mindedness.   Eliot A. Cohen of Johns Hopkins University was Counselor to the Department of State in 2007–2008. He recently wrote of his experience in government: "My first, sobering observation is that government pays only intermittent attention to talk on the outside. To a remarkable extent, in fact, government talks only to itself. . . . Government resembles nothing so much as the party game of telephone, in which stories relayed at second, third or fourth hand become increasingly garbled as they crisscross other stories of a similar kind."‡

In other words, in regard to *understanding* what is happening in the world, once a person is in power, he is out of the loop. He listens only to other members of the government, each of whom has his or her own personal agenda and pushes whatever analysis serves that agenda.

Obama makes no secret of the fact that he plans to escalate the war in Afghanistan and Pakistan—despite . . .

---

* "Global Economy Top Threat . . .," *New York Times*, February 12, 2009.
† "Popular Rage Grows . . .," Spiegel Online, February 9, 2009.
‡ "How Government Looks . . .," Eliot A. Cohen, *Wall Street Journal*, January 23, 2009, p. A15.

2. The Growing Failure in Iraq.   Many times in the 1990s, I pointed out that Iraq is an artificial country cobbled together by the British after World War I. The only person ever able to control its fractious groups was Saddam Hussein.

The Bush administration invaded Iraq and got rid of Hussein, but then failed to change Iraqi leaders into Patrick Henrys and James Madisons. It also failed to convert the Iraqi population into Sons of Liberty and Minutemen—big surprise.

Now the place is as fractious as it has ever been, and the three main groups—Shiites, Sunnis, and Kurds—hate each other bitterly.* Shiites are the majority, and dominate the south, which isn't far from the Shiite areas of Saudi Arabia, which contains oceans of oil.

Iraq is one of the most corrupt nations in the world, and the country has become a loose confederation of feudal states ruled by local gangsters.[†]

The only way the Bush gang could "win" the war was by putting a collection of Hussein clones in power, which they did. It's been years since I've heard anyone say something good about Iraq's leaders (or Afghanistan's). The best I've heard is, yes, they're crooks, but they're our crooks.

That's true, but the first Saddam Hussein was U.S. property, too, until he decided not to be. We no longer have one Saddam Hussein, we have dozens, and an unknown number of them are in bed with the government of Iran.

The Iraq war is not over. The only thing that has ended is Chapter One. To keep the frogs out of its new backyard swimming pool, Washington stocked the pool with sharks.

Look at a globe. Iraq and Iran together dominate the Persian Gulf, which reportedly contains two-thirds of all the oil in the world. And, Iraq's economy is a wreck. An estimated 28 percent of young males are out of work, and until oil goes back above $100, that's likely to worsen. Sixty percent of the Iraqi labor force "works" for the government.[‡]

In short, the place is like Germany in 1933, a political and economic cesspool ripe for a Hitler.

---

* "Take Them Home . . .," *Economist*, March 7, 2009, p. 17.

[†] "War-Hit Nations Head Corrupt List," BBC web site, September 23, 2008; "Biometrics Give . . .," *Defense News*, April 28, 2008, p. 30.

[‡] "Iraq's Young Jobless Threaten Stability . . .," *L.A. Times* web site, February 16, 2009.

None of this comes as a surprise to longtime readers of *EWR*, but, judging by his speeches, Obama thinks the Iraq "surge" worked. That's why in Afghanistan and Pakistan he is using the same policy as in Iraq, sending more troops to back any cutthroat who claims to be pro-United States.*

3. Pakistan.   Pakistan has long earned my vote as the single greatest danger in the world.

The government of Pakistan is a collection of professional ding-a-lings who own scores of nuclear weapons. This while Obama continues the Bush policy of bombing their western region (near Afghanistan), and plans to escalate the war there. The phrase "throwing lit matches at a powder keg" hardly seems adequate.

Pakistan is no more a real country than Iraq or Afghanistan. Like them, it's a patchwork of feudal states. There isn't even a real government in the sense that Americans think of one. It's a collection of factions who have their own policies and obey orders from the top only when they are in the mood. One faction is known to have spread nuclear weapons know-how to the regimes in Iran, North Korea, and Libya.[†]

In February, a popular former prime minister told a crowd to "Rise and revolt!"

EWR has long said Pakistan is the single biggest loose cannon on the planet. Now, as the economy grows worse, and as Obama puts more Pakistanis in his bombsights, we may find out just how loose that cannon is. This is another (nuclear-armed) country ripe for a Hitler.

4. China.   Since the Federal Reserve went into operation in 1914, the U.S. government has created trillions of fiat paper dollars out of thin air.

In the 1980s, China was undergoing a vast transformation, adopting some aspects of capitalism. U.S. officials knew full well that their phony dollars were flowing to the Chinese, who were amateurs at modern finance, and naïve.

The injections of dollars helped produce the great Chinese boom. The Chinese business model became: Work hard producing valuable goods and services, then sell them to a counterfeiter.

---

* "U.S. Courts Former Warlords . . .,"*Wall Street Journal*, March 20, 2009, p. 1.
[†] "Are Pakistan's Nuclear Weapons Safe?," BBC web site, January 23, 2008.

I don't think the Chinese knew what was happening to them until they were ensnared in the scam and awash in malinvestment. Instead of taking the depression that would be necessary to shake out the malinvestment, officials decided to keep quiet and go along with the scam. Today, in my opinion, nearly all of Chinese industry is malinvestment.

This insane scheme had to go bust eventually, and now it's happening. China is facing its worst financial crisis in a century, and I think the violence will likely be some of the bloodiest in world history; 670,000 small and medium-sized firms have closed.* Millions of unmarried young males roam the country jobless, and riots have broken out. This was predicted in my 7/05 and 2/06 articles about Ogs, Berserkers, and China's young male population. I suggest you review them.

According to the *New York Times* web site article entitled "Dragons, Dancing...," there were a reported 120,000 riots, strikes, and protests in 2008.

President Hu Jintao has asked the army to remain loyal.[†] Interesting; why would he feel the need to do that?

For the first time since the 15th century, the Chinese navy is operating along the Arabian Peninsula, near the oil-rich Persian Gulf (ostensibly to fight pirates). Hundreds of missiles line the Chinese coast facing Taiwan.[‡]

According to the Federation of American Scientists web site, China's arsenal of nuclear warheads could number as high as 2,000.

5. Russia.   The Russian nuclear weapons stockpile is reported to number at least 5,000, but no one except Russian rulers truly knows. And the rulers may not know, either. Russian accounting and inventory controls during the Soviet era were somewhere between awful and nonexistent, so no one has any idea how many nuclear weapons Russia is supposed to have or how many are missing.

What we do know is that Russia is one of the most corrupt countries in the world, and the theft and selling of everything including military items is routine.

---

* "China Crisis as Economy Crumbles," London *Independent*, March 6, 2009.
† "China Prepares to Clamp Down . . .," London *Independent* web site, February 22, 2009.
‡ "What Lies," *Economist*, January 24, 2009, p. 46.

In 2000, fascist Vladimir Putin became president, and the huge economic expansion that followed was bankrolled by the high energy prices. Russia is a chief producer of oil and gas. Now the energy boom has slowed, the protests have begun, and, opines Garry Kasparov in the *Wall Street Journal*, "there is ample evidence suggesting that the Putin regime is teetering toward collapse."*

I think it is highly unlikely the Russian social and political matrix—and control of the nuclear weapons—can stay intact unless we see a huge rise in energy prices.

Kremlin officials surely feel great pressure to find a secret way to wreck their chief competitor, the Persian Gulf.

In short, the country is already fascist, and every day looking more like Germany in the 1930s.

There's a lot more trouble brewing all over the world, but I think you get the picture.

If an unbiased observer from Mars were to lay the geopolitical situation of 1938 beside that of 2009, he would surely pick 2009 as the more dangerous. Yet, the mainstream press, fixated by the domestic economic crisis, and by sports and entertainment, says almost nothing about the hurricane that is forming.

East Europe—the Baltics (from the May 2009 *Early Warning Report*)

The psychology in Russia today is alarmingly similar to that of Germany in the 1930s: We have been impoverished and humiliated, and we will support anyone who restores us to our former greatness.

Putin desperately needs to make a comeback, and surely knows that if Hitler had stopped with Austria, Czechoslovakia, Poland, and Hungary, the Führer today would probably be regarded not as a madman but as one of the top leaders of the 20th century. German National Socialism would be called a great success.

In the 8/06 and 9/06 *EWR*s, I gave a lengthy explanation of conditions in Russia, and predicted that the Kremlin would first make a move in the former Soviet state of Georgia, then the Baltics.

In July 2008, the Russian Bear moved south, invading Georgia. Instead of taking a none-of-our-business attitude, Bush and NATO

---

* "Beware of . . .," Garry Kasparov, *Wall Street Journal*, March 5, 2009, p. A17.

stamped their feet at the beast. Putin thumbed his nose back and, of course, got away with it, so now he is undoubtedly looking west. I think the Baltics, beginning probably with Latvia, are next on his menu.

The Baltics are members of NATO. They are in deep economic trouble, and militarily weak. Putin knows it. He also knows the west Europeans are all bluff and are distracted by their own economies.

One of the Kremlin's oldest ploys is to secretly foment trouble in a country, then invade it for the purpose of "stabilizing" it.

Riots have broken out in Latvia and Lithuania.

Investors, watch the Baltics. If the Kremlin does make a move there, this will be one more excuse for Congress to pour money into the weapons industries I wrote about [in April 2009].

Also, raw materials including precious metals tend to do well during geopolitical turmoil, so a big blowup would multiply the profitable effects of the coming inflation.

Piracy (from the February 1998 *Early Warning Report*)

In the February 1998 *EWR*, I began writing about piracy. In that article, and many times thereafter, I warned that a feature of the approaching war between Washington and its Islamic enemies would be Muslim pirate attacks on ships traveling through the South China Sea, Indonesia, Bay of Bengal, Indian Ocean, Arabian Sea, Gulf of Aden, and Red Sea. I was widely regarded as having lost my marbles. Piracy? Today? In the modern world? Pirate attacks now are common in all those areas.

The piracy is caused mostly by gun controls. Civilian vessels are forbidden by international law to carry serious weapons,* because mistakes might happen. These ships are, therefore, nearly helpless, sitting ducks.

Since civilian vessels are required to be vulnerable, the whole burden of maritime defense falls on navies, which are spread so thin that the pirates can operate with near impunity.

The oceans are huge, and are used by 50,000 large vessels, plus millions of smaller ones. All the navies of the world combined could not possibly police them.

---

* "Old and New Threats: Piracy and Maritime Terrorism," www.southchinasea.org.

The U.S. Navy has 283 warships, of which only 153 are surface shooters.* This is much more than any other navy, and far more than enough to defend America, but it's pathetic for controlling a global empire.

In the widely televised April 2009 incident off Somalia, the Navy tasked a frigate, destroyer, and amphibious warfare ship—2 percent of their total surface shooter force—to save one man.

Of course, the rational approach would be to tell civilian ship crews they have the right to protect themselves, but I see little possibility of that happening. We live in a world where helplessness is considered a virtue—because, if people have the means to defend themselves, something bad might happen.

Persian Gulf (from the January 2007 *Early Warning Report*)

For more than a decade, I've pointed out that the key to understanding the whole mess in the Persian Gulf is to realize that Iran is Persia, and Persians are not Arabs. Persia owned the Persian Gulf for more than 2,500 years until the governments of Britain and the United States stole it from them in the 20th century. In a wholesale violation of the principle "do not encroach on other persons or their property," London and Washington gave most of the Gulf and its oil to their puppet Arab regimes on the west side.

Washington is and always has been fundamentally in the wrong to be in that area at all. The U.S. Navy unwittingly admits this when it refers to the Persian Gulf as the Arabian Gulf—we stole it, it's ours, so we have the right to rename it.

Look at it this way. Suppose a hundred years ago, a foreign government, say the Kremlin, had sent troops and warships into Chesapeake Bay, and established puppet governments in Virginia. The Kremlin then gave much of the Bay to these puppets. And, suppose today these puppet dictatorships backed by the Kremlin were still there. How would Americans feel? Would they *ever* stop fighting to evict these puppets and their foreign backers, and take back Chesapeake Bay?

The Persian Gulf belongs to Persia. Give it back, and buy the oil from them.

---

* "U.S. Navy Active Ship Force Levels," www.history.navy.mil/branches/org9-4 .htm#2000.

The Long-Term Outlook for the Mideast

Of course, Washington has far too much pride to do that, so no American alive today is likely to see the end of war in the Persian Gulf.

Investors should plan for a wartime economy for the rest of their lives, meaning an endless series of tax hikes, inflations, financial crises, booms in investments that do well in wartime, and the withering of those that don't.

As Washington and Tel Aviv now rush headlong toward war with Iran, a new juggernaut is quietly arising in Iraq. I think the Persian Gulf is much closer to total chaos than the investment markets realize.

The Gulf reportedly contains two-thirds of all the oil in the world. I could be wrong, but I'm sticking with my forecast. The evidence is very strong that in "real" (inflation-adjusted) terms, sometime in the next decade—probably earlier rather than later—we will see $300-per-barrel oil and $9-per-gallon gasoline.

If that forecast turns out correct, then practically any non-Chaostan energy investment is a bargain at today's prices.

The Coming War with China (from the June 2000 *Early Warning Report*)

A recent *Wall Street Journal* editorial expressed the prevailing view of China: "Beijing, for all its backwardness on such issues as religious freedom and human rights, is at least following a promising economic course . . . capitalism."*

This is a highly naive and dangerous view, and it masks a big threat that is now emerging. Here's the story.

I have often pointed out—most recently in the 1/00 *EWR*—that most of today's geopolitical strife is the result of Europe's past conquests of nearly the whole world. To understand what China's rulers are likely planning for the near future, we must understand what European rulers did to China over the course of three centuries.

China has an ancient tradition of distaste for foreigners, regarding them as barbarians, as most were, compared to the Chinese. China is one of the oldest civilizations; it had compasses and cast

---

* "Why It Would Be a Mistake . . .," George Melloan, *Wall Street Journal*, May 16, 2000, p. A27.

iron 10 centuries before Europe. The custom of shunning foreigners was made official policy in 1433 when China's rulers banned contact with the outside world. They burned the Chinese exploration fleet and sealed the records of the fleet's discoveries.

Just because you are paranoid it doesn't mean they aren't out to get you. In 1669, Russians invaded Chinese territory, beginning a long series of European and Japanese attacks on the Chinese.

The Chinese have never attacked or even threatened to attack Europe, but by 1897, most of China had been overrun and conquered by European invaders—carved up like a Thanksgiving turkey.

Here is a partial list of cases in which Europeans left their homes and sailed 13,000 miles to fight with the Chinese:

War Begins	Invaders
1840	Britain, France
1857	Britain, France
1860	Britain, France
1894	Japan
1897	Britain, Japan, Germany
1898	Britain, France, Japan
1900	Britain, France, Germany, Japan, Russia, United States
1911	Britain, France, Japan
1926	Britain, France, Japan, Portugal, Spain, Holland

Thanks to the Europeans and Japanese, the Chinese loathing of foreigners turned out to have been well founded. Further invasions of China by Japan during the two world wars reinforced these feelings.

After World War II, Washington's alliance with Japan and backing of Chiang Kai-shek, who murdered 10.2 million Chinese,[*] added fuel to the fire. Then, Clinton's (accidental?) bombing of the Chinese embassy in Serbia [in 1999] was, in the minds of many Chinese, the last straw.

---

[*] *Death by Government*, R.J. Rummel, Transaction Publishers, New Brunswick, 1994, p. 8.

Thanks to Washington's military alliances with Japan and Europe, the Chinese tend to paint America with the same brush as they paint Japan and Europe. It may not be much of an exaggeration to say they see us as savages with rocket launchers. If you were them, how would you see us?

Today an integral part of Chinese culture is the assumption that China has a score to settle with the outside world. The power junkies in Beijing have built on this assumption and made no secret of their desire to annex surrounding territories. They have recently taken Hong Kong and Macao, and clearly intend to take Taiwan. In 1996, they announced annexation of the entire South China Sea, and have placed military bases in the Spratly Islands.

Reinforcing Beijing's claims is the fact that waters around China have names reflecting China's ancient ownership of the area: the East China Sea, the Yellow Sea, and the South China Sea. Also, the peninsula to the south containing Vietnam, Laos, Thailand, Cambodia, Malaysia, and Burma is called Indochina.

Notice that Beijing's warlike intentions have little to do with "communism" or any other ideology. This is a vendetta and it goes back centuries. Communism, in China and elsewhere, has never been more than a simple-minded excuse for power junkies to do what they have been doing for thousands of years—play God.

The overwhelming force at work here is that at one time or another, the fertile valleys of China have been invaded by almost anyone who had a horse or boat to get there. Japanese have invaded China too many times to count. And, as I said, Washington is allied with Japan. The Chinese are fed up.

Until recently, Beijing's disdain for foreigners and desire for expansion and retaliation were not important. China had a large population but its socialist economy was so primitive that its army, navy, and air force were poorly equipped.

During the 1990s this changed. Twenty years ago, Chinese rulers began freeing the Chinese economy; by 1995, Chinese industry had become vast and highly capable.

Visiting a local Kmart to look for items produced in China, I was amazed. It seemed that half the high-tech equipment and precision instruments in the store carried the label "Made in China"—electronic cameras, binoculars, computer equipment, telephones, stereo tape decks, cordless electric drills, power saws, drill bits, sanders, digital watches, televisions, and tape recorders, not to mention more mundane items such as electric irons, mixers, blenders, and can openers.

Some of these, like miniature CD players and computerized answering machines, are so sophisticated that 20 years ago they did not exist anywhere at any price. Now the Chinese mass produce them for under $200 each.

Chinese factories even turn out Buicks, Audis, and airliners. If they can do that, they can make a lot of modern weapons.

A common assumption is that military equipment is more advanced than civilian goods. On the contrary, these days, markets are so smart and fast, and governments so slow and dimwitted, that the Kmart toy department contains items more advanced than many you would find on an air base.

My guess is that China is at or near the point where it can mass produce anything America can, and equip its army with the latest and best of everything. Yet pundits applaud China's moves toward capitalism.

I am sure more than one Chinese general has visited a Western-built plant in China and wondered, how can the barbarians be so technologically brilliant and so politically stupid?

Incidentally, at Kmart, if you can find "Made in Russia" at all it will be on cheap trinkets like the ones from bombed-out Japan in the 1940s and 1950s.

The main reason China's new manufacturing capability is so important militarily is China's population, the largest in the world. An old truism says that if all Chinese nationals were stood in a line, and the line began marching into the sea, the population would never diminish; it is that large and reproducing that fast.

Try to grasp China's population statistics—they are awesome. To give you a frame of reference, the total U.S. population is 273 million. The United States presently has 1.4 million active-duty military personnel. During the total mobilization of World War II, it had 12 million. Total U.S. deaths in World War II were 407,316.

China's population is 1.3 billion. If Beijing launches a total mobilization, the number of able-bodied military-age males available for drafting into the armed forces is 200 million. The most important statistic is that the number reaching military age (18) each year is 10 million.

Think about it. They can suffer 10 million casualties per year without diminishing their total force availability of 200 million. Imagine an army of 100 million Chinese troops armed with modern weapons. This possibility is no longer far-fetched.

Americans have become reluctant to accept any casualties at all. The power junkies in Beijing could throw away 100,000 men in one battle as comfortably as you or I discard an empty soda can.

I am sure that a Chinese threat to the American homeland is still at least 10 years away, and unlikely even then, for reasons explained in the 9/99 and 5/00 *EWR*s. Also, China is a land-power; its naval and air forces are short range and small, and the Pacific is 7,000 miles wide.

However, for China's neighbors, the threat is real and immediate. The 1996 announcement about annexing the whole South China Sea was a virtual declaration of war on the nations adjoining these waters. The mainstream press says little about it.

Control of Oriental seas would require aircraft carriers. Beijing has purchased three that were in poor condition and due to be scrapped. Two are Russian and one Australian.* The true status of these carriers is reportedly unknown. The largest, the 66,000-ton *Varyag*, once known as "the jewel of the Russian fleet," was purchased in 1998 by a shadowy Chinese company for use as a casino. *Far Eastern Economic Review* discovered the company's address was fake.

As the consequences of China's malinvestment grow, and unemployment spreads, Beijing's rulers will be sorely tempted to mask their economic problems the way Hitler masked Germany's. They will likely try to settle old scores by drafting idle workers into the army, invading nearby countries, and shifting idle factories to war production.

When will this happen? It's impossible to say, but the demise of the USSR left a vacuum in the slot for number-two superpower, and I think Beijing plans to fill this slot before Russia's Putin can produce a Russian comeback. If the beleaguered U.S. armed forces were tied up with Iraq and Iran in the Persian Gulf, Beijing would be free to run wild over the Orient.

Summarizing, the view that China's economic progress is a good thing is naive and dangerous. Thanks to the Europeans and others, the Chinese have a well-earned contempt for outsiders.

---

* *Army Times*, May 22, 2000, p. 3.

Given the Chinese regime's lack of interest in liberty, their moves toward capitalism during the past 20 years have really been moves toward war, and now the stage is nearly set.

If You are a Speculator (from the April 2009 *Early Warning Report*)

If you have the money to gamble, and you plan to buy and hold for three years or more, I think the time has come to get back into defense stocks. There are three reasons:

First, during economic downturns, companies are loath to lay off their trained workers. They know that when the recovery comes, they will go crazy trying to recruit and train replacements. This makes unemployment a laggard in the economic cycle, and that means, very likely, before this crisis is over, a lot more people will be losing their jobs. Pressure on federal officials to expand their porkbarrel to create jobs will continue growing for a long time, maybe years.

Congress writes the checks, and no one owns more congressmen than the military industries, so these industries are likely to receive a lot of "stimulus" as joblessness worsens.

Second, I've recommended mutual fund Fidelity Select Defense (FSDAX) off and on since 1994. FSDAX is back to where it was before the war began. This means—my key point—that *military stocks are priced as if there is no war*. But, as we saw in the previous articles, the war is much more likely to grow than to shrink.

Third, military industries are one of the few pork recipients that are darlings of both political parties. Leftists make speeches against the military, but when it comes to collecting votes and cash from military unions and firms, they don't complain much.

No guarantees, but defense stocks certainly look like a bargain to me, assuming you plan to hold for three years or more. There's no telling what will happen in the short run; another deflationary down leg, or two, may be in store. But in the long run, 2,500 years of economic history show that wars tend to overwhelm all other influences.

Two exchange-traded funds you might consider are:

1. iShares Dow Jones U.S. Aerospace & Defense Index Fund (ITA)
2. Powershares Aerospace & Defense Portfolio ETF (PPA)

Over their short lives, both have done better than FSDAX, and they've also done better since the economic crisis began in August 2007.

Interestingly, since the crisis began, they've tracked the S&P 500 almost exactly. I take this as further evidence that investors are ignoring the war and treating defense stocks as if they are part of the general economy, which they are not.

I've been in FSDAX since March 2000, when I suggested it because I thought the war was near. Since then, the fund is about 60 percent ahead of the S&P 500, so I'm satisfied with it and don't plan to incur the costs of moving to an ETF.

If you are not already in FSDAX, I'd be comfortable with either defense ETF.

What you might want to do is buy one ETF, and also pick up some General Dynamics (GD). GD is my favorite military supplier. It is extremely well run—meaning, among other things, its drovers herd its congressmen with great skill.

But GD's story runs deeper than that. Clinton and Bush bombed and otherwise angered so many governments that cooperation from these governments has diminished. Reportedly, flows of data from allies, spies, and embassies have been greatly reduced.

A primary tool in compensating for the shortfall is attack submarines. Attack boats are now equipped with a plethora of electronic gear that enables them to lie quietly submerged offshore and track what's happening on land.

Here's the math. Subs are unimaginably complex and difficult to keep in shape. The Navy calculates that it needs 5.8 attack subs to keep one continually on station. The 4.8 extras are undergoing maintenance, training, upgrades, trials, and other work.

We know that in July 2005, Navy commanders wanted 13.5 boats on station in six theaters. This was to handle two small wars (Iraq and Afghanistan) and several other areas of concern.

In the Reagan era, when there was no war to speak of, the Navy had 98 attack boats. By the end of 1998, they were down to 65. For a large war, they project a need for 35 on station, so under a ratio of 4.8 to 1, that's 203 attack boats, and these boats take years to build.

In 2008, the Navy had only 53;* 203 minus 53 is a shortfall of 150 hugely expensive vessels.

---

*All submarine figures are from "A Balancing Act," by Milan Vego, professor of operations at the Naval War College, *Armed Forces Journal*, February 2009, p. 30.

For over 100 years, General Dynamics has been the primary builder of U.S. subs.

Get the picture? There are revolutions and wars brewing all over the world, a shortage of jobs, a shortage of subs, and GD's corral full of congressmen hot to dish out pork. If I am right about the coming defense pork orgy, you will certainly be on the paying end, so you might want to try getting your money back, and then some, by also being on the receiving end—by owning GD stock.

Estimated risk levels of FSDAX, PPA, and ITA (on a scale of 1 to 5, with 1 being safest), are 2.5 for each, and estimated three-year profit potential of each, 200 percent; risk level of GD is 3.0, and three-year profit potential, 250 percent.

Closing Thoughts

Commentary and excerpts from my previous *Early Warning Reports* are noted in most cases and may be dated information now. Nevertheless, I believe that the geopolitical aspects and my opinions regarding Chaostan are still very valid.

Obviously, specific recommendations mentioned in this chapter are subject to change and their future performance and risk profile are a judgment call by me. Do your own research to verify their current attractiveness for your investment portfolio, or work with an investment advisor that is familiar with my newsletter. Martin Truax and Ron Miller have been subscribers for many years.

If my research on Chaostan and geopolitical commentary piques your interest, you can stay updated by subscribing to my *Early Warning Report* newsletter. If you mention this book when ordering, you will receive a year's subscription (10 issues) at half the regular price.

Voice: (800) 509–5400; (602) 252–4477

Fax: (602) 943–2363

Web: www.chaostan.com

The *New* Global Investing Strategy

Adrian Day

"What do they know of England who only England know?"

—Rudyard Kipling

When I first came to this country, in the mid-1970s, international investing was in its infancy, and was considered unnecessary, risky, and even unpatriotic. It was considered a strange concept, especially for retail investors. For many years, I and a small band of other zealots used to give speeches on "the benefits of international investing."

To me, it was startling that an investment advisor believes he has need to answer the question, "Why invest abroad?" and even more so that the question should be asked at all. In England, whence I hail, it is quite usual for a well-rounded investment portfolio to be diversified internationally, just as it is diversified among investment vehicles, among sectors, and among individual companies. A British investment advisor would just as likely recommend U.S., Dutch, and Hong Kong stocks as he would British. The same is true of continental Europe. A Swiss banker who suggested to a foreign client that he place all his assets inside Switzerland would not stay in business very long. This is also true for much of the world.

American Superiority

It is perhaps peculiarly American that the question is asked and need be answered. John Pugsley calls the typical reluctance of Americans to look abroad a "natural consequence of their heritage." Partially, of course, this derives from the sheer size and—certainly until recently—the dominance of the U.S. economy. But it also reflects a certain provincialism among Americans (by which I refer to citizens of the United States), a belief that everything American is the best—certainly the biggest—in the world.

Americans no longer feel quite so self-assured. None could argue that U.S. automakers or banks are the best in the world. But though international investing is no longer considered exotic, the myths and fears remain, and Americans for the most part do not perceive investing in foreign companies quite as naturally as buying U.S. stocks.

This sense of American superiority was once partially correct. The United States was, and in some ways still is, the most powerful country on earth, economically and militarily. At one time, not so long ago, even its currency was strong; "as strong as a dollar" went the saying. The U.S. stock markets once accounted for 70 percent of total world stock capitalization; 30 years ago they were still half the world's stock capitalization. Today, it is just one-third, while emerging markets—a mere speck 10, 20, and 30 years ago—now account for almost 20 percent of the value of the world's stocks. Some of the changes over time reflect changing fortunes in specific markets; in 1989, just at the peak of its bubble, Japan was the largest stock market in the world, representing over half the world's total, but today is less than 10 percent. (See Figure 9.1.)

But there are some fundamental shifts, and prime among them are the decline in the United States and the emergence of developing countries. Reflecting this, the mood among the U.S. investing public is slowly changing. The time is long past when most investors—still less investment advisors—feel they could safely put their money into only U.S. stocks. The big profits in the coming decade will be made outside of the United States, just as they were in the past decade. (See Figure 9.2.)

International market pioneer, the late Dennis Hardaker, saw a parallel between the "hard money movement" in the 1970s advising investments in gold and silver and foreign currencies, and international investing. "By the time the American brokerage community

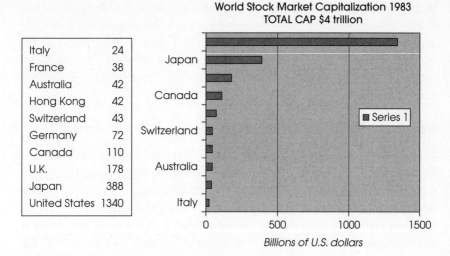

Italy	24
France	38
Australia	42
Hong Kong	42
Switzerland	43
Germany	72
Canada	110
U.K.	178
Japan	388
United States	1340

Figure 9.1   Stock Markets in 1983: U.S. Dominates

Source: International Investment Opportunities, Adrian Day, Morrow, 1983.

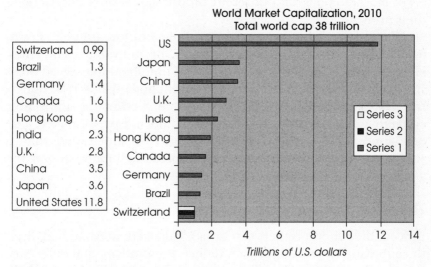

Switzerland	0.99
Brazil	1.3
Germany	1.4
Canada	1.6
Hong Kong	1.9
India	2.3
U.K.	2.8
China	3.5
Japan	3.6
United States	11.8

Figure 9.2   Stock Markets Today: Rise of China and Brazil

catches on to the merits of diversification on international stock markets, the big gains will have already been made." Few advisors today stick with the "buy American" approach, and articles advocating international investments are common. One theme is the decline in the value of the U.S. dollar and the obvious problems besetting many U.S. industries. That is not the only valid reason for pursuing an internationally diversified approach. Indeed, regardless of the health of the U.S. economy and investment markets, the sensible investor should always pursue a global approach. There are several reasons.

Reasons to Internationalize

Prime among them is diversification: Markets move in cycles, and by following, for example, 50 stock market cycles around the world, the investor is thus multiplying his opportunities. There are products or services we take for granted in the United States that are just beginning to penetrate foreign markets, such as fast food in emerging Asia, and high-end designer clothing in China. On the other hand, there are foreign products that are better or cheaper, and as they penetrate the U.S. and other developed markets, the profits of the local companies will grow. By gaining exposure to different market cycles, and different products, investors can increase their profits.

The risk-spreading advantages of diversification are well known, whether among markets, sectors, assets, or individual companies. However, in global investing as elsewhere, one shouldn't spread one's risk so much that one risks losing one's profit potential. Warren Buffett has suggested that diversification is often a cover for ignorance; certainly too broad diversification leads to bland performance. The best approach is with a carefully aimed rifle shot rather than a scattergun. I certainly do not advocate spreading money all over the globe just for the sake of it.

The Global Approach

Indeed, the difference between broad, balanced international diversification and the rifle approach reflects the fundamental difference between "investing abroad" and global investing. Today, the bold advisor will advocate 20, 30, or even 50 percent of an investor's portfolio be in foreign equities. But though this is indeed a major advance on the hesitant approach of 20 years ago or the ignorance of 30 years ago, it also reflects a flawed approach, in my view. I used to liken the "American-centric" view of investing to buying only stocks whose initial began with the letters *A* through *M* and refusing to buy the rest. That would limit opportunities and inevitably mean that investments were not made in certain sectors or industries.

Similarly, the idea that one should have, say, 20 percent of a portfolio in foreign stocks has similar flaws; but even if one says that 50 percent of a portfolio should at all times be in foreign stocks, apart from the fact that the United States now represents only 30 percent of global stock capitalization, it also means one is investing without regard to comparative value, without regard to growth potential, and so on. Again, if I suggested that half a portfolio should always be in stocks whose names begin with the letters *A* through *M* and the other half *N* through *Z*, you'd probably think I was a little peculiar or pedantic, if not downright crazy, and rightly so.

The distinction between U.S. companies and foreign in any event is becoming ever more meaningless in the increasingly global world. Nestlé is a Swiss company but generates the vast majority of its revenues and does most of its manufacturing in countries around the world, certainly not in Switzerland. What do we mean when we say Nestlé is a Swiss company? HSBC is based in London, but generates a third of its earnings from Hong Kong. Is it really a British company?

The global approach recognizes this: In contrast with the artificial "U.S." versus "foreign" dichotomy, global investors stand above the world and look for opportunities wherever they may be. They compare values and potential, comparing risk and reward of one market against another. If, for example, one wants to invest in the banking sector because of a view on global interest rates and growth, one would look at Swiss banks, at Asian banks, at Japanese and Brazilian banks, in addition to U.S. banks. One would compare the risk/reward profile of each in relation to their value, and one might determine, for example, that Brazilian banks generally offered the best risk/reward prospects over the next three to five years, while Canadian banks, without such strong prospects, offered lower risk and better current yields. It would most certainly not be a case of putting most of one's allocation into the U.S. banking sector and adding one or two names from abroad.

In comparing the risk/reward of the sector in different markets, a discount would be placed on different markets, depending on growth potential, regulation, overall market and currency risk, and so on. In the past, an American might apply various discounts to all foreign markets, a small one for, say, Switzerland, and larger ones for emerging markets. Whether today some markets should have *premiums* over the United States is a different subject, but one must assess the risk and potential in each market as objectively as possible and handicap in each market in which there is value.

At the same time, each investor must look at his own risk tolerance. Regardless of how favorable the risk/reward equation may be, a certain risk in absolute terms may be too great for some investors. Nine-in-ten odds of, say, doubling one's money against a one-in-ten chance of losing 50 percent represents objectively and mathematically good odds. But that one-in-ten risk of losing 50 percent may be too much for some investors.

But whatever the risk tolerance, the global investor does not see the dichotomy between U.S. investments and foreign investments, and thus will not have a "balanced" portfolio reflecting market weightings. John Templeton, the true pioneer of global investing, had in his flagship international fund at different times a majority of his investments in Canada, in Japan, and even in the United States. That's right; a global investor does not eschew the United States. He invests there when the values are there.

Where to Find Bargains

The global investor will also utilize both the bottom-up and top-down approaches to investing. The top-down approach looks for a theme, whether a global economic theme such as rising inflation or a specific market. An investor, for example, might believe that Thailand is a good market in which to invest. He believes the economy has long-term potential and the market is cheap. He will then ask himself which sectors are likely to prosper if the economy grows, and may decide that banks, newspapers, mobile phones, and beer brewers would all grow along with the economy. He then selects the best, perhaps the biggest, in each sector, and by thus doing has broad exposure to a growing economy.

A more specific example might look at Brazil, and rather than the very broad trend of economic growth in that country, there is the specific trend of the emergence of a middle class. This economy has seen a fundamental transformation over the past decade. In the 1990s and before, one thought of Brazil as an economy with runaway inflation and a depreciating, indeed frequently vanishing currency, as one currency was replaced with another, despite high interest rates. However, a series of economics ministers introduced discipline to the nation's finances, initially raising interest rates to over 50 percent to wring inflation from the system. Over the past decade, as rates have come down steadily to around 12 percent, inflation has come under control, falling below 5 percent, while the currency has appreciated. Indeed, the Brazilian *real* has been one of the strongest currencies in recent years, so much so that the government imposed a tax on inward capital movements in an attempt to stem the advance. But these fundamental changes to the economy mean other changes: People can save (no one did when the currency was depreciating daily) and firms can offer long-term loans, including mortgages (again, no one would make long-term loans in a vanishing currency and no one could afford them at 50 percent interest rates). Given the characteristics of Brazilian culture and the economy, this leads the investor to look at consumer goods and department stores, at airlines serving the domestic market, and at mortgage providers. (Everyone wants a home, but until recently, without a domestic mortgage market, only the very rich could afford to buy their homes.)

The bottom-up investor, on the other hand, does not care where the specific company is based or even what it does, but rather looks for good companies selling at discounts to their intrinsic value, *wherever* they may be based. Of course, each company's intrinsic value is partly a reflection of where it is based, and of the prospects for the industry in which it operates.

Part of this analysis involves looking at currencies. To my knowledge, there is not a case in which a country has succeeded in having a strong economy over a sustained period with a weak currency. Strong currencies beget strong economies. Nonetheless, of course, if one believes a country's currency is likely to appreciate in coming years, one might want to avoid emphasizing export companies, particularly if the products are produced from domestically sourced materials, and favor importers or companies with largely domestic sales, which will benefit from the stronger currency. This might include department stores or newspapers and other media.

Although some global investors hedge their currency exposure, I do not believe this is generally advantageous, nor feasible for the individual investor. The theory is that by hedging currencies, one is a pure value investor, comparing the intrinsic value in one company versus another, without the overlay of currency movements. However, hedging on a consistent basis can be expensive, removing part of one's gains. I prefer to factor a long-term currency outlook into the decision whether to invest in any given market and what sectors to buy or avoid in that market.

The Balance of Power Shifts East and South

Though I firmly believe in being a global investor at all times, there are special reasons to be looking abroad in these times. A major theme in the global marketplace over the next decade or two is the relative decline of the United States (and Europe) and the absolute rise of China, other parts of Asia, and some other emerging countries.

Figures 9.1 and 9.2 illustrate this: first, with the strong relative decline in economic power of the United States over the past decade, and second, showing China's dominance of the central banking sector. The United States, which only a few years ago had 7 banks in the top 20 (including the top 2), now has only 3 (the largest of which ranks fifth, and 2 of them are really investment companies, not banks at all).

Some might object that the U.S. banking sector is more dispersed than elsewhere, distorting the table. Not so! China's banking industry in aggregate is now the world's largest banking sector, approximately 50 percent larger than that of the United States. Similar tables of a range of other industries produce similar results.

Throughout Asia, as in Brazil and some other emerging economies, more and more direct capital investment in the economies comes from within or from other emerging economies, while trade patterns increasingly show great trade among emerging economies to the relative detriment of trade with the United States. As an example, just a decade ago, almost 20 percent of all emerging Asia exports (ex-Japan and China) went to the United States, and only 7 percent went to China. Last year, less than 10 percent were destined for the United States and over 25 percent went to Asia. More Asian products are going to Japan, and trade within emerging Asia is increasing dramatically as well. Similarly, whereas prior to the Asia crisis in 1997, over 70 percent of Foreign Direct Investment into Asia outside of Japan came from the United States, today it's well under 50 percent, with increasing levels from China, Japan, and other Asian countries. As for the stock market, there is increased investment by locals around the region and in other emerging countries, boosting trading volumes and reducing dependence of fickle global funds, as well as limiting dependence on the United States. Both the economies and the markets are increasingly decoupling from the United States.

While clearly, when the U.S. economy enters a recession or the stock market falls significantly, we should expect declines in Asia and other emerging markets, those corrections are increasingly shallower and more importantly shorter than in the United States. Following the major global market declines precipitated by the U.S. credit crisis in September 2008, Asian markets led the recovery.

Just as we were shown by Copernicus and Galileo that the geo-centric view of the universe was false, so too we need to see the standard view of the United States as the center of the economic and investment world as false. The investment winners in the period ahead will be those who understand this sooner than others.

The Decline in the Dollar

Along with this decline in economic dominance comes a long-term decline in the purchasing power of the dollar. This is partly a reflection of the financial condition in the United States as opposed to other countries. The accumulated savings and strong balances of governments, companies, and households in China (and, for example, Singapore) contrast with the fiscal irresponsibility in the United States. This did not start in 2009, of course, but at the government level has certainly taken a quantum leap toward oblivion since then. U.S. households present an even stronger contrast, with the U.S. consumer living off the savings of other countries for many years.

The long-term reasons for the dollar's decline are well known: the U.S. financial situation, high debt levels, and low savings rates. But foreign central banks still hold about 70 percent of their nondomestic reserves in U.S. dollars. The level is so high partly because of lack of alternatives—who wants to hold the euro as insurance?—and because of a heretofore trust in the fundamental health of the U.S. economy. But as we can see from Figure 9.3, it is precisely the newly developing countries that tend to have the largest reserves, and since these countries have only recently built up their international reserves, they tend to hold the vast majority in U.S. dollars, because they built them up at a time when the dollar was dominant. (It is also

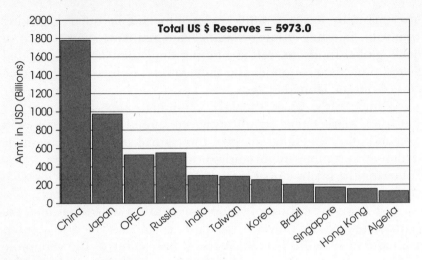

Figure 9.3   Foreign Exchange Reserves

precisely these countries, incidentally, that tend to have the lowest allocation to gold in their reserves, but that's a different matter.)

Global officials are realizing that such concentration is imprudent, all the more so given the overleveraged economy. A widely publicized article in the Chinese *People's Daily* called for "a new financial and currency order that is no longer dependent on the United States and the dollar," and said that "the world urgently needs to create a diversified currency system." The pressure has stepped up recently, as the BRIC countries (Brazil, Russia, India, and China) in particular continue to advance the concept of replacing the U.S. dollar as the world's reserve currency. In 2009, for the first time, the leaders of the four BRIC countries met in Russia to discuss their growing clout in the world economy as well as the specific issue of the dollar.

Brazil and China have agreed to use their domestic currencies for bilateral trade, instead of the dollar, something the Brazilian government said was "unthinkable 10 years ago." And Russia and India are discussing a similar arrangement.

With over $4 trillion in U.S. dollar paper held by the world's central banks—at least half of it by those who are not necessarily friendly with the United States (China, OPEC, and Russia)—a move to become "less dependent" on the dollar is not to be taken lightly.

In my view, we can draw lessons for the United States today from the position of Britain at the end of World War II. Britain had been the world's dominant economic, political, and military power, with the world's reserve currency. But by 1946, it was militarily stretched beyond its capacity, and highly indebted. The United States took over the number-one spot. Britain fell from the world's dominant economic power to a point where, in the 1960s, it was forced to go begging to the IMF for emergency aid. The standard of living fell steadily over the decades. The dollar became the world's reserve currency, with the pound falling from five-to-one in 1946 down to parity four decades later.

The problem with being the world's reserve currency is that more money is created than is necessary for the domestic economy's needs. For decades, the United States has created far more dollars than it needs, but it didn't matter so long as other countries were prepared to buy and hold those dollars. But those dollars still exist. As other countries lose confidence and diversify, those dollars eventually come back: Too many dollars and too little demand equal a lower price.

Growth from Emerging Countries

Certainly, the growth internationally is mostly coming from emerging countries. In the 15 years to the end of the first quarter of 2009, the United States and U.K. saw GDP growth of 5 percent or less per annum. This is no doubt strong growth and well above long-term historical standards, boosted by excessive leverage. Over the same period, however, many emerging economies saw double-digit annual growth. Despite the huge devastation in the Asian crisis at the end of the 1990s, China's GDP grew an average of over 15 percent and India's by over 13 percent. For the most part, stock market returns over the longer term follow economic growth: In the United States and U.K., stocks returned 6 to 7 percent annual growth. In India, with GDP growth 13.2 percent, stock markets returned 13.3 percent. Only China's market underperformed, but this partly reflects over-valuations at the starting point, and partly reflects a lack of global confidence in the domestic markets. Moreover, with a price/earnings multiple in the mid-20s, Shanghai's stock market is trading well below its long-term average multiples, approaching 40 times.

Today, emerging markets generally are in a far stronger position than they were a decade ago, before the Asia crisis, and stronger even than the U.S. and some other developed economies. For the most part, banking systems are resilient, savings strong, government finances prudent, and currencies undervalued. Taken together, emerging economies now account for one-third of total world GDP. China, the fastest growing economy in recent years, is at the "takeoff" point through which most economies develop, promising many years of growth ahead as it becomes the world's dominant economy. India, the world's fourth largest economy (measured by GDP), is also the second-fastest growing. One billion new consumers throughout emerging economies imply long-term growth in consumption, everything from automobiles and refrigerators to fast food and designer clothes. They also imply massive infrastructure investment in roads, rails, ports, and airports. At the beginning of the decade, there were just 19 companies from emerging markets on the Fortune 500 list, and many of them were producers of the cheap goods for the American marketplace. Today, there are world beaters, global blue chips—a total of 75 companies from emerging countries on that list, and the number is growing each year. The world is changing indeed, and investors need to get on board.

Ways to Invest Internationally

Although options for international investing have become incomparably greater in the past couple of decades, investors still need to be on guard. One can buy a mutual fund, but be aware of whether it is a global or international fund (the latter of which invests outside the United States only). An increasing number of market ETFs investing in just one country or a group of countries (there is a BRIC country ETF, for example) have attractions, but also pitfalls. In many foreign markets, one or two large companies may dominate and this is reflected in the ETF. Royal Dutch Shell dominates the Amsterdam index, almost 40 percent of the total market. An investor might want to invest in the Netherlands stock market, but may not want so great an investment in oil, and one oil company at that. In Switzerland, one-third of the market is health care and another third is financials. Buying the index ETFs does not allow the flexibility to choose. Similarly, with the BRIC ETF, the investor may like the growth prospects of major emerging markets, but be nervous of Russia, for example. One can say these ETFs add to the options available for the global investor, but one needs to know what one is buying.

If one wants to be exposed to individual companies, it is critical to use a manager or broker who understands global markets. In buying individual shares the investor has the choice of ordinary shares or ADRs. Ordinary shares are the underlying issues on the home market. Many international companies have American Depository Receipts or International Depository Receipts to facilitate trading in those shares on the U.S. or other major international exchanges. Not all ADRs trade on the major exchanges, however, particularly if they are not sponsored by the company itself. Nestlé's ADRs, for example, are unsponsored and trade over the counter, with wide bid–ask spreads and illiquid trading. My general advice is that if shares are listed directly on an exchange—such as HSBC's shares listed on the New York—or if ADRs trade on the New York, I buy those rather than the ordinaries. But generally, I avoid ADRs trading over the counter, and prefer to buy the ords. For example, there is absolutely no reason to buy Nestlé over the counter rather than in the highly liquid and efficient Swiss exchange. In the case of Taiwan or Korea, for example, retail investors can have difficulty buying directly on the local exchanges, so one should stick with ADRs. However, be aware of the often enormous premiums at which these ADRs can trade.

Again, it would be impossible to point out here all the pitfalls and all the ramifications of various investment vehicles. The conclusion for the investor wanting to buy individual stocks is clear: Use someone who knows what he is doing. It is far better to use a broker with knowledge of global markets than to use a discounter with low commissions, but wind up paying excess fees, spreads, and currency conversions.

It's a wonderful world of opportunities, and a changing world, and the successful investor needs exposure to these opportunities.

10

High-Yield Investing in the Shadow of the Big W

Roger S. Conrad

Inflation and credit concerns: These are the two basic risks of income investing.

If you want to live off portfolio income, you've got to stick around long enough to capture the dividends and interest. That leaves no alternative but to successfully deal with both threats.

For the better part of two years, credit risk has been the primary danger. Wall Street always produces for investor demand. And before the 2008 market crash, that craving was for high yields. The Street launched a plethora of new securities to capture it, ranging from the more traditional, such as master limited partnerships and real estate investment trusts, to entirely new derivatives like income deposit securities, which combined equity with debt into a single security.

Unfortunately, when the credit crunch hit, many of the new issues weren't up to the challenge. Yields that tempted many vanished overnight amid an avalanche of dividend cuts and even bankruptcies. For many of the failures, the key was that the underlying businesses were ill-suited for any structure paying out big dividends. For others, the blame lay with piling on too much debt to fund growth. But whatever the cause, the results have been the same: cratered share prices and a loss of income that will never be recovered.

Not even the strongest companies' stocks, bonds, and preferred stocks have wholly avoided the extreme volatility and risk that's prevailed since mid-2007. In fact, most are underwater for the past two years. Some in more cyclical industries like oil and gas production have cut dividends and may not be so quick to restore them.

The difference, however, is that they're still very much in the game for a full recovery. In fact, that rebound is assured, provided they stay strong as businesses.

What makes a strong company? When it comes to income-generating stocks, the most important thing is the ability to maintain and grow dividends over time. There are several business numbers found in earnings reports that provide valuable clues.

The gripping recession that's followed the credit crunch and market crash of 2008 has made the payout ratio a more important metric than ever. Basically, the payout ratio is the dividend as a percentage of profitability needed to pay it. A company can pay out more than its profits in dividends for a time. Sooner or later, however, it has to either cover or else pull in its horns.

For most corporations, "earnings per share" is the best point of comparison. Master limited partnerships and Canadian trusts, however, pay distributions from pre-tax cash flow. As a result, the best metric is "distributable cash flow" rather than earnings per share, which are intentionally minimized for tax reasons. Rural phone companies' payouts come from "free cash flow," which is cash flow less what's needed for capital expenditures.

Strong companies don't necessarily eschew debt entirely. In fact, even the most powerful companies do borrow. The difference is their debt burdens don't impede their ability to grow. And their access to credit is unfettered—no matter what's going on in the economy, they can borrow.

Most of the income stocks I recommend have one other great strength. They operate in niches that are generally recession resistant, and they hold commanding market positions in them. Owners and operators of energy pipelines, power plants, communications networks, water systems, and so forth may not be the most exciting industries to own in good times. But as the 2008–2009 recession has proven once again, nothing holds its own in bad times so well—and that's the key to maintaining income streams.

So long as strong companies stay strong, their market prices will eventually recover. We may have to wait a while for that to happen, particularly if the overall economy has a relapse. But as long as we're patient—and provided the underlying businesses stay strong—recover we will, even as we continue to garner a hefty stream of income.

Recovery or Relapse

The global stock market is in perpetual fear that we're nearing another down-leg of a "Big W" recession. So the theory goes: Late 2008 and early 2009 were the first down-leg, as the credit crunch knocked the economy and stock market for a loop. The first up-leg of the W has been the stock market recovery since March 2009 and the modest improvement in economic growth during the last half of 2009 and the first quarter of 2010, after the 6 percent declines in the fourth quarter of 2008 and first quarter of 2009.

In this third leg of the W, the U.S. economy will supposedly resume its contraction and the stock market plunge once again. This could occur during 2010. The logical downside for the Dow Jones Industrial Average is roughly 6,000, and 600 or so for the S&P 500. At that point, we'd start the fourth leg, with the economy and stock market at last cycling out of trouble.

No matter how patient an investor you are or what you're invested in, the Big W scenario is not pleasant to contemplate. And for many investors, the possibility of living through another horrific selloff like late 2008 is just too much to bear. The result is the current bifurcated market we find ourselves in now.

On one side we have U.S. Treasury bonds, the U.S. dollar, and, somewhat surprisingly, gold. On the other side is virtually everything else, from energy and technology to dividend-paying stocks that have proven to be recession resistant thus far.

When the news on the economy seems to indicate a positive direction, the action is positive and often greatly so. However, when the news on the economy arouses fears of a Big W, everything sells off, often with stocks of the most recession-resistant businesses leading the way down. Adding to the confusion, the action on any given day is more often than not completely reversed the next.

I'm not convinced this is a time to run for the hills. In fact, it's unlikely we'll see another late-2008-style meltdown in the stock market. Selloffs of the magnitude of the one that occurred after the September 2008 fall of Lehman Brothers occur only very rarely in market history. That's because they require a thankfully unique combination of relatively high stock valuations—that is, high investor expectations—and a series of extremely unfortunate events.

Despite the run-up we've seen in many stocks since early March, it's hard to make the case that investor expectations now are anywhere close to as high as they were a year ago. Rather, the violence of selloffs in the face of bad economic numbers is a clear sign of the opposite. Mainly, investors great and small fear a Big W and another day of reckoning for stocks across the board.

The U.S. economy is admittedly still weak. Unemployment especially is a worrisome indicator and we're not likely to see any dramatic improvement soon, with companies continuing to tighten their belts. Much of the good news we're seeing, meanwhile, is thanks to the unprecedented federal government stimulus, both fiscal and monetary.

On the other hand, while things may be slow to get appreciably better, neither are there real catalysts for things to get markedly worse. That's the pattern evident in economic data across the board, including from the housing market.

There are still U.S. financial institutions at grave risk, as the CIT Group's recent restructuring clearly demonstrates. Meanwhile, the Federal Deposit Insurance Corporation (FDIC) has seen its reserves drop dramatically as it's been forced to rescue the largest number of banks in decades.

However, global monetary authorities, including the U.S. Federal Reserve, have been on the job of rescuing the financial system for more than a year now. Bank capital ratios are getting stronger, even in the most affected countries. Perhaps more important, officials know where vulnerability lies and potential accidents are now being cleared up almost before they occur.

On top of that, cash is flowing to creditworthy borrowers, both corporations and individuals. The spread between yields on newly minted A-rated utility bonds and the 10-year Treasury note has again sunk below 150 basis points, as low as it's been since early 2007. Coupled with the lowest Treasury yields in years, the result is the lowest interest rates paid for borrowing corporations in years. Even non-investment-grade or "junk" bonds have surged.

The credit market is still largely frozen to those who really need to borrow cheaply. Fairpoint Communications, for example, defaulted on its credit agreement. That's the likely first step in a wholesale reorganization likely to wipe out all but a sliver of shareholder value. The financially strong, however, are taking advantage to cut interest costs and strengthen balance sheets. Even companies involved in aggressive acquisitions like Frontier Communications have been able to refinance debt at preferential rates.

The situation in the credit market is perhaps the biggest difference between now and September 2008, when the fall of Lehman Brothers was the last straw to teetering financial institutions, freezing credit markets and driving the economy and stock market off a cliff. The bottom line: If there is to be another catastrophe for the stock market, the credit market won't be the catalyst.

That means something else will have to emerge. And with investor expectations so low, it will likely have to have even greater power to wreak havoc on the economy and stock market than the credit crunch of a year ago. Fortunately, that's not very likely and it means that whatever corrections we see going forward will almost surely be worth riding out for the eventual recovery, again provided you're in strong positions.

In my view, the next big risk for income investors is not going to be on the credit front but with an upsurge of inflation. At this point, only one historically reliable indicator of inflation is flashing red: gold prices.

Gold's recent high of around $1,200 is still well below the 1980 high adjusted for inflation. But it appears institutions as well as individuals are reportedly taking positions in the metal at an unprecedented rate. Even Yahoo! Finance, which long ignored the gold market, has begun posting the per-ounce price of the near-term futures contract on its homepage.

At a minimum, gold's move means investors are seeking alternatives to the U.S. dollar after so much easy money in recent years. From 2003 to 2007, inflation fears stirred every spring and early summer like clockwork, triggering a spike in interest rates and a corresponding selloff in prices of income investments from utilities and bonds to real estate investment trusts. Every summer, those fears were eventually quelled. Interest rates headed lower again and income investments rallied, wiping out the previous losses and in most cases moving on to new highs.

Next time around, however, is likely to be much, much different. And gold's ability to hold around $1,200, even with Treasury yields so low, is a clear sign things could get ugly for many income investments, which tend to move countercyclically.

Fortunately, rapid inflation is not going to happen until the economy rebounds. Moreover, income investments outside of Treasuries are now trading cyclically—they're profiting from any news that the economy is strengthening. That means a lot more upside for almost everything paying a yield, before inflation becomes a real threat again.

In the Sectors

Here's a look at where the various income-producing sectors stand in the current environment. Note that you'll always do far better by taking the time to identify the best positioned in any sector, than simply taking a bet on an exchange-traded fund (ETF) or ordinary mutual fund.

In the short-term, the stock market is a popularity contest. Huge institutions slosh money around into popular stocks and even more so sectors. Today's profits are more often than not tomorrow's losses.

In contrast, in the long-term the markets act as a weighing machine. Growing, healthy businesses become more valuable over time and therefore gain value in the stock market. You can build wealth even as you collect generous dividends. And buying only the best of a sector also enables investors to avoid the worst risks of a sector.

Happily, the key to building wealth is also the same as avoiding the worst of both credit and inflation risk. That's to focus on securities backed by healthy, growing businesses. Healthy growing businesses not only hold their dividends in tough times, they increase them. Their bonds and preferred stocks earn higher credit ratings, or are redeemed at substantial premiums.

In contrast, those who are lured by a high current yield into buying a weak business will suffer at best stagnation and erosion of value in the face of inflation pressure. At worst, they'll be the victims of dividend cuts, plunging share prices, and, as we've seen more than once over the past year, potential bankruptcies and total wipeouts.

Buying only from good businesses is as essential to surviving future inflation risk as it's been to surviving credit risk over the past couple of years. That's because growth offsets inflation, particularly if it translates into a growing dividend yield.

Equally important is maintaining diversification and balance. My approach is to own securities issued by first-rate businesses from a range of sectors. Some will outperform in inflationary times, others when the economy is slumping and credit risk is a worry. If you're investing to build wealth, such moves are largely irrelevant. But if you're living off those investments, you can't afford to be in the position where you have to eat your seed corn—that is, being forced to sell good positions at rock-bottom prices to raise needed funds.

Obviously, there are times when you can't help when you sell. But by diversifying among many sectors and keeping the dollar value of your holdings roughly balanced, you can ensure that your overall portfolio maintains a certain baseline value where funds will be available.

Earnings always slump during recessions, even for the most creditworthy companies. That begs the question of how anyone could infer any of these businesses are still building wealth. And this is where the "buying the business" strategy gets tricky. Put another way, it's pretty easy to tell if a business is getting more valuable and building wealth in good times when everyone's earnings are rising. It's another matter entirely to be able to reach that conclusion when the headline profits-per-share number may not look so good.

Of course, there are plenty of companies that have continued to grow earnings in the bad times. In my universe of companies, reverse-osmosis water provider Consolidated Water turned in blockbuster second-quarter numbers, as it completed new plants and put them in operation selling water in its Caribbean Islands service territory.

For the rest, however, underlying signs of wealth are considerably more subtle. They involve delving below the headlines to ascertain whether a company is putting the pieces in place for growth when better times return, how well its business is standing up to economic pressures, and how well its financial strategy is preserving cash flow and balance sheet strength.

- *Canadian trusts.* Any trust that's been able to hold its dividends steady over the past three years has proven itself a winner in almost every possible condition. They coped not only with reduced access to capital and a credit crunch but also with volatile energy prices and the North American recession, which has hit every Canadian company doing business in the United States. Particularly impressive are energy-producing trusts that have held dividends steady. Even 2011 taxation is not nearly the risk some fear, as a growing number of trusts are converting to corporations and leaving their dividends the same. The best trusts have one other key advantage: They're priced in and pay dividends in Canadian dollars and the "Loonie" follows oil prices, making it an excellent inflation hedge. In the non-energy-producer trust camp, I like trusts like Bird Construction (TSX: BDT-U, OTC: BIRDF) and Macquarie Power & Infrastructure (TSX: MPT-U, OTC: MCQPF). For energy producers, you won't go wrong with Enerplus Resources (TSX: ERF, NYSE: ERF), the oldest and arguably most conservative of its breed.

- *Energy.* Energy stocks are among the best hedges against inflation. They've had a tough time since mid-2008, as the global recession temporarily crimped worldwide demand. But the best have continued to hang in there and are poised for a massive recovery. My favorites are always those with rising production, as they have the longest futures and greatest upside. The safest for income investors, however, are the super oils that have balance sheets stronger than most countries and truly global reach. My favorite is Chevron (NYSE: CVX).

- *Financials.* Small banks are the best and only picks in this sector. Deposit-focused institutions with solid loan growth may be tough to come by. But those that boast these characteristics are very-low-risk ways to play the eventual recovery of the U.S. financial system and economy. My favorite in the group is Arrow Financial (NSDW: AROW), which has proven its mettle once again in this credit crunch/recession by boosting deposits, reducing loan losses, and increasing dividends.

- *Master limited partnerships (MLPs).* On a tax-equivalent basis, even the very strongest MLPs' current yields are as high as 10 percent. That's in large part because they're high to begin with, as MLPs push their pre-tax cash flow directly to investors. But it's also because they pay such little tax at all. Anything that is owed is almost entirely return of capital (ROC), on which no current tax is due. Rather, the ROC dividend is deducted from your cost basis until you sell. MLPs suffered an extreme crisis of investor confidence in late 2008. That's because many of the initial public offerings from the new issue flood of early 2007 buckled under credit and recession pressures. Other MLPs—including the popular Alliance Bernstein—are basically financial constructs that are in the crosshairs of the Obama Administration on the so-called "carried interest" issue. Should they wind up being taxed, they'll crash and burn. None of those risks, however, apply to MLPs that own and operate energy infrastructure like pipelines, processing centers, and storage facilities. Rather, these earn their cash flow from fees that are unaffected by the ups and downs of energy prices. Even throughput—the energy moved through these assets—is little affected, as the infrastructure is absolutely vital even in recession. And many earn fees tied to "capacity" rather than throughput, meaning that customers must pay the fees whether they ship, store, or process the energy or not. These MLPs have continued to expand assets and therefore cash flows during the past two years, despite tight credit and the recession. Some have benefited from "drop-downs." These are effectively transfers of assets from diversified parent companies organized as corporations to affiliates that are organized as MLPs, in order to boost cash flow to the parent. My favorite MLP for long-term investors over the past decade has been Enterprise Products Partners (NYSE: EPD). Management has boosted distributions for 23 consecutive quarters and there's a lot more to come.

- *Real estate investment trusts (REITs)*. This group has been beaten black and blue by a combination of tighter credit, rising vacancies, falling rents, and declining property values. But some in the sector are still thriving, mainly in the apartment rental sector and Canada. Those who kept their debt under control earlier in the decade are also having the last laugh, as their peers flounder. Along with financials, REITs have been the kings of the dividend cut over the past year and there's still more room for downside in commercial property values, which are already off more than 30 percent over the past year and more than 40 percent of the cycle. But valuations are also as low as they've been since the 1990s, and that means opportunity. In the safe category, I like Home Properties (NYSE: HME) and Canadian Apartment Properties (TSX: CAR-U, OTC: CDPYF). Those who want to take on more risk should check out Vornado (NYSE: VNO), which is aggressively attempting to buy properties cheap.

- *Utilities.* Regulated power, gas, and water utilities' resiliency has been particularly apparent during the bear market/recession that began in mid-2007. Despite the worst economy in decades, all but a handful continue to post earnings that cover distributions handily, maintain balance sheet strength, and lay the groundwork. In fact, after eight years of cutting debt and operating risk since the fall of Enron, the industry has rarely been stronger. The key to keeping that going is maintaining positive regulation. The recession has weakened the regulatory compact in some states, notably Florida, where Governor Charlie Crist has stacked the state Public Service Commission to boost his chances of election to the U.S. Senate. But most states are still positively regulated, despite the economic pressures. And even in riskier states, most companies are well protected against a relapse to the negative regulation of the past, thanks to successful unregulated enterprises and the strongest overall operations in decades. Florida's biggest utility, FPL Group (NYSE: FPL), for example, won't suffer much from weaker Florida regulation due to the rapid growth of its unregulated NextEra Energy unit, America's largest wind and solar power producer. My top picks in this group are almost all from the states of the old Confederacy, which still boast the most favorable regulatory climates and therefore have consistently maintained the nation's lowest power rates. This is also the region where industrial companies continue to migrate to, another plus for utilities. Dominion Resources (NYSE: D) and Southern Company (NYSE: SO) are top candidates for sleep-easy returns. FPL is a great pick for growth, thanks to renewable-energy mandates in 33 states.

11

The Case for Growth

Elliott H. Gue

Many investors assume that stocks paying dividends are inherently safer investments than growth-oriented names that offer no yield. The logic goes that companies with dividends offer steady income while gains from growth stocks are ephemeral, based solely on ever-shifting expectations of future earnings prospects and economic conditions.

Investing for growth and capital gains is all too often associated with painful memories of the technology bubble in the late 1990s, during which investors shunned value and dividend-paying stocks, bidding up valuations on growth-oriented names to unprecedented levels. After all, those who drank the New Economy Kool-Aid projected that the Internet would offer companies limitless growth opportunities.

Some concluded that dividends were totally anachronistic; companies should reinvest their cash to grow the business further. The folly of that growth-at-any-price mantra became all too apparent after the 2000 tech wreck.

But, the easy money policies of the Federal Reserve after 2001 helped to inflate an income stock bubble that was every bit as pernicious as the tech boom and bust that preceded it. As Figure 11.1 shows, amid a series of rate cuts the U.S. national average yield on a 1-year certificate of deposit (CD) collapsed from more than 6 percent at the beginning of the decade to less than 2 percent, an insufficient payout for most investors looking for regular income from their savings.

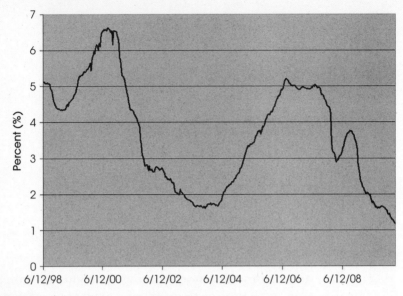

Figure 11.1 Effect on CDs amid Rate Cuts

To compensate for the paltry yields available on CDs, government bonds, and other traditional income groups such as real estate investment trusts (REITs), investors became enamored with high dividend yields; far too many yield-seekers had little regard for underlying business risk.

Bonds rated B by Standard & Poor's are two levels below investment grade and are considered highly speculative. But at the height of the income bubble from 2005 through 2007, 10-year bonds of industrial companies rated B–, an even lower rating than B, offered a yield less than 300 basis points (3 percent) over the 10-year Treasury bond (see Figure 11.1). That means investors were willing to accept considerable risk in exchange for only a slight yield premium.

The Great Recession has proven conventional wisdom on the "inherent safety" of dividend payers and the "income-at-any-price" paradigm just as devoid of reason as the growth-centric, "New Economy" mantra of the late 1990s. Contrary to their safety-first reputation, income-oriented stocks largely underperformed the broader market averages in the bear market of 2008.

Investors who purchased the 50 highest-yielding stocks in the S&P 500 at the end of 2007 would have lost just under 40 percent of their investment by the end of 2008, compared to a 37 percent decline in the S&P 500. Even worse, 5 stocks in the high-yielding group discontinued their dividends entirely by the end of 2008, 1 filed for bankruptcy, and 17 cut their dividends by an average of more than two-thirds by year-end. Investors who focused on yield without thoroughly examining the underlying businesses were badly burned.

Even worse, Wall Street created an alphabet soup of preferreds, exchange-traded mini-bonds, trust income securities, and income deposit securities to meet investors' insatiable thirst for yield. While not all of these securities are inherently a poor investment, many were issued by fundamentally weak companies looking to raise capital cheaply in a yield-hungry market. Predictably, hare-brained, over-indebted businesses offering high-yields performed just as poorly as the dubious dot-coms of the late 1990s.

Some investors may also find it equally paradoxical that some of the best-performing sectors since the October 2007 market highs have been groups traditionally thought to be growth oriented. For example, the S&P 500 Information Technology Index outperformed the S&P 500 by roughly 12 percent in the two years after the 2007 market highs. The Energy and Consumer Discretionary Indices—both offering a lower-than-average yield—also beat the market by around 5 percent in the 24 months after the 2007 top.

I don't recount these facts to disparage income investing; in fact, income stocks should form a core part of every investor's portfolio. But, just because a stock offers a yield doesn't mean it's a safe investment—selectivity and a careful analysis of the underlying business is every bit as important for income-paying securities as it is for growth stocks. Similarly, companies that don't pay dividends aren't necessarily riskier; investors buying technology and retail stocks actually outperformed more income-oriented players in the two years after the 2007 market highs.

It's high time for investors to abandon faddish, flavor-of-the-month approaches to the market and adopt time-tested principles of portfolio construction. The only way to flourish in this volatile market is to buy a well-balanced and diversified mix that includes exposure to quality income and growth themes.

The Growth Shift

On June 4, 1968, the S&P 500 first broke through the psychologically important 100 barrier and breached 108 that November. In the preceding two decades, the S&P had returned over 500 percent, a historic rally at the time. Not surprisingly, many expected America's postwar prosperity to continue indefinitely.

But more than 14 years later, in August 1982, the S&P 500 traded at just over 102, still under the high achieved in 1968. To make matters worse, the intervening years brought high inflation, high unemployment, and four recessions that averaged more than a year in duration. With the ravages of inflation, an investor who bought the S&P 500 in 1968 lost more than half his or her purchasing power by late 1982.

But although the 1970s were a disaster for buy-and-hold investors, the decade wasn't all doom and gloom. Nimble investors who bargain hunted when the economy weakened caught several multiyear cyclical bull markets that offered gains of as much as 100 percent.

Investors willing to identify sectors and markets in true up-cycles also profited handsomely. For example, Japan's Nikkei 225 rose 365 percent—close to 19 percent per year—during the 1970s. Meanwhile, crude oil prices jumped to over 25 times their initial value between 1970 and 1982, and gold prices soared from around USD35 per ounce in 1970 to more than USD800 per ounce in 1980. Not surprisingly, commodity-related stocks caught fire in that environment; gold-mining names were the bread and butter of many newsletter editors.

No two periods in market history are exactly alike. But the 1968–1982 secular bear market is in many ways analogous to the current environment. The trading pattern in the S&P 500 since 1998 broadly resembles that of the S&P 500 from 1968 through the 1970s; the index has experienced some wild swings but remains relatively unchanged.

This comparison goes beyond superficial chart patterns. Although the fundamental reasons are different, the current decade, like the 1970s, has ushered in a significant rally in commodity prices.

There's also reason to expect a pattern of frequent recessions and recoveries—short economic cycles—similar to the 1970s, and markedly different from the bull market that occurred between 1982 and 2000.

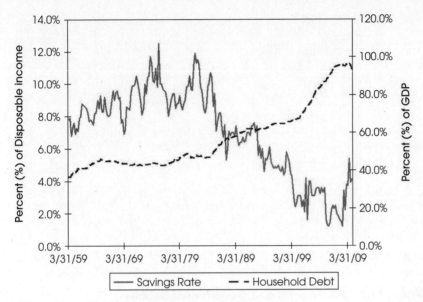

Figure 11.2   U.S. Personal Savings and Debt Rate

Throughout that period, the ever-resilient consumer proved a reliable growth engine, shopping the U.S. economy out of every economic downturn. Thanks to the consumer, the 1991 and 2001 recessions were among the shortest and shallowest in history.

As depicted in Figure 11.2, the U.S. personal savings rate hovered around 7 to 10 percent of disposable income from 1968 to 1982. But from 1982 through 2007, that savings rate steadily dropped, falling to less than 1 percent earlier this decade.

In addition to saving less, U.S. consumers borrowed at unprecedented levels. As you can see in Figure 11.2, in the late 1950s, total U.S. household debt—such as mortgages, credit cards, and auto loans—stood at less than 40 percent of gross domestic product (GDP). That ratio rose to roughly 45 percent by the mid-1970s. But just as the savings rate dropped precipitously post-1982, debt levels steadily increased and were near 100 percent in 2007.

The pattern is clear: Americans cut their savings and borrowed money to fund consumption. This alone accounts for the consumer's resilience and willingness to buy the country out of every contraction over the past 25 years.

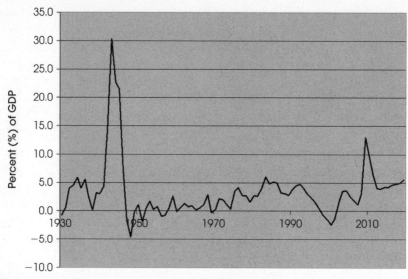

Figure 11.3   U.S. Federal and Government Deficits

But that trend has ended abruptly. The U.S. savings rate jumped to as high as 6.2 percent during the financial crisis, and the household debt-to-GDP ratio has begun to decline as Americans pay down their debt. Because the excessive debt burdens of the past few years are unsustainable, this pattern of deleveraging is likely to continue for at least a few more years. The U.S. consumer isn't spent, but will no longer drive global economic growth.

Another key challenge facing the U.S. market and economy is massive federal government deficits. As Figure 11.3 illustrates, the U.S. deficit hit 13 percent of GDP in 2009 and is expected to average over 5 percent of GDP through the end of 2019. Accordingly, the Congressional Budget Office expects the U.S. debt to increase from 40 percent of GDP to 70 percent over the same time period with much of that debt likely to be held by foreigners. With the exception of war-related spending in the 1940s, this level of spending is unprecedented in American history.

Even amid the worst financial crisis since the Great Depression, foreign buyers have exhibited an unfailing appetite for U.S. government bonds. China, in particular, has been an aggressive buyer of U.S. government debt in recent years, helping to keep U.S. interest rates near multi-decade lows.

But with the U.S. dollar generally weak and America's fiscal condition deteriorating, the nation's creditors will ultimately demand higher interest rates to compensate for growing risks. Higher interest rates are bad news for over-indebted American consumers and for a still-shaky U.S. real estate market.

With the U.S. consumer focused on paying down debt, the U.S. economy entering a period of more modest growth, and the U.S. markets rangebound, buying and holding a diversified portfolio of S&P 500 stocks is no longer a viable strategy. Investors will need to be selective, picking sectors and markets that can buck U.S. markets' secular bear trend and generate real growth.

The primary engine of global economic growth is shifting from the United States and the American consumer to developing nations. The largest and most profitable U.S. companies have recognized that simple fact (see Figure 11.4 for a closer look).

Companies in the S&P 500—the largest U.S. corporations—are deriving an ever-growing proportion of their earnings from outside the country. In 2001, less than one-third of S&P 500 profits came from outside the United States; now that ratio is more than half and growing steadily.

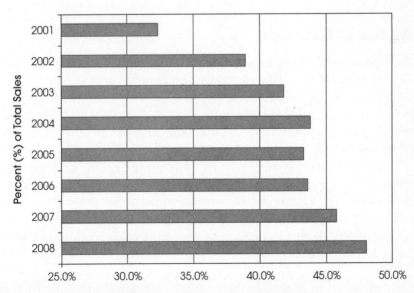

Figure 11.4   U.S. Companies and Developing Nations

If the largest and best-known U.S. firms see better opportunities for growth abroad, investors need to follow their lead by putting their money to work outside the United States and in sectors and companies that benefit from growth in the developing world. Stocks leveraged to key growth trends abroad will outperform in spite of what's likely to be a prolonged period of subdued American growth.

One sector that fits the bill is Energy. Whereas the United States is still the world's largest oil consumer, it's no longer the key to global oil demand—nor, for that matter, are other developed markets. Consider that from 1998 through 2008 oil demand from companies in the Organization of Economic Cooperation and Development (OECD)—a proxy for the developed world—increased their total crude oil consumption by around 734,000 barrels per day. However, countries outside the OECD increased their consumption by 10.1 million barrels per day. In other words, the developing world accounted for more than 93 percent of global oil consumption growth over this time period.

That trend is likely to continue. Literally billions of consumers in China, India, Brazil, Russia, and other developing countries are now reaching a tipping point, a level of income where per-capita demand for energy skyrockets. That spells more demand for oil to run cars, and natural gas, uranium, and coal to generate electric power.

The End of Easy Oil

On September 2, 2009, London-based super oil BP Plc (London: BP; NYSE: BP) announced the discovery of a large oilfield, dubbed Tiber, located in the deepwater Gulf of Mexico. The field is 62 percent owned and operated by BP, while Brazil's Petrobras (NYSE: PBR) and ConocoPhillips (NYSE: COP) own 20 and 18 percent of the find, respectively.

The technical challenges BP encountered in drilling this prospect have been immense. The field is located in waters more than 4,000 feet (1,220 meters) deep, and the total length of the well itself is more than 35,000 feet (10,685 meters)—more than 6.5 miles long from the bottom of the drilling rig to the bottom of the well.

The pressures and temperatures encountered at such depths tested the physical limits of drilling materials and technology. Temperatures in a deepwater oilfield can exceed 300 degrees Fahrenheit (150 degrees Celsius) and pressures can top 10,000 pounds per square inch (psi); for comparison, normal atmospheric pressure on Earth at sea level is just 14.7 psi. In fact, just a few years ago most producers and industry pundits felt drilling such a long well in deepwater was technically impossible.

In the deepwater Gulf of Mexico, BP is the largest leaseholder, has the largest remaining reserves, and is the largest producer, pumping 400,000 barrels of oil equivalent per day.

The company suggested that Tiber will be bigger than another discovery made in the region, the so-called Kaskida find. Since Kaskida is estimated at around 3 billion barrels, this implies that Tiber could be one of the largest oilfields discovered anywhere in the world in the past two decades. Tiber could rival in size some of the major deepwater discoveries offshore from Brazil over the past three years, such as Tupi.

Not surprisingly, soon after BP announced its discovery headlines screamed about a giant new oilfield with reserves equal in size to an entire year's worth of Saudi Arabian oil production.

Some pundits predicted that this surge of new supply would put downward pressure on oil prices, the huge reserves in the Gulf of Mexico seeming proof that global oil production can rise fast enough to meet long-term growth in demand.

As impressive as the Tiber discovery is, the latter argument just doesn't hold water; take great care when absorbing sensationalist headlines about new discoveries. The basic problem is that many confuse oil reserves with oil production, and reserves can be a misleading concept.

The reserve estimates you often hear quoted in the news are for estimates of original oil in place (OOIP), the total amount of oil contained in the reservoir. But oil and gas aren't found in giant underground caves or lakes. These substances are actually trapped in the pores of rocks.

Some of this Tiber oil is stranded in sections of the field where the rock is impermeable—the oil can't flow into the well. And some will simply be left behind during production; there's no way to "pump" it out as if it were in storage.

Typically, a producer won't recover anything close to 50 percent of the OOIP even after many decades of production. In the case of Tiber, it's likely that even if OOIP is more than 3 billion barrels, producers will extract only 500 million to 1 billion barrels of oil, a recovery rate of as high as a third. And this production will come over decades. Don't make the mistake of assuming that 500 million barrels of recoverable oil means producers can extract 1.35 million barrels a day over a one-year period.

The reality is that the Tiber field won't go into commercial production until around 2019. And estimates are that BP's newer deepwater discoveries will allow the firm to boost output from its 2009 level of 400,000 barrels a day to more than 600,000 by 2020. Thus, the real impact is an incremental 200,000 barrels a day of production, a nice boost for BP but barely a drop in the bucket when you consider global oil consumption of more than 80 million barrels of oil per day.

But 200,000 barrels a day of incremental production a decade in the future just doesn't sound as exciting as more than 3 billion barrels of oil in 65-million-year-old rocks under the seafloor; that reality doesn't get much media attention.

This brings me to another common misconception about the oft-used term *peak oil*. Many investors I speak to appear to be of the impression that "peak oil" means that the world is literally running out of oil. That's not the case. "Peak" refers not to the amount of oil in the ground but to the rate at which it can be produced. In other words, the world consumes more than 80 million barrels of oil per day, and demand is likely to grow long-term due mainly to increased consumption from developing countries.

The real question isn't how big global oil reserves are or how much can ultimately be recovered. The question is how quickly they can be produced. If the world demand grows to 90 million barrels per day over the next five years, one of two things must change: Either prices will need to rise enough to choke back demand, or producers will need to ramp up capacity to 90 million barrels a day.

But new production from fields like Tiber in the Gulf and Tupi offshore Brazil is counterbalanced by declining production from existing, older fields.

Consider Figure 11.5, which shows oil production from the U.K. and Norway, the two main producers in the North Sea.

Production of oil from these two countries approximates North Sea production. The U.K.'s two major fields, Brent and Forties, went into production in 1975 and 1977, respectively. Norway's major fields started going into production in the early 1970s and underwent major rehabilitation programs to boost production in the 1980s.

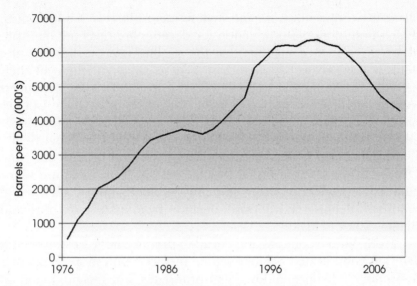

Figure 11.5   Oil Production from the U.K. and Norway
Source: BP Statistical Review of World Energy.

At any rate, Figure 11.5 shows that not long after these giant fields entered production, North Sea oil production began to soar. The initial growth in production was rapid; the North Sea finally entered a sort of plateau period in 1995. Production peaked early this decade and has since fallen precipitously.

Although these fields will still be yielding oil (and gas) for many years to come, the production rate will continue to fall. That's despite the fact that some estimate that many North Sea oilfields still contain 70 percent of their OOIP.

Most fields follow some version of this "bell curve" production profile. In other words, production ramps up quickly when a field is first produced because underground pressures are high; natural geologic forces drive production. But at some point, as pressures fall, production hits a plateau. This occurs long before all the OOIP is recovered. At this point, the producer can use certain techniques to stabilize pressures and increase production. However, these factors are unlikely to do much more than simply stabilize production at relatively high levels.

Simply put, the world isn't running out of crude oil but it is running out of "easy" oil. That is, the massive, technically easy- and cheap-to-produce onshore and shallow-water oilfields that have been the bastion of global production for decades are reaching maturity. Mounting evidence suggests that the decline rate on these mature fields is a good deal higher than analysts usually include in their models. The faster the decline rate, the harder it is for producers to generate real production growth; companies must first offset lost production. To compensate, producers are tapping complex, distant, and expensive-to-produce oil reserves such as BP's Tiber field.

Supply concerns are at the heart of the end of easy oil. Non-OPEC oil production will, at best, remain steady in coming years; additional production from nonconventional sources, such as oil sands and deepwater, will offset declines from mature onshore and shallow-water fields.

Production from easy- and cheap-to-produce large onshore fields with less complicated geology will be replaced with more expensive-to-produce offshore fields. That translates into rising marginal costs for crude oil production and elevated oil prices to incentivize undertaking the massive investment needed to produce oil sands and deepwater projects.

In coming years, the amount of oil OPEC must produce to balance demand (the so-called "call") will increase gradually as demand from developing countries rises and non-OPEC supply declines. OPEC countries have a number of planned projects slated for completion in the next seven years that should increase the organization's production capacity. The bulk of this new capacity will come from Saudi Arabia. Of course, there remains a big question mark as to whether these planned expansions ultimately will increase capacity to the extent expected.

And even if production capacity does rise, the combination of flat-to-declining non-OPEC supply and rising demand will increase the call on OPEC to make up the difference. In short, OPEC's spare capacity—production capacity that can be ramped up quickly and maintained—will likely continue to drop gradually over the coming five to ten years. Figure 11.6 offers a closer look.

Figure 11.6 shows the call on OPEC dating back to the mid-1960s. To facilitate comparison between different periods, I expressed that call as a percentage of global consumption. Beginning in the late 1970s, the percentage declined, and that downward trend accelerated into the mid-1980s. This was a period when OPEC's spare capacity grew sharply due to increased non-OPEC supply from regions such

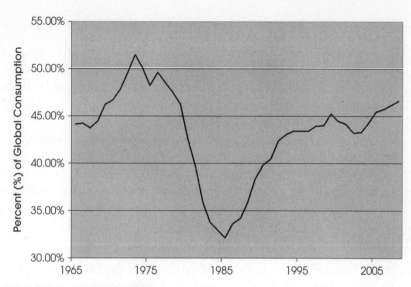

Figure 11.6   Call on OPEC

as the North Sea and Mexico. In 1985, it's estimated that OPEC's spare capacity hit highs above 15 percent of total global demand. In other words, back then the world truly was awash in plentiful crude. Generally speaking, this was also a period of weak oil prices.

The period after 2002 is also noteworthy. As the call on OPEC gradually increased after 2002, spare capacity as a percentage of global consumption declined, hitting lows of roughly 2 percent of global demand in 2005. At that time the oil market literally had only a razor-thin margin of excess capacity. Any shocks to oil supply or demand were enough to send prices soaring. This is the main reason oil prices rallied so much during this period.

The global credit crisis prompted a drop in demand for oil in 2008 and 2009 and corresponding cuts in OPEC output. In other words, the call on OPEC fell with oil demand, and OPEC's production cuts increased spare capacity. But nothing really changed on the supply side; in fact, a severe decline in spending on drilling and exploration will ultimately hasten the fall in non-OPEC output.

Even within OPEC, low oil prices late in 2008 and early 2010 have prompted the delay or outright cancellation of many projects. In other words, the increase in spare capacity in 2008 and 2009 was wholly a function of a short-term drop in demand; as demand returns, spare capacity will decline once again.

This basic theme suggests two key investing angles:

1. *Oil services and equipment firms that have the advanced technologies required to produce more complex fields in regions such as the deepwater Gulf.* Drilling such wells requires far more participation from service and equipment companies than drilling in onshore regions of Texas or the Middle East.

2. *Oil producers with the capacity to increase oil production meaningfully in coming years.* In a world where most of the mammoth integrated oil companies are likely to show declining or, at best, flat production, there's a handful of producers that have the capacity to grow production meaningfully in coming years.

An End to Easy Oil

Here's a rundown of a handful of companies that represent plays on the end-of-easy-oil theme. Investors should consider accumulating shares gradually over a period of time rather than in a single purchase and buying shares after short-term corrections. This discipline will help to ensure the best possible average price.

Schlumberger (NYSE: SLB) is far and away the world's largest oil services company with operations in every imaginable oil- and gas-producing region of the world. Schlumberger is known as a technology leader in many key oilfield services needed to produce the increasingly complex reservoirs that are the key to global oil production. And the company's massive research and development budget ensures that it will maintain its technological leadership in the future.

An example of the type of service Schlumberger performs is reservoir evaluation—evaluation involves determining the quality of a particular field being drilled and type and presence of hydrocarbons (oil or natural gas). For example, logging-while-drilling (LWD) technologies allow producers to evaluate the quality of their reservoir as they're drilling a well; detailed data about the well and nearby rock formations is transmitted on a real-time basis from the drill-bit to operators on the surface.

Schlumberger's WesternGeco unit provides advanced seismic services—the use of sound and pressure waves to map subsurface rock formations. Schlumberger has particularly advanced seismic technologies to map formations in deepwater environments; detailed seismic data are a must in the deepwater as wells are expensive to drill and producers need to ensure wells are placed for optimal production.

Schlumberger also wins points for its geographic and product line diversification. The company has a long history of operating in regions such as the Middle East and Russia and has a significant presence in these key producing countries. In most cases, Schlumberger hires a large local staff rather than simply deploying workers from the United States or Europe. This longstanding presence and local knowledge gives the firm a leg up when it comes to winning new contracts.

Even more important is the rising importance of integrated project management (IPM) and bundled service contracts. Under such deals, producers contract with a services firm to manage projects on their behalf. This might include, for example, arranging for drilling rigs and drilling a certain number of wells in a particular field. Because Schlumberger is a market leader in so many different types of services, it's a natural when it comes to providing bundled deals on complex projects.

Weatherford (NYSE: WFT) is a far smaller services company than Schlumberger but is the fastest growing major oil services firm in the world. Just a few years ago, Weatherford was primarily a North American services firm; the North American drilling market is known for wild cyclical swings in profitability.

But Weatherford has been scaling back its U.S. and Canadian businesses and beefing up its international operations. North America is among the most mature oil- and gas-producing regions of the world; Weatherford has long had a reputation as an expert in maximizing oil and gas production from these older fields. But fields outside the United States and Canada are also aging rapidly; Weatherford is in an excellent position to bring the knowledge and experience honed in North America to other markets.

Weatherford also recently acquired the oilfield services division of TNK-BP, BP's Russian oil joint venture. Weatherford made this acquisition at an opportune time—with oil prices weak in late 2008 and early 2009, the services giant likely got a far better price than it would have during the height of the energy boom in 2006 and 2007. The deal also makes Weatherford a much larger player in Russia, one of the largest and most promising oil- and gas-producing regions of the world.

Weatherford, like Schlumberger, is also becoming an increasingly important player in IPM deals. Examples include the company's multi-year deal in the Chicontepec field in Mexico.

Oil country tubular goods (OCTG) producer Tenaris (NYSE: TS) is a play on rising production from deepwater fields. OCTG are essentially pipes and casing that are used in the construction of wells. Casing for example, is a thick, large-diameter pipe that's cemented in place underground to prevent undesirable liquids, such as water, from seeping into a well and to prevent the well from collapsing.

Although manufacturing pipe might seem like a low-tech, low-margin business, that's not the case. Drilling in deepwater environments exposes pipes and casing to extreme temperatures and pressures that can cause pipes to fail. Tenaris produces advanced, seamless OCTG. Traditional welded pipes are made from a sheet of metal that's formed into a circular shape and then welded closed—an obvious stress point that will fail under extreme pressure. Seamless pipes made from advanced, super-strong metal alloys are needed to effectively drill and produce deepwater fields.

The global rig count—the number of rigs actively drilling for oil and natural gas—fell sharply in late 2008 and early 2009 due to weak natural gas pricing and a pullback in oil prices. Less drilling activity spells less demand for OCTG and, therefore, was bad news for Tenaris.

However, the company's business remained more resilient than most expected; spending on deepwater and other complex international projects remained a lot more robust than expected amid the drilling downturn of late 2008 and early 2009. Deepwater projects call for Tenaris's most advanced pipes and tubing, the company's highest profit margin goods; even as total volumes of OCTG sold have declined, Tenaris saw its mix of products sold shift toward the higher-margin, advanced OCTG used in deepwater projects. This is proof of the power and defensibility of its advanced OCTG franchise even in the midst of a market downturn.

Many investors seem to believe that in a deepwater field, all the equipment used to control a well is located on a floating production platform. But that's just not the case—producers install equipment directly on the seafloor, and this equipment is aptly named *subsea equipment.*

Dril-Quip (NYSE: DRQ) has two divisions: Drilling Equipment and Services. The company's drilling equipment segment, accounting for about 85 percent of revenues, manufactures subsea products used primarily in deepwater offshore field developments.

Subsea trees are key pieces of equipment used in all deepwater oil and gas developments. When onshore wells are completed and ready for production, producers install a network of valves and pipes on top of each well. Subsea trees are infinitely more complex. Such installations include equipment that allows producers to control the flow of oil and natural gas remotely from the surface. In addition, subsea trees have to be able to handle the extremes of pressure, temperature, and other harsh environmental conditions endemic to deepwater oil and gas plays.

As the name suggests, *subsea risers* are a sort of pipe that acts as a conduit between subsea wells and surface production and drilling equipment. Obviously, risers are required during the drilling process and to actually bring produced oil and gas to the surface.

Dril-Quip primarily operates as a backlog business, booking orders for new subsea equipment and then filling those orders over time. Therefore, one widely watched metric of the stock's fundamental health is the size of its backlog, which had continued to rise despite the slump in exploration-and-production spending late in 2008 and early in 2009.

Brazil is unique among global producers in that the vast majority of the nation's oil production comes from offshore fields. The national oil company (NOC) Petrobras (NYSE: PBR) accounts for more than 95 percent of Brazil's production, and 88 percent of this output comes from offshore fields. The contribution of offshore fields to total production has risen steadily in recent years from just over 70 percent in the mid-1990s; offshore and, in particular, production from ultra-deepwater fields is expected to yield most of Brazil's production growth in coming years.

In aggregate, Petrobras now plans to spend a total of $179.4 billion from 2009 through 2013. Roughly 60 percent of that amount will go to exploration and production, while 25 percent will go to downstream/refining operations. That works out to more than $104 billion to be invested in exploration and production in Brazil over the next few years, a major boon for oilfield services and equipment companies that specialize in the technology needed to produce these complex offshore fields.

Petrobras has grown total production roughly 5.6 percent annually since 2001. Management expects annualized growth to reach 8.8 percent through 2013 and 7.5 percent from 2013 to 2020.

If Brazil meets its goal of producing a total of 5.729 million barrels of oil per day, its oil production will be more than double current levels. To put this into perspective, consider that Petrobras projects it will produce more oil than giants Total (NYSE: TOT), Chevron (NYSE: CVX), Royal Dutch Shell (NYSE: RDS.A, RDS.B), and ConocoPhillips (NYSE: COP) by 2013.

Even more impressive, if Petrobras meets its 2020 production targets it will eclipse ExxonMobil (NYSE: XOM), which currently produces around 4.25 million barrels of oil equivalent per day. Its total reserves would be between 25 and 30 billion barrels of oil equivalent, also well above Exxon's reserve base. Given these statistics, it's not hard to see why there's so much excitement about Brazil's deepwater oilfields and Petrobras.

Petrobras is also emerging as a leader in deepwater development, not just in Brazil but in other parts of the Deepwater Golden Triangle. According to management's estimates, Petrobras operates nearly one-quarter of the world's total deepwater production. That's 8 percentage points more than ExxonMobil. In addition to Brazil's deepwater plays, the company owns stakes in deepwater wells in both Africa and the U.S. Gulf of Mexico. Every well that Petrobras drills in the deep adds to its reputation and real-world knowhow, making it a valuable partner in deepwater projects all over the world.

Deepwater is perhaps the most direct play on the end of easy oil, and Petrobras is undoubtedly among the top operators in this area.

Many investors believe that contract drillers actually produce oil and natural gas, but that's not the case: Contract drillers merely supply energy producers with rigs, which include the basic equipment and personnel required to drill an oil or gas well. The producers pay a daily fee known as a *day rate* to lease the rig. Day rates are the main source of revenue for contract drillers and bear no direct relationship to the value of the oil or natural gas extracted from these wells.

Floaters are offshore drilling rigs used in deeper waters. Rather than attaching legs or columns to the seafloor, floating rigs usually rely on a combination of mooring and *dynamic positioning* systems. Whereas mooring systems hold the rig in place using large-diameter rig cables, dynamic positioning systems activate computer-controlled thrusters on a rig to counteract even the choppiest of seas.

Today there are two main types of floating rigs in use around the world: *semisubmersibles*, often referred to as *semis*, and *drillships*. Semis consist of a platform with two large pontoons. Crews tow these rigs to the desired location and fill the pontoons with water, sinking the lower part of the rig to the requisite depth. Pontoons can sink to more than 100 feet below the ocean's surface. Semis are typically moored and dynamically positioned, while the submerged pontoons offer additional stability. Despite these advantages, maneuverability concerns often preclude operators from using semis in remote locations.

The drillship is the other class of floating rig currently in use. These rigs resemble normal oceangoing ships and move under their own power rather than relying on another vessel to tow them—a distinct advantage over semisubmersible rigs. Offering greater maneuverability and equipped to drill to great depths, drillships are used to exploit remote reserves that aren't easily accessible to semis.

Some contractors will use terms like "sixth-generation floaters" to describe their rigs during conference calls, but *ultra-deepwater,* *deepwater,* and *midwater* are the designations usually used to categorize rigs by drilling capabilities.

Although the terms are subject to some interpretation, ultra-deepwater rigs usually can drill in water 7,500 feet or deeper; deepwater rigs can drill to depths of 4,500 to 7,500 feet; and midwater floaters can drill to depths of around 1,500 to 4,500 feet.

Norway-based driller Seadrill (OTC: SDRLF) owns a mixture of primarily ultra-deepwater rigs and high-specification jackups. In total, Seadrill owns 12 ultra-deepwater semis and drillships, one deepwater rig, and one midwater rig. These rigs all have multiyear contracts, many signed in the high-rate environment of 2006 and 2007. Five of these rigs are signed under long-term deals above or near $600,000 per day. The next Seadrill deepwater rigs roll off contract starting in late 2011.

Finally, Seadrill owns a fleet of so-called *tender rigs.* These rigs are used to transport equipment and act as work platforms offshore. They tend to earn lower day rates, but all are under long-term contracts. Suffice to say, this is an attractive asset base. Seadrill's average day rate on ultra-deepwater floaters is higher than what Transocean pulls in, and it's a dominant player in this market niche.

Another source of upside leverage for Seadrill: further normalization of global credit markets. Seadrill has a heavy debt burden. Although a rock-solid backlog of contracts on ultra-deepwater rigs ensures that this debt is serviceable, Seadrill's stock was slammed when investors aggressively sold any company with heavy debt last year. That prompted Seadrill to cancel plans to pay dividends in an effort to conserve cash and shore up confidence in its stability.

To make matters worse, some executives and institutional buyers owned Seadrill stock using what's known as a *total return swap*, a leveraged way to own the stock. The crumbling debt markets meant these trades had to be unwound, further pressuring share prices.

And while Norway is an oil power, it's still a small market; when the U.S. and U.K. debt and equity markets are troubled, those same markets in Norway essentially disappear. But credit spreads have improved markedly, and Seadrill's debt is no longer a major negative. The company's solid backlog of signed contracts essentially guarantees strong cash flows that are more than sufficient to service its debts. It's likely that Seadrill will eventually reinstate a significant dividend backed by these ongoing cash flows.

The ongoing boom in demand for energy from the developing world will continue to surprise most pundits on the upside just as it has over the past decade. But, the real surprise will be supply— global oil production will not be able to grow quickly enough to meet all that new demand. And, in their struggle to boost output, global producers will be forced to tap more technically complex and expensive-to-produce fields.

The spike in crude oil price to $147/bbl in the summer of 2008 wasn't the final move in the energy bull market but the opening salvo in what promises to be an even bigger move.

Epilogue: The BP Mississippi Canyon Block 252 well in the deepwater Tiber field in the Gulf of Mexico blew out on April 20, 2010, after this chapter was written. A resulting rig explosion, sinking, and loss of life ensued. As of July 1, this well is still spilling oil into the Gulf with unprecedented environmental and economic consequences. Attempts to plug the well have so far been unsuccessful. The hope is that two offset wells expected to be completed in August will be able to stop the oil flow. A massive cleanup of the environment and recovery of the regional economy will likely take years. The ultimate impact on BP and the oil industry in general is yet unknown. Elliott Gue discussed "The End of Easy Oil"—little did he know at the time how soon and how profoundly this would prove to be true.

—Ron Miller

CHAPTER 12

Gold Facts

Duane Poliquin

Gold is the earliest metal to be used by humans. Imagine humankind's first encounter with gold when an early human spotted a bright yellow nugget in a creek and picked it up. Gold's luster is not dependent on reflected light, so no matter how he turned it the nugget remained the same beautiful color. It did not tarnish or diminish in any way with time. Most likely he attached it to a leather thong and it became the first gold neck ornament, maybe a gift to his lady.

However this occurred, every society on earth that has had access to gold has valued it very highly, and this happened independently in many places. A culture based in what is now Eastern Europe began to use gold to make decorative objects around 4000 B.C. The gold used was probably from the Mount Pangeon area in northern Greece or from the Transylvanian Alps (the area of Gabriel Resources Ltd.'s Rosia Montana deposit).* The ancient Egyptians thought of gold as a divine and indestructible metal, associated with the brilliance of the sun, with almost supernatural qualities. The skin of Egyptian gods was believed to be of gold and so the Pharaoh wore a lot of gold in order to appear more godlike.[†] There are many references to gold and silver in the Bible and in ancient Greek, Roman, and Persian literature.

---

*The National Mining Association, www.nma.org/pdf/gold/goldhistory.pdf.

[†] "Ancient Egypt: The Mythology," www.egyptianmyths.net, p. 1.

An early reference from India is from a Vedic text written about 1750 B.C.:

> A hundred gold pieces from the fame-seeking king, Together with a hundred horses as a present have I received.*

These pieces of gold were most probably used as money.

The Native American societies, most notably the Incas and Aztecs, prized gold highly and became master craftsmen working with gold. Indeed, whenever one views ancient gold jewelry from some long-lost culture in a museum, the astounding skill and detailed work of these ancient artisans cannot fail to impress; many techniques developed then are still very much in use now. By 3000 B.C., the Sumer civilization in Iraq was making very sophisticated jewelry with some styles still in use today.

Gold Facts

Gold is the 72nd most abundant element in the earth's crust. The chemical symbol for gold is Au, its atomic number is 79, and its atomic weight is 196.96. Gold melts at 1064.43 degrees Centigrade. The specific gravity of gold is 19.3, which means that gold is 19.3 times as heavy as an equal volume of water, an important fact used in gold recovery. Gold is measured in grams or troy ounces. There are 31.1 grams in one troy ounce and one troy ounce is equal to 1.1 ordinary or avoirdupois ounces. One avoirdupois or ordinary pound equals 453.59 grams and one troy pound equals 373.2 grams. One ounce per short ton is equal to 34.3 grams per metric ton. Gold can occur in natural form or it can be tied up within compounds of sulfur and metals called sulfide minerals, such as pyrite, an iron sulfide. Rocks and soil average about 0.0000005 percent gold. Many open-pit heap leach mines make a profit mining rock that contains one gram of gold per metric ton, which is 0.0001 percent gold. That is about one-thirtieth of an ounce in 2,200 pounds! One ounce of gold per metric ton is about 0.0031 percent gold; this would be considered as very high-grade ore.

---

*John Keay, *India: A History* (New York: Grove Press, 2000), p. 30.

Mining and Production

About 2 percent of the world's total gold was produced prior to 1492, when Columbus discovered America. Most of this came from streams that contained gold washed down from the mineral deposits in the area drained by the stream. These are called *placer deposits*. Over time, the rocks are weathered and, as a result, the complex minerals containing the gold break down, liberating the gold, which then gets washed into the streams draining the area. The gold is moved along until it reaches the slow-moving portions of the stream. Where the energy of the stream is lower, it cannot continue to move the heavier minerals along and the gold gradually accumulates until enough has been deposited to make its recovery worthwhile. Ancient gold prospectors and miners wandered far and wide for the precious metal. Strabo, in A.D. 10, wrote, "the mountain torrents are said to bring down gold and these barbarians catch it in troughs perforated with holes and in fleecy skins."

Far earlier, the Egyptians, Greeks, and others had also been using sheepskins to catch the gold in their sluice boxes. Modern placer miners' techniques have not changed much. Bulldozers and pumps move gravel and water now in much bigger volumes and cocoa matting has replaced the fleece. Egypt had many small miners scattered through the Nubian Desert (*nub* was their word for gold). They and other ancients had tunnels and shafts into the deeply weathered parts of bedrock gold deposits. Much of this material could be extracted by pick and pry bar, but harder material like quartz was broken down by first heating it by lighting a fire against the face of rock and, once it was hot, quenching it with water, which caused the rock to crack. This must have been slow work, and these must have been high-grade deposits, although many were operated with slave labor, which resulted in very low mining costs (sad but true). The Egyptians mined about 5 tons per year while the Romans produced about 5 to 10 tons per year. Grave robbers were important in the Egyptian economy because they kept gold in circulation. The Roman coinage was significant because previously the metal had never been abundant enough to underpin a far-reaching money system. To keep the gold in circulation, there were laws limiting the amount of gold that could be buried with the dead.* The Romans

---

* "Gold Avenue Encyclopedia," http://info.goldavenue.com.

particularly wanted the mines of Spain and so they fought the Carthaginians for it. They also invaded and conquered Dacia (now Romania) to gain its rich gold deposits for the empire.

After the so-called Dark Ages, mining and extraction of gold from bedrock deposits gradually became more sophisticated and new techniques for breaking down gold-bearing sulfide minerals were developed. Gunpowder allowed much more rapid extraction of the gold-bearing rock. All of these methods were available when the New World was discovered by Europeans, and abundant new gold sources began to lubricate world commerce. Obviously, much of this was plundered gold, but the Spanish were good prospectors and soon found many new mines to exploit.

Some calculations suggest that prior to the discovery of gold at Sutter's Mill and the California Gold Rush of 1849, total world gold production was only about 10,000 metric tons. This means that more than 90 percent of the world's gold has been produced since 1848.*

Productivity rose because the industrial revolution rapidly developed many useful things. Steam power could run pumps, so mining below the water table became easier (although the Romans had developed manpowered waterwheels to raise water from underground workings). New and bigger milling machinery as well as techniques such as concentration of sulfides by flotation and the use of cyanide to dissolve the gold from rock and then precipitate it again using zinc dust also allowed for larger scale production. After California, fabulous new gold fields were found in the Klondike and Australia and elsewhere. Much of this new gold was from placer deposits and, although rich, their rate of production soon diminished. However, in this same period, several large hard-rock gold districts were also discovered. The most notable of these was the huge Witwatersrand deposits (discussed in the following), discovered in 1886, which have now been producing for well over 100 years. In North America, the Homestake mine in South Dakota and the Kirkland Lake, Timmins, and other camps in Ontario, Quebec, and British Columbia also became very important producers. This rapid rate of development was emulated in Australia, Russia, South America, and many other countries.

Even so, about 50 percent of the world's total gold was produced after 1980. This new era for the yellow metal came about after the

---

* www.goldipedia.gold.org.

price of gold in U.S. dollars rose to its highest level ever until very recently. New gold came from the rapid expansion of production at known deposits, from the mines of the Carlin and other trends in Nevada, from new mines in South America based on a newly understood deposit type, by product production from rich open-pit copper mines such as Grasberg in Indonesia, and by further new techniques in open-pit mining and heap leaching of low-grade ores.

The prolific mines in the Witwatersrand area of South Africa are a unique type of deposit, thought by most (but not all) to be buried ancient placer deposits where the gold has been somewhat remobilized as the placer deposits were deeply buried and then transformed into hard rock. These mines are both very deep and hot, so keeping the workings cool enough for the miners to work is a major mining issue. Other matters affecting South African production are black empowerment legislation and the high cost and availability of electrical power. South African gold production is in serious decline. In 1970, South Africa produced 47.5 million ounces of gold, which was 67.7 percent of the world's gold production; by 2008, this was down to 7.46 million ounces, which was 9.8 percent of total world production.*

For some years now, the overall trend in mining has been toward open-pit mining and recovery of the gold by heap leaching; this has allowed many new companies to enter the ranks of producers because of the lower capital costs involved. Heap leaching was developed by researchers Potter and Salisbury, working in the Salt Lake City branch of the U.S. Bureau of Mines, which, despite the good work it did, was subsequently closed down. This process involves first building a large (in acres) impervious pad of clay with a gentle slope. This is covered with plastic, which in turn is covered with gravel to protect the plastic from punctures. Then either run of mine-broken rock or the same ore crushed to a size determined by testing to be optimum for leaching is heaped on the pad. The pad is then sprinkled with a weak cyanide solution and this trickles through the broken material, dissolving the gold and carrying it down through the gravel to the plastic and along the slope to a collecting pond. This gold-rich solution is then stripped of its gold and recycled through the pad until recovery is determined to be reaching its limits. Further lifts of ore can be piled on top and the

* "Gold Sheet Mining Directory," http://goldsheetlinks.com/production.htm.

process repeated until the property is mined out. The heaps are then sterilized, and rehabilitated by being contoured, covered with topsoil, and seeded with appropriate plants.

This recovery method has been adopted around the world and has allowed for efficient recovery of the oxidized or weathered portions of low-grade deposits and the halo of low-grade material around mined-out high-grade zones. There was a heyday for these deposits because no one had been searching for them until heap leaching changed their economics. The world was scoured for heap-leachable deposits, and they were relatively easier to find because they were near surface and many deposits were quickly identified. It now appears that the most obvious ones have been found and exploration focus must turn to other types of deposits. Other very large gold deposits quickly entered production in this era. Some were known but mothballed through the previous long period of low gold prices; others were known but either very risky or off limits because of their political situation. The end of the Communist era opened up many areas, and not just behind the Iron Curtain. Now, many parts of the world are again becoming very risky for explorers.

Carlin-type deposits have kept the United States in the ranks of the largest gold-producing countries. Around 2000, when U.S. gold production was peaking, Carlin-type deposits were producing over 8 million ounces of the country's total annual production of over 11 million ounces of gold. The first mine was, of course, the namesake Carlin mine, found by large-scale rock sampling to find the source of placer gold in the local streams. The discovery of the Carlin was an excellent piece of work because the fine-grained nature of the gold mineralization made the deposit less obvious than other types and so a whole new type of gold deposit was identified. The second mine discovered became the first Cortez pit, found by sampling in the Cortez hills area by United States Geological Survey personnel. Some samples from this preliminary work ran in the multi-ounce range. Gold has now been produced from more than 40 Carlin-type deposits in Nevada and Utah, and total ounces mined and in reserves is estimated at over 120 million ounces.* The early Carlin-type deposits were mining high-grade zones in open pits, and gold recovery was in conventional cyanide mills with crushing

---

*Steven Castor, "Carlin Type Deposits: An Overview," *SMEDG Talk*, 2001.

and grinding circuits, but heap leaching gradually became the most important recovery method. Then, because the mines became deep enough that they reached unoxidized rock and because some very rich deep deposits were discovered where the gold was locked up in complex sulfides, underground but large-scale mining came back into use with the refractory sulfides being broken down in mills using autoclaves. This type of mining and processing has much higher capital costs and so requires higher-grade ore.

Much of the earliest underground mining was for gold in quartz veins. These deposits are generally narrow, but high grade. They are more labor intensive than open-pit mining, and it can be difficult and expensive to define reserves, so that, in many cases, the mine operator works with only a few years of reserves proven at any one time and the total number of ounces in a deposit is not known until totaled up when the mine is finished.

Nevertheless, over time, vein-type deposits have been one of the most important sources of gold worldwide. There are two main types of vein. *Low sulfidation epithermal veins* are near surface filling of fractures by upwelling waters near volcanic centers. Groundwater flows by gravity down fractures to areas where pressure is great and temperatures are very high. It cannot boil because the pressure at these depths is too high. In this state, the fluid can pick up a load of metal from gases rising from magma. The hydrostatic head caused by more cold, dense water descending causes this superheated fluid to rise up another fracture to the point where, approaching atmospheric pressures and at about 250 degrees Celsius, the hydrothermal fluid boils violently and drops its load of gold and other metals.

Over time, this process repeats with quartz vein material sealing up the fracture as it is deposited. Pressure builds up again and the seal is again burst so that further boiling and deposition occur. Epithermal veins are near surface and the usual vertical range where the boiling could occur is in several hundreds of meters. Such gold deposits can be formed in very short geological time.

Another type of vein deposit is called *mesothermal*. These fracture fillings form above 350 degrees Celsius at depths of more than three kilometers below the surface and they appear to be associated with upward migration of fluids from deeper within the earth. They usually form along cracks subsidiary to major fault lines or fractures of the earth's crust and can have great vertical extent and contain very large deposits. Mesothermal deposits include major vein camps in eastern Canada, the mother-lode district in California, and districts in Australia and other parts of the world. Gold in *banded iron formations* is found in Pre-Cambrian rocks and consists of sedimentary layers or bands of chert alternating with iron-rich layers. The iron can be present either as magnetite (iron oxide) or pyrite (iron sulfide). Most geologists believe the gold was introduced from the same sources as mesothermal veins and deposited due to chemical reaction between these fluids and the iron-rich rock.

Most low-sulfidation epithermal veins are young and most mesothermal veins are old. This is probably simply due to the fact that over time the near-surface epithermal veins are eroded and it takes a long time for Mother Nature to erode the three or more kilometers of rock down to where mesothermal veins will be exposed for discovery. Both can be very high grade with lower grade haloes around them.

High-sulfidation epithermal deposits are another very important source of gold. High and low sulfidation refer to the ratio of sulfur to metal in the sulfide minerals found in each type. These are formed in the near-surface part of a volcanic center. Rather than involving much groundwater, these deposits form in two phases: First, acidic fluids rise along fractures from a hot magma chamber in the core of a volcano. These hot, corrosive fluids spread out, dissolving the rock-forming minerals around the passageway and leaving only the silica, resulting in a sponge-like residual rock called *vuggy silica*. Later, gold- and copper-bearing brines also rise from the magma chamber and fill the spongy rock spaces, forming a gold or gold-copper deposit. These deposits are sometimes large, open-pittable deposits such as Pierina or Pascua Lama in South America. Examples in Nevada include Goldfields, Paradise Peak, and Santa Fe.

Porphyry copper deposits can be another important source of gold. These deposits are formed in the core of a volcano at the top of the magma chamber and usually about one to four kilometers below the surface at the time of emplacement. They would be more or less vertically below a vuggy silica zone and the level of erosion would determine which, if either, might be exposed. The gold is produced as a by-product of the copper mining operation. These are very large, usually lower grade operations. The low-grade aspect is overcome by large tonnages of daily production. This needs high capital costs and a long lead time for feasibility, permitting, financing, and construction. These operations are sensitive to high fuel prices and power costs. The gold grades may be low, but the huge volume mined annually results in significant production. In fact, the Grasberg mine in Indonesia has become the largest goldmine in the world, producing about 2.5 percent of the world's annual gold production. It is also higher grade than many goldmines, averaging over 1.5 grams per ton gold. Grasberg usually produces about 1.4 million ounces of gold annually along with over 4 billion pounds of copper. Some of the ore is in granitic rock intruding into limestone beds, but some very large, rich zones are in rock at the contact between intrusive porphyry and limestone chemically altered by the heat and fluids associated with the intrusion. These are called *skarn* deposits. As these mines get older and deeper, there is a developing trend toward underground block caving. This is also a bulk-tonnage mining method with costs approaching those of open-pit mining. This method of mining requires even more time and up-front capital to prepare the deposit for production.

Analysis for Gold, Associated Scams, and Quality Control

The Babylonians developed the *fire assay* method to determine the purity of gold in about 1350 B.C., and this is still the definitive assay method for gold today. This might be an appropriate place to put in a warning to investors: Do not *ever* believe stories about gold that cannot be detected by fire assay. Generally, these scams run with claims about some special litharge (the flux used in fire assays) or a very secret proprietary method that detects the gold in order to lure the hapless investor into putting money into some worthless project. Often the potential investor is invited to watch the assay process and, of course, a gold bead is produced for the investor to see with his or her own eyes. It is there only because it was *put there* by human hands; *there is no gold that cannot be detected by fire assay*. Further, if the gold can be detected only by a secret means, then obviously no milling equipment currently available could recover the gold in a full-scale operation. Strangely enough, many people who should know better have been taken in by these tales and, even when told it is a fraud, they still want to believe because they saw some gold with their own eyes. Fraud can also be perpetrated by adding gold to samples; this is called *salting*. The infamous Bre-Ex scam was a very sophisticated salting operation where thousands of samples over a long period of time had placer gold added to them in a way that made the assay results consistent and believable to the extent that many experts were fooled. Salting can be subtle, such as putting gold in solution into sample bags using a hypodermic syringe, or not so subtle, such as replacing the shot in a shotgun shell with grains of gold and firing it at the area to be inspected and sampled.

As part of quality control, the engineer in charge of a drill or other sampling program will insert a number of samples known to have no gold (blanks), duplicate samples, and standard samples (samples prepared by a specialist laboratory that, after multiple assays, can certify the precise amount of gold per ton that the sample contains) into the flow of samples going to the laboratory. The samples are kept under secure conditions until the laboratory doing the analyses takes delivery of the samples. If any of the blanks, standards, or duplicates yields analyses different from what is expected, a warning flag goes up and the discrepancy is tracked down for explanation.

Gold as Money and a Measure of Wealth

Gold has been the final settlement mechanism for trade for at least 3,500 years. Even in barters, if the bartered products were not equal, the difference could be made up in a gold exchange. Somewhere around 1500 B.C., the mines of Nubia (modern-day Sudan) made Egypt a wealthy nation as gold became recognized as the standard medium for international trade. The *shekel*, a coin originally weighing 11.3 grams of gold, became a standard unit of measure in the Middle East. It contained a naturally occurring alloy called *electrum* that was about two-thirds gold and one-third silver. Around 1091 B.C., little squares of gold were legalized in China as a form of money, followed independently by the Asia Minor-based kingdom of Lydia, which produced the first coins made purely from gold.

About 360 B.C., Aristotle pointed out that gold was the best thing to be money because of three qualities: First, it is durable and will never tarnish or rust away or be diminished in any way by use. Your wedding ring might have been part of some ancient king's crown, melted and remelted and refashioned many times over the centuries so that its provenance is lost in time but the gold remains the same. The only gold lost to use is that buried or in sunken ships. Second, gold is portable; it has high value in a small size so that one can carry a lot of value of money on one's person. Third, it is divisible. A diamond can be more valuable for the same weight, but if the big diamond is divided, the value for each piece goes drastically down, whereas a smaller weight of gold has the same value per ounce as a larger piece. In addition to these qualities, gold has intrinsic value because it has many uses beyond money, jewelry, or decorative application that the ancients never even suspected. For instance, gold's high conductivity makes it a must-have for electronic uses such as the contact points in your computer and television set, and it is used in the electronics of your car's airbags to ensure reliability.

As trade and communications became more sophisticated, some form of note backed by or exchangeable for a defined amount of gold was sometimes used. This was easier to carry around but depended on confidence in the bank or party holding the gold in trust. When there was confidence in these notes, trade and prosperity flourished; but when the bank decided to profit more by printing more notes than the gold held, people gradually lost their confidence and drops in trade and prosperity would follow.

The same holds true for governments. Virtually no government throughout history, whether despotic or democratic, has been able to resist for very long the desire to grow and spend more every year. To finance the growth in bureaucracy, monuments, military adventures, or buying votes with more and more and sillier social spending, tax revenue is never quite enough and so the existing money has to be diluted without causing too much concern among the people. When gold and silver were the only money, one way to achieve this was by clipping edges off the roughly made coins. When enough clippings were assembled, a new coin with the same face value was made. So, the coins weighed a bit less but still had the same face value. There were probably still some unclipped coins in circulation, so no one noticed right away and the government got the same bang for less gold. However, when most were clipped, the more sophisticated people would notice and prices would start to creep up and the first inflations were born. The same thing was done by some rulers who gradually diluted the gold by alloying it with silver or copper but keeping the same face value, with the same long-term results. There is no possible shenanigan to dilute the money and spend it before the public notices that some government hasn't tried. We can read of the same methods being repeated in different ages by different peoples. Even outlawing gold as money is not new but has failed in history and will ultimately fail whenever tried.

Throughout time, rulers have always claimed a monopoly on gold and gold mining. Some governments had their own mining operations and some farmed out the right to mine in return for a royalty. This is still the case with mining rights obtained by staking a claim, or acquiring a lease or concession. This right is always subject to some form of royalty or taxes, so mining companies seek out jurisdictions with the most favorable rates. Many regimes today are not much better than the despots of ancient times. Too often, regulations that sound reasonable are put in place to attract investment but when a valuable mineral deposit is found the rules change, or the investment contracts suddenly need renegotiation, or some problem (pick a favorite) is found with the mining companies' work or reporting, and the discovering company is out of luck. Then the newfound gold deposit winds up in government or government cronies' hands.

After World War II, the United States had three-quarters of the world's gold, so international finance was arranged under the Bretton Woods system, whereby other currencies had a more-or-less fixed exchange rate to the U.S. dollar and it in turn was tied to and exchangeable for gold at the rate of $35.00 per ounce. The cost of the Vietnam War and domestic policies began to result in trade and budget deficits for the United States in the 1960s. Other countries, particularly France, began to worry about the dollar and began to turn in their dollar holdings for gold.

Richard Nixon unilaterally and "temporarily" suspended the dollar's convertibility to gold on August 15, 1971. The closure of the gold window led to the dollar's devaluation in terms of gold in both 1972 and 1973. In order to prevent further devaluations, the tie to gold was broken and the IMF's articles were amended so as to prohibit members from denominating their currencies in terms of gold. Ironically, although it was the weakness of the dollar relative to gold that brought about the collapse of the Bretton Woods system, it was gold that was removed from its primary position as a monetary asset while the devalued dollar became even more central to the smooth operation of the international economy.*

---

* Mark Duckenfield, editor, *The Monetary History of Gold: A Documentary History, 1660–1999* (London: Pickering and Chatto, 2004), pp. 324–327.

In the years since Nixon closed the gold window, gold's role as money has been forgotten by many and is considered a quaint, old-fashioned notion. Governments continue to print more paper money and exchange between currencies is mostly with floating rates. We are told that currencies are backed by the economy, but the currency is a government monopoly and the economy is surely made up of enterprises owned by individuals and corporations. If the government wants the economy to back its currency, it has to do so by taxing the economy for what it needs.

No matter what economists or politicians might want, it seems certain that gold will continue to be a long-term store of wealth for individuals for a very long time to come.

Outlook for the Gold Mining Industry

In the past few decades, the gold industry has grown mostly by mergers and acquisitions. Former major mining companies, such as Dome, Placer, Homestake, and Lac, and a host of smaller companies now make up Barrick Gold Corporation. It used to be that the large companies did grassroots exploration, because only they could afford it, while junior companies focused on old showings because at least they were starting with some kind of mineral-bearing zone. Now, most major company exploration budgets are focused on the areas around their existing mines, trying to develop more reserves near their established operations, and virtually no money goes into early stage exploration. The juniors also seek advanced properties because these are what they can raise exploration money on. So the juniors often option noncore properties from a major, and this has been well rewarded in the marketplace.

In the meantime, total world goldmine resources are in decline and the production rates of many companies are in a downward trend. An acquisition may make a company and its total reserves larger, but there are no new ounces of reserve as a result. The same ounces simply have a new owner. There are few discoveries in the pipeline and those that are new are often in politically unstable jurisdictions. New discoveries are needed, and the main incentive to seek them and to finance this type of exploration is probably a very sharp rise in the price of gold. There is no doubt that many new deposits remain to be discovered, and these will continue to satisfy humankind's need for gold.

The Rare Coin Market

UNDERSTANDING HOW IT WORKS

Van Simmons and David Hall

The rare coin market is one of the oldest and most exciting of all the collectibles markets. The Romans collected Greek coins! There has been an active coin market in this country since just prior to the Civil War.

For the past 40 years, the rare coin market has been extremely active, prices have soared, and the market for rare coins has grown to annual sales of approximately $5 billion, not including what the various government mints sell, and not including pure bullion coins.

For many decades, rare coins have been a superb inflation hedge and a great store of value. Rare coins are the most information rich (there is tons of information both from the U.S. Mint and private sources on rare coins) and liquid of all collectibles. And of course rare coins have a very strong connection to the gold and silver markets. Rare coin prices have performed superbly for the past 10 years. Although the rare coin market, like all free markets, has its ups and downs, the long-term trend has been up.

The world certainly has a lot of financial challenges today, and rare coins offer a superb hedge against one of the biggest challenges of all: the declining purchasing power of the U.S. dollar.

In the rare coin market today, the name of the game is *rare gold*. And considering what is going on in the world, this makes total sense.

Since the financial crisis that started around mid-2008, many commodities, including oil and (very telling) platinum, dropped in price for a while until late 2008. Since then, gold bullion has risen to new highs and for the first half of 2010, has traded in the $1,000 to $1,200-plus range. The world obviously is looking to gold, and the smart money doesn't have a lot faith in the U.S. dollar.

I was in Rome recently, taking a tour of the ancient sites—the Coliseum, Forum, and so on—and the tour guide mentioned that the great Emperor Trajan did not inherit the throne but rose to the title when there was no heir available because he was the greatest general of the time. Since he wasn't an heir, he had to prove himself to the Senate and the people, so he gave away a lot of money and favors and immediately became very popular. The fact is, all of our politicians, on the right and on the left, curry favor with the voters and even more so the special interests by giving away money and favors. But it's money that doesn't exist. It's not gold; it's just printed paper and entries in computers. The U.S. dollar is deteriorating and the world knows it. Worse, the deterioration is accelerating. Gold remains the safe haven, and one extremely interesting little corner of the gold market is rare gold coins, and their rare silver sisters.

How to Participate in the Rare Coin Market

This should be simple—just call up a coin dealer and buy some coins, right? Well, you can do that, but like all markets there are good strategies and bad strategies. We'll define "good strategy" as actions that will increase the potential for monetary gain and decrease the potential for headaches and problems. Here are the *do's* and *don'ts* of the rare coin market:

Basic Strategy #1: Buy the Right Coin

The easiest thing to do in the coin market—and maybe the easiest thing to do in life—is to spend money. But if you want to maximize your potential, you have to buy the right coin. First, you should buy gold and silver coins. The world understands gold and silver. There are some wonderful rare copper and nickel coins, but unless you're a serious long-term collector, you are better off sticking with gold and silver coins.

Second, you should buy the classic, nonesoteric market. As I stated earlier, this is an information-rich market. Any dealer who tells you he has a "super-sleeper" coin is probably lying to you about other things as well. Stick to the classics: top-quality examples of the major gold types (circa 1840–1933), proof gold coins (1860–1915), early gold (1795–1838), silver type coins (circa 1795–1916), Morgan and Peace dollars (1878–1935), silver commemoratives of the classic era (1892–1954), and Walking Liberty half-dollars (1916–1947).

Basic Strategy #2: Buy the Right Grade

In the collectibles markets, quality is a big component of value and demand. You can buy beachfront property or property in the ghetto, but the slum-landlord approach to rare coins is not the way to go. Only buy top-quality coins. That's where all the demand and action are. Rare coins are graded on a 70-point scale, where 70 is the highest grade. Coins graded 65 or better are considered *gem quality*. With the exception of early issues (pre-1840) and generic bullion-related gold, you should buy 65-or-better-quality coins exclusively. Again, this is where most of buyer demand has been focused for the past 40 years and it will probably continue this way.

Specific Coin Recommendations

There are all kinds of great coins you can buy, and some not-so-great coins you shouldn't buy. Here are a few of the rare coin market's current best bets.

The two types of rare gold coins that have the most potential are *proof* gold coins and the 1838–1908 *Liberty* gold coins. Proof gold is the beachfront property of the rare coin market. These coins are very rare with some dates having original mintages of as few as 20 to 30 coins.

Interestingly, there is very little high-quality proof gold available. The supply is extremely thin, especially for Professional Coin Grading Service (PCGS)-graded coins. Gem-quality examples of circa 1860–1915 proof gold coins start in the $10,000-to-$20,000-per-coin price range, so it's an area for those with a sufficient budget, but you receive a tremendous amount of rarity and importance per dollar spent. This is one of the areas that has my highest recommendations.

Rare-date Liberty gold coins constitute one of the few actually underpriced areas of the rare coin market. The rare coin market is relatively mature and there is a ton of information available about each rare coin issue, so the pricing structure of the market is pretty rational. But Liberty gold has often taken a backseat to the glamorous 20th-century issues, such as the $20 St. Gaudens and $10 Indian, when in fact many of the better date Liberty gold coins are much rarer. Take a good look at the $2.5, $5, and $10 Liberty series. There are great coins available starting at about $3,000 per coin.

There were 144 different silver commemoratives; all but two were half-dollars, issued by the U.S. Mint between 1892 and 1954. These have been avidly collected for decades. Recently, at least as of this writing, prices have come down on these numismatic classics. They are beautiful, historically important, relatively scarce, and fairly inexpensive. Consider putting together a 50-piece type set or a 144-piece date and mint mark set of these beautiful coins.

The classic 19th-century silver type coins is an area that has enjoyed good demand and price action for decades. These are extremely beautiful, very important coins that are rare in top condition. Some of the key issues are:

- Trade dollars (1873–1885)
- Liberty Seated dollars (1840–1873)
- Proof Morgan dollars (1878–1904)
- Liberty Seated half-dollars (1839–1891)
- Twenty-cent pieces (1875–1878)

Buy these coins in mint state or proof 65 or better condition.

What Not to Buy

There are definitely coins you should avoid. The two major areas to avoid are ultramodern issues and very common, mediocre-quality coins. The ultramodern coins—coins that were struck after 1970 or so—were made in huge quantities and a high percentage were saved. The closer to present time you get, the truer this axiom becomes. Coins from the 1990s and 2000s, for example, are readily available and there is not very much after-market demand. I highly recommend you stick to prewar (World War II) issues and avoid the modern "television shopping" coins.

Be certain the coins you purchase really *are* rare. So avoid mediocre-quality, relatively common coins. You want true rarity and you want high quality. And this should be a concept that's easy to understand.

Two Final Very Important Tips

Here are two tips to help you get what you pay for in the rare coin market: First, when you do business with a dealer, make sure you are dealing with the person who owns the company. If you're talking to an "account representative," a "senior numismatist," or anyone other than the owner(s) of the company, you are talking to a salesperson. In the coin industry, sales reps typically get a 6 to 10 percent commission on sales.

And guess who pays the sales commission? You do, in the form of a higher price for the coin. Some firms have 40 to 50 people working the phones. Those firms also have sales managers who get a commission override on the sales staff. Look for the firms owned by a true coin dealer/expert and deal directly with that person. You don't want to buy coins from a commissioned phone sales rep.

The second way to increase your odds of getting what you pay for is to make sure you buy PCGS-graded coins exclusively. The PCGS is the third-party "gold standard" among the coin-grading services. Since 1986, PCGS has graded over 17 million coins with a declared value of over $20 billion. PCGS coins are worth more than coins graded by other grading services. Some dealers may tell you that coins graded by XYZ Grading Service bring the same as PCGS coins in the market, but it's just not true. Dealers will try to sell you non-PCGS-graded coins for *one reason only*: The profit margins are bigger on non-PCGS-graded coins.

The rare coin market should do really well in the next few years if any or all of the following happen (and all of these scenarios are interrelated): The gold bullion market remains strong in the $1,000-per-ounce range, the gold bullion market makes a significant run above $1,000, inflation increases, and/or the U.S. dollar continues its value slide.

The rare coin market is a good inflation/dollar deterioration hedge, and a good bet on the upside for gold prices. Buy from true experts, not sales reps, buy PCGS-graded rare coins, and look only at high-quality rare gold and silver coins.

Other Currencies versus the Dollar

Frank Trotter

The investing world is extremely set in its ways.

Since the advent of enterprise, people have invested time, labor, intellectual property, and money (when it came into existence) in business. At first, this took the form of throwing in your lot with a friend or neighbor. The two of you would shoe horses, or bake bread, or plow fields in exchange for some other service. In time, some metals began to act as a medium of exchange and a storehouse of value. We think of gold and silver today, but tin, cattle, rocks, diamonds, and other portable elements acted as a clearinghouse for services in different regions and at different times.

Eventually, some people accumulated enough wealth as measured in the local community to invest in other businesses. Initially, this was done directly, person to person; since exchanges developed it has been possible to invest in equities nearby or far away, either to benefit from their success or lose your shirt along with the owner when the bubble bursts or the market turns. Over time, investing in stock markets has provided investors the world over with what are considered superior returns on the capital invested.

On the borrowing side, first monarchies and then companies obtained funding from the community in the form of loans. As more money was needed from a wider audience, these became subdivided like stock into shares called *bonds*. Bondholders own the opportunity for full loss of principal like stockholders, but have traded many other risks away in return for interest payments and a more senior position in liquidation. Bonds provide stability and much relative security.

Since the pioneering work of Markowitz in the 1950s, investing professionals and most individuals have focused on building diversified portfolios. While the strict academic components of the theoretical process are often unknown or misunderstood, most investors understand the basic concepts of diversification and have attempted to include assets from different classes in their portfolios of risk assets.

But at the same time, even today, as we talk with friends and colleagues you might hear them respond to a question about diversification with something like, "sixty-five percent stocks, thirty percent bonds, and five percent cash." If you probe deeper, they'll probably answer that their stock portfolio consists of various classes of U.S. equities, and that the bond portfolio is laddered for maturity using U.S. Treasuries and mortgage-backed securities. Many would consider owning the latest S&P exchange-traded fund to be a complete diversification of their portfolio.

Well, that's a start.

Since World War II, the markets here in the United States have progressively become inclusive for individuals in all walks of life. Not only are the wealthy participants in the markets, but today a broad sweep of the population has a stake in our economy. The advent of individual retirement accounts (IRAs) and investing at work in 401(k)s and the like has extended the level of participation.

Over the past 40 years, improvements and innovation in mutual funds and collective investing have developed so that all major and many minor asset classes are covered and for most there are many choices of approach.

One of the key results has been that returns in these investing alternatives have become efficient to the point that they cluster almost exclusively around the asset class index. Despite the protests of market professionals, studies have consistently shown that selecting asset classes is far more important than selecting managers or attempting market timing.

One example is "False Discoveries in Mutual Fund Performance: Measuring Luck in Estimated Alphas," by Laurent Barras, Olivier Scaillet, and Russ Wermers. This study shows that over a long period of time, 75 percent of managers have enough skill to approach their measurement index after fees and expenses, 24.4 percent do not make the index, and only 0.6 percent are skilled enough to outperform for over five years. Since we haven't met an investment advisor or asset manager who doesn't claim to beat his or her index, this must mean that everyone is one of that 0.6 percent!

The rational result of this is to build portfolios around asset classes that provide risk diversification and opportunities for return. In the process we have seen a burst of activity toward the democratization of the global marketplace. Today, you can choose from equity investments from markets around the world, bonds in many markets and many currencies, and commodity and other alternative classes to spread risk and gain when each asset class comes into the light.

Currency Investing: Adding an Asset Class with Global Clout

August 15, 1971, was otherwise a dog day of summer with nothing to commend it. Swirling around the edges were the Vietnam War, oil price pressures, increasing inflation, and the first U.S. trade deficits of the 20th century.

Since World War II, the United States and its major trading partners had been managing currency prices under the Bretton Woods system, put in place at the end of the war to provide financial stability to the world. Under this system, currencies were pegged in price to gold, and participating countries were required to follow policies that maintained the relationship of their currency to the price of gold.

This controlled-exchange-rate environment, akin to a multilateral version of what China does unilaterally today, did provide for years of relative stability compared to some of the financial disasters following World War I.

But it is the nature of governments that they want to control the world around them. Historically, as modern finance developed in the West, this mostly meant controlling the flow of gold in or out of the country. Countries that could export valuable products would see gold flowing into their kingdoms, and net purchasers would watch it literally sail away to other shores.

As a relatively fixed-quantity commodity, gold served as a governor on the potential pace of growth the world could attain. And through time, while governments sought to violate the laws of trade, often cooler (and in this case arguably remarkably better) heads prevailed. The following shows that balance of trade and payments has been a source of contention throughout our modern history:

> The safety & encrease of the coyn depends principally on the ballance of trade. If the ballance of trade be against us the money will be melted down & exported to pay debts abroad & carry on trade in spight of laws to the contrary, & if the ballance of trade be for us such laws are needless and even hurtfull to trade.*

This discipline, however, while the friend of restraint and rationality, is not a comfortable companion to rulers wishing to extend beyond their means. After nearly 10 years of the escalating costs of the Vietnam War, and the first few years of the Great Society, and through inflation pressures it was too much for the United States.

On August 15, 1971, President Nixon unilaterally removed the U.S. dollar from convertibility to gold. In one stroke this ushered in an era where financial restraint became passé. Over the past 40 years, this has resulted in a system of governing, by both major parties, where running fiscal deficits and ignoring trade imbalances has become the norm. This has also led to the creation of a new asset class and a way to profit from relative government behaviors and hedge against a fall in global purchasing power. One of his chief advisors for this move was Paul Volcker, who will appear again in our saga.

When we look at currency behavior since 1971, we see a number of long-lived trends of U.S. dollar decline and advance. (See Figure 14.1.) Looking further into research, academics note that currency prices do move in long trends that are based on fundamental relative government policies. So, what are the key factors in determining currency prices?

Whether you do this explicitly like an equity analyst, or subjectively like most retail investors, the price of a stock is determined as the present value of expected future cash flows, discounted at an appropriate risk-based rate of return. While that is quite a mouthful, it is based on things like the quality of management, effectiveness of sales and operations, and the general health of the industry.

---

*1702 July 7 Report of Isaac Newton to Sidney Godolphin, Lord High Treasurer of England, concerning the values of various foreign gold and silver coins.

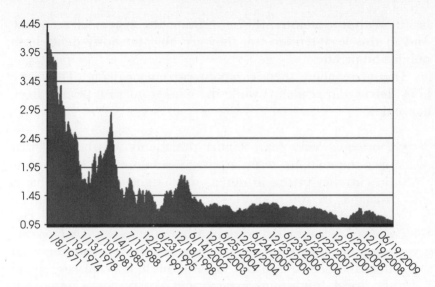

Figure 14.1 U.S. Dollar versus the Swiss Franc (1971–2010)

In short: Is this a potentially growing industry with adequate net income potential, and is the management good at the business?

Currencies in the modern world do not have this luxury. Everything is relative because nothing is fixed. A satirical piece in *The Onion* hits uncomfortably close to the truth:

> The U.S. economy ceased to function this week after unexpected existential remarks by Federal Reserve chairman Ben Bernanke shocked Americans into realizing that money is, in fact, just a meaningless and intangible social construct. . . . "It's just an illusion," a wide-eyed Bernanke added as he removed bills from his wallet and slowly spread them out before him. "Just look at it: Meaningless pieces of paper with numbers printed on them. Worthless."*

At the end of the day, currencies are in fact a belief system that is more a medium of exchange than something of real value. They float based on the market's assessment of relative strength gained from government policy and business activity. Within a political entity, they are the scorecard for labor, production, expense, and

---

* *The Onion*, February 19, 2010, http://www.theonion.com/articles/us-economy-grinds-to-halt-as-nation-realizes-money,2912/.

profit. Within a country, they constitute the system of accounts. And in this legal-tender era, they are able to satisfy debts both public and private.

There are many theories about currency pricing. These are hotly debated in academia while the market goes on pricing from day to day.

- *Purchasing power parity.* Under this theory it is believed that over the medium term, arbitrage cannot occur based solely on currency prices. In other words, a good or service that is available in two countries under consideration cannot be priced differently for long before arbitrageurs drive the currencies' prices to parity. For illustration purposes, *The Economist* publishes what they call the "Big Mac Index" showing what this sandwich costs in U.S. dollar terms in many places around the world. If it is more expensive in Norway, for example, it is an indication that the Norwegian currency is overvalued, and if it is cheaper in China, then the Renminbi is undervalued.
- *Quantity theory of money.* In this case, from a starting point the relative change in the quantity of money between two countries will drive the reset of exchange rates. For example, if the money supply growth in the United States is greater than the money supply growth in Norway, then the U.S. dollar should lose value against the Norwegian krone. This is the primary theory for the monetarist camp of economics.
- *Labor price of money.* Something that can only change in the long run combines the two theories noted above. Within a market, labor costs drift toward a level that can be sustained locally. With active substitution of labor, similar jobs will price near the same level; a skilled factory worker will earn similar amounts within an economy in different geographies. This becomes the median income figure quoted across countries. This level is driven in part by the quantity of money in an economy, which changes the level of prices; in the end, the job will buy a similar basket of goods over time. After this has stabilized, purchasing power parity will drive currency prices to equilibrium (for an instant) based on costs and values on a global scale.

In our view, valuing currencies is much like going to a low-end used car lot. No currency today has any intrinsic value—all are arbitrarily priced. Each government and economy has blemishes. In car terms, investors seek to choose the used car that is likely to start most days and get them to work and that drives a little longer, better, and faster than the others. Since governments are involved, the quality of the car can change at the whim of those in power at the moment, but since policy tends to move slowly, the car will tend to continue in one direction, weaving along the way, until something substantial changes.

Looking back to 1971, we see that the U.S. dollar has endured five trends. Let's break these down and see what some of the underlying causes were to help us look into the future.

1971-1978

Recall that prior to 1971 the U.S. dollar price was fixed by the Bretton Woods agreement and was essentially fixed, or at least managed, within a range. The contributing factor for Nixon to remove the United States from the gold standard was that with all the deficit spending for the Vietnam War, and the Great Society, and with inflation rising investors and governments around the world believed that the U.S. dollar was overvalued.

As it turns out, the market continued to think this way. Over this seven-year period, the U.S. dollar lost 65 percent of its value against the Swiss franc, an annual rate of 12.6 percent. (See Figure 14.2.)

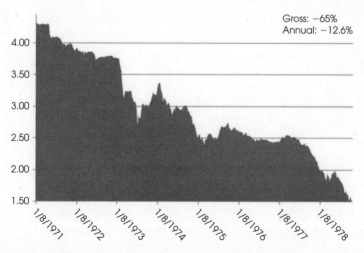

Figure 14.2   U.S. Dollar versus Swiss Franc (1971-1978)

This was a period of continued fiscal problems, inflation, and slow growth. *Stagflation* became the word of the day and we were wearing Whip Inflation Now (WIN) buttons in order to combat this insidious problem.

We regard this as weak dollar trend, one that ratcheted down the value of the dollar, in a jerky sort of way, across three administrations from both sides of the aisle.

1978–1985

After clicking around the same level for about a year, in October 1979 the United States in particular and the world in general experienced the Volcker Shock Therapy. Applying a monetarist approach, the U.S. Federal Reserve Bank led by Volcker (there he is again) decided to focus its attention on money supply growth as its chief policy tool. Already in the midst of stagflation, the U.S. economy entered a genuine recession as interest rates spiked. The prime rate rose as high as 21.5 percent and U.S. Treasury bills traded in the high teens.

While the U.S. dollar rose 93 percent from its lows in 1978, it remained 30 percent lower than where it began in 1971. (See Figure 14.3.) Other factors played heavily in this rise. Ronald

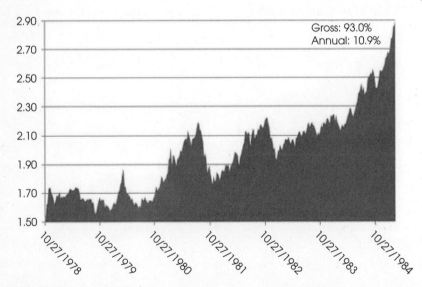

Figure 14.3   U.S. Dollar versus Swiss Franc (1978–1985)

Reagan was elected president and began to change the regulatory framework of government, and at the same time created with Congress hitherto unheard-of deficits. With the world's reserve currency providing extremely high interest rates with no default on the horizon, investors the world over bought dollars to buy U.S. Treasury issues and company stock as the great stock market gain commenced.

We consider this period of U.S. dollar strength a technical anomaly due to the unusually high rates available at the time.

1985–1995

As the United States became less and less competitive in the global marketplace, with the U.S. dollar climbing higher and higher, the Group of Five, as it was known at the time, came to an agreement to reduce the value of the U.S. dollar. This Plaza Accord, with the United States represented by Paul Volcker among others, contained both jawbone (rhetoric) and currency market intervention. Within two years, the U.S. dollar had declined by slightly over 50 percent, a trend that flattened but continued for another eight years. (See Figure 14.4.)

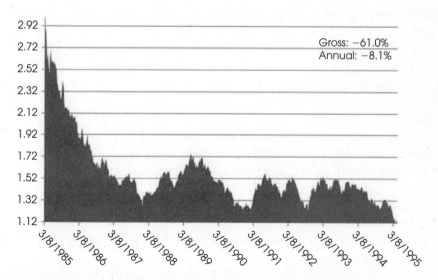

Figure 14.4   U.S. Dollar versus Swiss Franc (1985–1995)

This period was also accompanied by the realization that the fiscal policies put in place in the early 1980s would not be sustainable in the long run. The theory went that at some points on the utility curve, a reduction in taxes provides an incentive that increases business activity so much that even at the lower rate total tax collections will increase.

As currency observers, we strongly agree that less government interference in the economy is best. We agree that a lower tax burden provides a significant incentive for companies. We also agree that at some points on the curve this will occur, and we agree that tax rates had to decline after becoming draconian in the late 1970s. But we also think that this approach ignores the inflationary impact of fiscal deficits to the point that while nominal collections may rise, real collections fall.

When you are running a budget—government, corporate, or personal—there are only three dials to turn when seeking to balance a budget. In government terms these choices are:

1. Reduce spending.
2. Increase revenue.
3. Continue to run a deficit and pay it back later with a depreciated currency.

In the life of a politician these days, cases 1 and 2 seem to be off the table for both ideological and political reasons. So, what we have had in most administrations since 1980 is the final choice—kicking the can down the road.

It was the post–Plaza Accord period that kicked off the intense focus on relative fiscal policy in currency price evaluations. It was also in this period that some countries, in particular New Zealand and Australia, came fully into the spotlight. In both cases, economies that had been heavily dependent on and controlled by Commonwealth policy were breaking free of those shackles and progressing toward a modern state. Like the United States, high interest rates existed through the mid-1980s, but for both New Zealand and Australia these high rates extended past the fall in U.S. rates as the risk in each economy required a higher rate to attract foreign investors.

As a result, while the U.S. dollar decline against its major trading partners occurred mostly within two years of the Plaza Accord, advances by the Pacific Rim and other currencies continued well toward 1995.

1995–2001

The period from 1995 through 2001 contained two key factors that drove the U.S. dollar higher. (See Figure 14.5.) First, the sometimes-uneasy partnership between the Gingrich Congress and the Clinton presidency produced fiscal policy that reigned in the fiscal deficit printed by the United States to the point that there were surpluses and forecasts of a reduction in outstanding U.S. debt going forward.

Second, the tech revolution and ultimately stock market bubble produced an investment environment where the world wanted to own U.S. stocks and had to buy U.S. dollars to do so.

Like a company that had finally gotten its balance sheet into shape, the market rewarded the U.S. dollar with an appreciation of nearly 50 percent. During this period, the United States had not only better fiscal management but also a strong dollar policy under Robert Rubin. Unfortunately, since 1987, the Federal Reserve was moving away from policies that contained money supply growth to more political policies to promote growth. This will be a major contributor to the next trend.

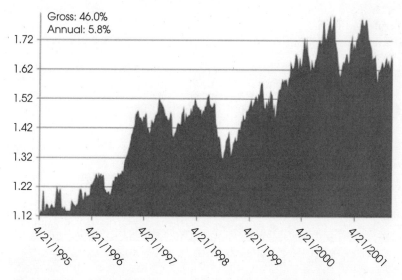

Figure 14.5   U.S. Dollar versus Swiss Franc (1995–2001)

2002–2010: The Present

One of the benefits of being currency market analysts and bean counters is that either side of the aisle can make things worse for the U.S. dollar, and both sides do. After being set up beautifully with a balanced budget and a growing economy in 2001, the combination of a small recession, the 9/11 terrorist attacks, and a pent-up-demand single-party budget set off a significant decline in the U.S. dollar.

After the announcement that the 2002 fiscal budget deficit might reach 5 percent of GDP, along with a trade deficit in the same range, I began to tell everyone I knew that the strengthening U.S. dollar trend was over and was going to reverse quickly. And so it did.

Against the Swiss franc, the U.S. dollar lost about 37 percent over the next eight years, and closer to 60 percent against the euro and the Australian dollar. (See Figure 14.6.) Congress and the administration stumbled along with large budget deficits, joined by a political Federal Reserve Bank headed by Alan Greenspan that kept rates remarkably low for an extended period of time. With Greenspan apparently having misplaced his predecessor Paul Volcker's understanding of money supply, a liquidity bubble was created that resulted in the mispricing of real estate assets. As we stand today, politicians on both sides of the aisle continue to say

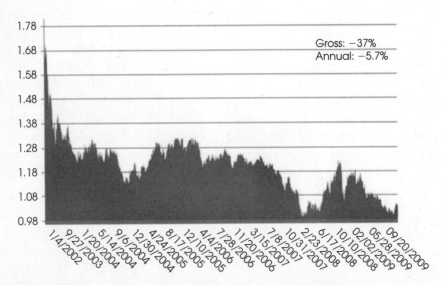

Figure 14.6   U.S. Dollar versus Swiss Franc (1995–2001)

that the current Great Recession was caused by the real estate industry and bad lending practices that have come undone.

Whereas this has great popular appeal, the politicians are mixing cause with effect. The late economist Hy Minsky is currently required reading at central banks around the world since his theories describe the past two asset bubbles pretty much to a *T*.

In short, his "financial instability hypothesis suggests, when optimism is high and ample funds are available for investment, investors tend to migrate from the safe hedge end of the Minsky spectrum to the risky speculative and Ponzi end."*

Put another way, when asset prices are rising, investors begin to believe that they will always rise. As this mind-set takes hold of the market, more participants enter, propelling the market even further. In just the past 15 years, this has occurred for tech stocks, real estate assets, and oil prices. Looking further back into history, we see this again and again: tulip bubble, South Seas bubble, and so on.

Liquidity in the 2000s was provided by outsized federal budget deficits, expansive money supply, and an ample source of funds from foreign investors as a result of the large trade deficit.

Banks make money renting money. They rent money from depositors at retail rates, and rent out money as loans at a higher rate that must reflect the costs of doing business and a risk premium for potential loss.

Imagine sitting around the credit committee of a bank in the mid-2000s. You are flush with cash from depositors as the liquidity in the market is absorbed. Your lenders tell you that competition is driving rates and credit standards on loans down as more banks compete for the business. You know you have to invest the money and cannot make enough in bonds for a decent return at the bank.

Finally, someone says, "Well, it may not make much sense but we need to put the money to work—I move for approval. And anyway, we are secured by real estate and they aren't making any more of that, are they?"

---

* Janet L. Yellen, president and CEO, Federal Reserve Bank of San Francisco, presentation to the *18th Annual Hyman P. Minsky Conference on the State of the U.S. and World Economies*: "Meeting the Challenges of the Financial Crisis," organized by the Levy Economics Institute of Bard College, New York City. For delivery on April 16, 2009.

This scene was played out in bank, investment bank, and institutional investor boardrooms over and over again. Real estate prices had risen well above their traditional link with inflation, but the sense was that even though high, real estate prices were unlikely to decline or would only decline a little. After all, right there in the 2002 FNMA Annual Report, there was Alan Greenspan saying, "Even though we have been having some fairly strong gains in home prices, it is our conclusion . . . that it is unlikely that we are confronting a housing bubble."

Even as late as April 2007, Treasury Secretary Hank Paulson said, "All the signs I look at show the housing market is at or near the bottom."

At this point, Hy Minsky would have stood to say that we were in a liquidity bubble and that it was only a matter of time before the crash. And crash we did.

Diversification

Earlier in this chapter we touched on asset classes and their role in investing. Since becoming free floating in 1971, currency has become known as a legitimate asset class with a volatility profile and returns that are separate from equities, fixed income, commodities, and real estate.

Since currencies price primarily reflects relative governmental policies, their price behavior is different from stocks and other asset classes. Technically, currencies have a low covariance with other assets classes, which means that they do not follow the same price pathways as these other alternatives. This also means that currencies are well placed as a diversifying asset class.

Some commentators suggest that investing in global equity mutual funds is a good substitute for adding currencies to a portfolio as an asset class. We think that this misses the point. As we said before, the price performance of a stock is based on management's execution within an attractive industry. Currencies move based on relative governmental policy execution. And in many stock mutual funds managers hedge away the currency risk to focus on the performance of the selected equities.

When we are asked how much of a risk portfolio should be allocated to currencies, we naturally say that one size does not fit all. This depends on how much overall risk someone is willing to take, what amount of his or her future spending patterns will be dependent on global purchasing power, and other considerations. For those able to appreciate portfolio diversification, however, allocations between 5 and 20 percent seem to be the levels suggested by many commentators.

How to View Currencies

When considering currencies, there are many things to take into account:

- *What is your base currency now, and what will it be?* For a U.S. investor, the answer to both of these questions is usually the U.S. dollar. But for a growing number of people there is a desire to retire outside the United States, and this decision can drive how to view a portfolio of currencies.
- *What is the fiscal balance situation of the country under consideration?* Generally, budgets are quoted as a percentage of GDP and any surplus and most low-digit deficits can be something to be sustained. One of the reasons we have consistently stated that the U.S. dollar is likely to decline in the intermediate to long term is that the fiscal deficits we feared at about 5 percent of GDP have exploded past 10 percent, and the total debt outstanding will soon cross 100 percent of GDP.
- *What is the county's balance of trade?* As Newton said earlier, having a positive balance of trade allows money to flow into a country, thereby boosting its reserves and financial situation. Exporting countries have a leg up on others when looking at prospective currency price changes.
- *Central Bank policy plays a large part in the strength or weakness of a currency.* The European Central Bank has historically performed well, for example, bolstered by the German attitude toward inflation and money supply control. Recently, the U.S. Federal Reserve appears to have abandoned its primary roles of defending the currency and focusing on the control of inflation to provide excess liquidity outside of the congressional budget progress.
- *Something the world wants can be one of the strongest drivers of currency prices.* Oil, commodities, agricultural products, or intellectual property can be the determinant in the demand for any given currency. This isn't a perfect indicator since government policies can eradicate any benefit, but energy

resources and commodities in particular can provide the basis for a long-term, sustained rise in the currency.

- *General business climate may indicate where the global investor may seek to profit from an expanding economy.* Given a choice, individuals will place funds where the largest risk-adjusted returns appear to be found. A fast-growing economy attracts funds, which bolsters the currency.

Which Currencies Should We Consider for the Long Run Now?

Placing a short list of currencies to study for long-term appreciation in a book is a very difficult matter. Governments change quickly and currency prices are driven by the long-term policies of governments. That said, here are a few to consider as a relative value opportunity:

- *Norwegian krone.* Norway is somewhat unique in that while maintaining a somewhat traditional European welfare state it has the money to do so. A bit like that uncle who spends too much on the kids, but can because he owns oil wells, Norway is the third-largest exporter of oil in the world. It maintains a positive balance of trade, a fiscal surplus, and has substantial reserves. All in all, it's a solid choice.
- *Australian dollar.* Australia has integrated itself into the Asian economy over the past 30 years, and is well placed to be the source of commodities that fuel the growth in China and the greater region. While running a small trade and budget deficit, the Australian dollar continues to remain strong based on purchases of energy and other commodities, alongside of a reasonably strong central bank.
- *Emerging markets.* Currencies from emerging markets often provide investors with a superior return as newly rational government policies can create a stable and positive situation within a growing nation. In addition, emerging markets are often just gaining the capability to exploit some national resource and provide for superior growth.

  Unfortunately, these currencies have a long history of good returns followed by severe and serious crashes. A new government comes into power through the ballot box or through a coup and changes all previously existing structure.

The government returns to a crony economy or worse. And often some other country has issues and the market sells all emerging markets' currencies at once.

A country like Brazil seems to have all the features for appreciation of currency. Good growth and a significant rationalization of its economy have boosted this currency over the past several years, and may for some time to come. However, as with any emerging market, enter here only at your own risk since there can be a large drop in value, creating losses in the currency, if any of the dire situations listed earlier occur.

- *Always diversify.* In any event, within an investor's allocation to currencies, a portfolio containing exposure to various regions and market drivers should be built. Some European, Asian, South Pacific, Canadian, and other currencies can be added, and, if the tolerance for risk exists, then add in some emerging markets currency in smaller proportions.

The Future of Currencies

In the modern era, currencies generate a lot of conversation. Congress is voting to censure China for manipulating its currency. Rumors have swirled for 30 years that the trucks are full of Ameros and are ready to pull out of the garage next week (every week). One-world-currency organizations come and go. We have no doubt that at some point in the future each of the existing currencies will reach its intrinsic value of zero (as Doug Casey likes to say).

At the same time, currencies serve the role of a medium of exchange and an agreed storehouse of value for the 21st-century economy. It is doubtful (until things change radically) that a single world currency will come into being; in effect, with full convertibility it really isn't necessary.

We are just beginning to see the discipline that even a "meaningless and intangible social construct" can provide as the major economies slide further into debt. In the era of a gold standard countries went bankrupt, and we expect to see more countries join that club in this epoch of fiat currency as well.

For the individual it remains important to understand that building an allocation to currencies within a risk portfolio is critical to the retention of purchasing power and protection against bad government policy.

15

The 2010 Estate Tax Law: Here to Stay or Going Away?

Gary Kashdan

When Congress passed the Economic Growth and Tax Relief Reconciliation Act of 2001 (also known as EGTRRA), they had to use some legislative maneuvering to make the potential loss in tax revenue fit into the federal budget. While the act eliminated the federal estate tax entirely in 2010, it also contains a "sunset provision" that reinstates federal estate taxes in 2011. As of 2011, the lifetime estate tax exemption that had increased in steps to $3,500,000 per individual in 2009 is scheduled to permanently reset to $1 million, and the top tax rate, which was 45 percent in 2009, will increase to 55 percent with an additional 5 percent surtax for some larger estates. Although the estate tax is repealed as of January 1, 2010, the gift tax remains with the same lifetime exclusion of $1 million per person. However, the tax rate on cumulative lifetime taxable gifts over $1 million has decreased from 45 percent in 2009 to 35 percent in 2010. For 2010, the annual gift tax exclusion amount remains unchanged at $13,000 per donee.

Everyone expected Congress to enact a legislative "patch" during 2009 that would extend the $3.5 million estate tax exemption and 45 percent top tax rate until they decided what to do for the long term. Alas, Congress failed to act and so made it impossible for attorneys, accountants, and financial planning professionals to give their clients estate planning advice that could be relied upon in the future. There is talk that Congress could act in 2010, but no one can say when and whether any changes would be made retroactive to January 1, 2010. For now, we can state only what we know to be true under current law:

- As of January 1, 2010, there is no federal estate or generation-skipping transfer tax.
- The lifetime exclusion on taxable gifts is $1 million and the top tax rate is 35 percent.
- As of January 1, 2011, the federal estate tax exclusion will be $1 million and the top rate will be 55 percent.
- The step-up in basis from the decedent's cost basis to fair market value at date of death in the hands of heirs that applied to all property in a decedent's estate is now limited to a total step-up of $1.3 million for property passing to non-spouses plus an additional $3 million for property passing to a spouse. This limitation on step-up of cost basis only applies to 2010. Unless new legislation changes the law, there will be no limitations on the step-up for all assets inherited once again beginning in 2011.

Where do we go from here? For now, there appear to be four possible outcomes:

1. Total estate tax repeal remains effective for 2010 and thereafter (very unlikely).
2. Repeal stays effective for 2010 and the changes scheduled for 2011 take effect next year.
3. Repeal stays effective for a period of time in 2010 but Congress eventually reinstates the estate tax using the 2009 exemption of $3.5 million and top tax rate of 45 percent.
4. The estate tax is reinstated retroactive to January 1, 2010, using 2009 rules.

It is also possible that Congress could pass legislation that would make significant changes in estate tax rules. Bills have been proposed that would raise the estate tax exemption to $5 million per individual, index the exemption for inflation, and enable a surviving spouse to utilize any portion of the exemption not used by the first spouse's estate.

If Congress has acted to resolve the current uncertainty relative to estate planning by the time you read this, some of the following topics may or may not be relevant. However, you may wish to give some consideration to some of the following issues.

Asset Titling

For estate planning purposes, it is generally considered a good idea for ownership of property to be divided equally between spouses. The objective is to ensure that, regardless of which spouse dies first, the decedent will be able to protect up to the maximum amount of taxable estate that can pass free of estate tax by virtue of the lifetime estate tax exemption (i.e., $3.5 million in 2009 and $1 million in 2011). The usual way of utilizing the lifetime estate tax exemption is to have a will that provides for property with cumulative value not exceeding the existing exemption amount to be placed in a trust. The trust is often referred to as a *family trust* or a *bypass trust*. The surviving spouse is usually given the right to all income realized by the bypass trust plus a limited right to invade the corpus of the trust for support and maintenance. When the surviving spouse dies, the corpus remaining in the trust passes to designated individuals (usually children and/or grandchildren) and bypasses taxation in the surviving spouse's estate.

Since there is no way of knowing which spouse will die first, it is important for each spouse to own property that could be used to fund a bypass trust.

As of 2010, however, there is no estate tax and, at least as important, a new treatment of the basis of inherited assets. Under estate law prior to 2010, heirs were able to step up the basis of inherited assets to their fair market value on the date of the decedent's death (or six months after the date of death in certain circumstances). Thus, if an individual bought a stock for $10 per share and the fair market value of the stock was $100 per share on his or her date of death, the basis of the stock in the hands of heirs would be stepped up to $100.

Under the new carryover basis rules, heirs will inherit assets that retain the same cost basis that existed in the hands of the decedent. The likely result of the new rules is potentially large capital gains when heirs sell inherited property. There are two important exceptions to the general carryover basis rules. Non-spouse heirs will be able to increase the basis of inherited property up to a total of $1.3

million. The total amount of step-up available can be allocated to any combination of property inherited. On assets passing to a surviving spouse, an *additional* $3 million of step-up is available.

Prior to 2010, the usual approach was to try to divide the property of a married couple approximately equally by value. Now, rather than allocating assets by value, each spouse should own assets that have approximately equal amounts of unrealized appreciation. But what if Congress does nothing in 2010 and the estate tax and unlimited step-up of inherited assets return in 2011?

Here is one solution: Retitle all of your nonretirement accounts as "tenants in common," so that no matter which spouse dies first, half the assets will be eligible for inclusion in a bypass trust.

Formula Clauses in Wills

Among the many issues that have arisen because of the current uncertainty in the estate tax arena is the use of formula clauses in wills. For example: Joe's estate is worth $10 million. Joe's will provides that his children from his first marriage are to get the maximum amount he can bequeath without triggering estate tax. Wife number 2 is to receive the remainder of his estate. In 2009, Joe's children would have received $3.5 million. Since there is no estate tax in 2010, the formula in Joe's will could result in his entire $10 million estate passing to his children, and his wife would receive nothing.

One method of preventing an unintended disinheriting of a spouse could be the inclusion of a *disclaimer trust* in the will. With a disclaimer trust, a spouse could leave his or her entire estate to the other spouse and give the survivor the ability to disclaim all or a portion of the inherited assets into a bypass trust. Doing so would cause the disclaimed assets to pass to heirs more tax efficiently if the estate tax is reinstated prior to the death of the surviving spouse.

For a disclaimer to be recognized for estate planning purposes, strict technical requirements must be met. Before making this or any other changes in your will, *you should consult with an experienced estate planning attorney.*

Gifting

Although there is no federal estate tax as of this writing, there is still a federal gift tax. However, there is also a gift tax credit that is designed to offset the tax on up to $1 million of taxable gifts made during your lifetime. A taxable gift is any gift to a non-spouse in excess of the annual gift tax exclusion, which is a maximum of $13,000 ($26,000 for a married couple) per donee. The good news is that the tax rate on cumulative lifetime gifts that exceed $1 million has decreased from 45 percent in 2009 to 35 percent in 2010.

For those individuals who are able and willing to use their $1 million gift tax exemption, using a *grantor retained annuity trust* (GRAT) could be a very effective gifting method. A GRAT provides the grantor (the person transferring property to the trust) with a "qualified annuity interest," which is the right to receive a fixed amount, payable at least annually, for a specified term of years. Because the annuity is a "qualified interest," the value of the grantor's retained interest is valued under IRC Section 7520, an assumed interest rate that is published monthly by the IRS. The value of the gift to the holder(s) of the remainder interest in the trust (usually a younger generation) is the fair market value of the property transferred to the trust less the assumed present value of the retained annuity interest.

The annuity interest is generally described as a percentage of the initial value of the assets transferred to the GRAT. If the grantor is living at the end of trust's term, any property remaining in the GRAT after the last annuity payment is made passes to the remainder beneficiaries, either outright or in trust for their benefit. If the return on the assets in the GRAT is less than the applicable 7520 rate, all of the trust property will be distributed to the grantor as part of the annuity payments during the trust term, and nothing will be left to the remainder beneficiaries. The grantor will be no worse off than if he or she had not created the GRAT, except for the cost of creating the GRAT and any gift tax paid upon funding the GRAT. If the return exceeds the applicable IRC Section 7520 rate, the property remaining in the trust at termination will pass tax-free to the remainder beneficiaries.

The IRC Section 7520 rate is also referred to as the *threshold rate*, because any appreciation of the assets, net of the annuity payments to the grantor, is passed to the younger generation, rather than being taxed in the grantor's estate. GRATs are particularly attractive now because the IRC Section 7520 rate as of March 2010 is only 3.2 percent.

Take the case of John, for example. John, age 65, transfers $500,000 to a GRAT in return for an annual payment from the GRAT of $35,000 (7% of $500,000) for 10 years. John's children are the remainder beneficiaries. Using the IRC Section 7520 rate for March 2010, the taxable gift to the children is calculated to be $204,467. If the assets in the trust were to produce average annual income of 3 percent and average annual growth of 3 percent, when the trust terminates in 10 years, the children would receive $436,928, and no additional gift tax would be payable by John.

In the example, by using a GRAT, the value of the $500,000 transfer is reduced by approximately 59 percent in calculating the amount of the taxable gift to John's children. Thus, gifting through a GRAT makes it possible for John to pass more property to his children under the $1 million lifetime gift tax exemption. The amount of the taxable gift resulting when the trust is created ($204,467) would be included in John's estate at death, but any future appreciation in the assets in the GRAT would be shifted to John's children. John will receive $350,000 back from the GRAT, and any net appreciation in the value of the assets in the GRAT will not be taxed in John's estate.

It is important to note that a transfer to a GRAT is irrevocable. In addition, if John were to die before the 10-year term of the GRAT ends, a portion of the assets would be subject to inclusion in John's estate. Thus, when choosing the term of a GRAT, it should be a term that the grantor is, absent unforeseen circumstances, likely to outlive.

A *qualified personal residence trust* (QPRT) is another type of trust that can be used to make a discounted gift to children and remove assets from the grantor's estate. A QPRT is similar to a GRAT, but in the case of a QPRT, the grantor transfers his or her residence to a trust and retains the right to live in the residence. When the trust ends, ownership of the residence passes to the remainder beneficiaries of the trust (usually children). In the case of a QPRT, the intervening interest that reduces the taxable gift to the remainder beneficiaries is the right to live in the residence, as opposed to a retained income interest in the case of a GRAT.

For example: Bob, age 68, transfers his home, with a fair market value of $750,000, to a 10-year QPRT with his children as remainder beneficiaries. Using the IRC Section 7520 rate for March 2010 of 3.2 percent, the taxable gift to the children is calculated to be $397,755, a discount of 47 percent from the actual fair market value of the home. Assuming the home appreciates by 3 percent per year for 10 years, it would be worth approximately $1,008,000 when the trust ends and ownership passes to the children. The taxable gift of $397,755 would have to be added to Bob's other assets in calculating his taxable estate at death, but the appreciation in the value of the home would pass to Bob's children. Assuming Bob's estate is in the 50 percent marginal federal estate tax bracket when he dies, the transfer to the QPRT would save approximately $305,000 in potential estate tax.

In the example, it should be noted that once the home is in the QPRT, it can be sold and another house can be purchased, or the sale proceeds can be turned into an annual annuity for the grantor, without losing the gift and estate tax benefits of the QPRT. It is also possible for the grantor to retain the right to rent the home from the remainder beneficiaries when the trust terminates, and payment of rent would further reduce the grantor's potential taxable estate.

As in the case with a GRAT, for a QPRT to be effective the grantor must outlive the term of the trust. If the grantor dies before the trust ends, the value of the residence will be included in the grantor's estate at its then fair market value. However, if the grantor does die prematurely, the end result in terms of estate taxes would be no worse than if the residence were never transferred to a QPRT.

Summary

The discussion in this chapter is intended only to give the reader a sense of the uncertain nature of federal estate taxes as of this writing. The gifting techniques described are in no way intended to be an all-inclusive discussion. *Before making any changes to any existing wills and/ or trusts or engaging in any gifting, you should consult with an experienced estate planning attorney.*

Epilogue

THE TRUTH ABOUT DEFICITS, DEBTS, DELEVERAGING, DEFLATION, AND DERIVATIVES

Martin Truax

Since this book's contributors last met in early 2009, the stock market has risen, but the financial fundamentals have gotten worse. The U.S. federal government has entered "tilt" mode, racking up *$1.5 trillion* in annual fiscal deficits for each of the latest two fiscal years, 2009 and 2010. That is an almost unbelievable number, inconceivable just two years ago. The previous record for a single-year's budget deficit was $455 billion, set in 2008.

In addition to a bankrupt federal government, at least 40 of our 50 states are in similar financial shape, running record deficits. There is one major difference. States are not allowed to print fiat money to make up the shortfall. Most states are not authorized to run budget deficits, so they must face harsh realities. Meanwhile, our federal government shows no signs of facing its irresponsible deficit spending addiction, as the following analysis makes clear.

The Growing Government Deficit Dilemma

What we see in the news reports is only the tip of the iceberg. The official deficit calculations we see in the press vastly underestimate government's total obligations. Economist John Williams of Shadow Statistics (www.shadowstats.com) calculates that the actual annual federal fiscal deficit in 2008 was more like $5.1 trillion, not the $455 billion reported. Using the kind of generally accepted accounting principles (GAAP) that apply to any other corporation, Williams said that we must add in the unfunded liabilities for Social Security and Medicare.

For fiscal year 2009, Williams calculates that the actual shortfall likely was "around $8.8 trillion, instead of the official cash-based

$1,417 billion." He then calculated that "the total federal debt and obligations at the end of the 2009 fiscal year [ending September 30, 2009] were close to $75 trillion, or more than five times the total U.S. GDP. The $75 trillion includes roughly $12 trillion in gross federal debt with the balance reflecting the net present value of unfunded obligations."*

Just counting the federal government's cash debts, ignoring any unfunded obligations, the U.S. government (meaning us taxpayers, our children, and our grandchildren) will owe almost *$14 trillion* at the end of 2010, and there is no end in sight. Just since early 2009, the federal government has taken over or assumed the debts of several massively large organizations—including AIG, GM, Chrysler, and Bear Stearns—while offering unlimited financial support to Fannie Mae and Freddie Mac. Debts from those two quasi-governmental entities alone could reach $8 trillion in taxpayer liabilities (according to the *Campbell Real Estate Timing Letter*).

Fannie and Freddie currently fund 90 percent of U.S. mortgages while guaranteeing 97 percent of them (and losing $94 billion in 2009 alone). Contractual Social Security future payments exceed *$45 trillion* and Medicare adds another *$55 trillion*. We can't conceive of a number like $100 trillion, but that's enough $100 bills to reach the sun—93 million miles away—with enough left over to circle the globe 72 times. And that doesn't include government pensions, veterans' benefits, or cushy congressional retirements. With that, the total could exceed *$120 trillion.*

The Census Bureau mailed forms to 120 million households in 2010. Thus, each household's share of the unfunded debt load would be $1 million. How many U.S. households have $1 million net worth to spare? So, how can the promises to Baby Boomers (retiring between now and 2029) be kept, much less the promises to their children? Even if you kick in *all* the net worth of all corporations, and *all* U.S. assets net of debt, that amounts to barely $50 trillion. And many government commitments are indexed to inflation, which will raise costs even further.

The official deficits over the next 10 years, not counting unfunded obligations, will add another $11 trillion, bringing total deficits to about $24 trillion, according to the Congressional Budget Office (CBO) in their latest estimation of the effect of the Obama Administration's budgets:

---

* http://www.shadowstats.com/article/hyperinflation-2010.

Year	CBO Deficit Projection
2010	$1.500 trillion
2011	$1.341 trillion
2012	$ 915 billion
2013	$ 747 billion
2014	$ 724 billion
2015	$ 793 billion
2016	$ 894 billion
2017	$ 940 billion
2018	$1.001 trillion
2019	$1.152 trillion
2020	$1.253 trillion
Total:	$11.26 trillion

The lowest projected deficit in the next 10 years ($724 billion in 2014) will be greater than any single deficit year before 2009. But the deficits don't just *stop* in 2020. It gets worse as the interest on that debt compounds and increases, probably at rapidly rising rates. Even at the current average rate of just 1.4 percent on Treasury bills, bonds, and notes, the CBO projects that 45 percent of government revenues will go to interest payments in 10 years. What if borrowing rates rose to 5 percent or more? Where would another $10 trillion of loans to the government, *or possibly much more*, come from? Our total U.S. stock market value (counting all exchanges) is just $11 trillion.

And don't forget, we have to roll over much of the existing $14 trillion of debt along the way. Why would other countries continue to lend money to us? Where would they get the funds—from their stock markets? They need to raise about $3 trillion a year for their own deficits, and all their stock markets combined will not cover our mounting projected cumulative debt.

"Guaranteed Lifetime Security" Undermines Most State Budgets

Our 50 separate states must balance their respective budgets annually, but they have less tax revenue coming in than it costs to run the state—not to mention their unrealistic retirement packages. The biggest gaps are in California, Illinois, Arizona, Nevada, New York,

Alaska, and New Jersey. The core deficit problem stems from the high wages and benefits of government employees, including generous retirement packages. According to the Bureau of Labor Statistics, average wages and benefits in state and local governments are $26.24 per hour versus $19.45 per hour in the private sector. Add $13.06 and $8.06 in benefits, respectively, and the total hourly cost is $39.30 for states and municipalities versus $27.51 for businesses.

Government retirement is usually available after just 20 to 25 years' service, at 70 to 90 percent of the highest-salary years, plus health benefits for the rest of their lives (and for a joint survivor, too, in most cases). Most of those early retirees have a 30-year (or more) life expectancy in retirement. In California, it's not unusual to get $100,000 per year in retirement, and $200,000 if you were a department head or administrator. To meet the cash flows needed, government pension funds are often invested in high-yielding, higher-risk investments, many of which are now under water. To make up for those losses and early retirements (forced or voluntary), many states and municipalities are having to cut essential *existing* services and personnel.

Boomers Building Castles of Debt

An estimated 10,000 Boomers will reach retirement age every day for the next 20 years. The average Boomer (born 1946 to 1964) can expect to live to age 83. There are now over 75 million U.S. Boomers in the pipeline waiting to retire in style. The government has promised each Boomer an average $14,000 in Social Security and $11,000 in Medicare benefits each year, for $25,000 per person per year in 2010 alone, indexed to inflation. Ignoring inflation for a moment, consider 75 million times $25,000 and you get nearly $2 trillion per year in benefits.

Those kinds of numbers put most household calculators into an error mode. Put simply, those transfer payments must result in either massive wealth confiscation or broken promises or some of both. Inflation makes the indexed CPI entitlement and interest rate calculation even worse: It won't compute. That's why each one of us will have to go refigure our retirement according to the realities of broken government promises and future taxation or confiscation.

In the revised calculation, do we just forget about the other budget items after entitlements and interest? Do we abandon all spending on national defense, nationalized health insurance, education, homeland security, state and local government aid, space missions, national science, low-cost housing, roads and other infrastructure, the justice system (judges, jails, etc.), and the millions of government employees, from park rangers to IRS agents? It's not adding up. There is a continuing series of brick walls ahead. Each one could prove more difficult to climb over than the one before it.

Last year, before the first Baby Boomer reached 65, Social Security inflow was already far less than outflow, by $129 billion. With more unemployed this year, the inflows are shrinking while the outflows grow. Previous to 2009, the reversal of outflow versus inflow wasn't forecast to happen until 2017. Thanks to the deepest recession since the 1930s, it has already happened.

It has been fun while it has lasted, but we'll now need backup plans for when the reality of these brick walls confronts us. The consumer society is dead and gone. Through commercialization, Madison Avenue has conditioned U.S. consumers to buy two or more of most luxuries, now rather than later. The list included second homes, cars, TVs, appliances, and luxury kitchens and baths. Buy now, pay later. Now, later has arrived. A generation ago, we typically saved 10 percent. In the credit binge of the past 20+ years, our net savings rate dipped below zero. (It is now 5 percent.)

The median American household net investment worth was less than $30,000 last year, according to the Employment Benefit Research Institute. Most people feel, according to that same poll, that they are on track to retire, when combined with Social Security promises. About half have never put a pencil to paper (or fingers on calculators) to check this assumption. Perhaps now is the time to face the future with our eyes wide open, and then plan accordingly.

Deleveraging Leads to Asset Price Deflation

Deleveraging is a painful side effect of debt implosion. Real estate values have declined and short-term loans are being called or written off. New loans are hard to come by. Banks are tougher on credit standards because securitization (the passing off of loans into packages to others) is almost dead. This deleveraging feeds on itself and *deflates* asset values.

Most estate planning and retirement planning projections need to be reviewed in this new light. What assumptions are more realistic? Are "guaranteed" fixed annuities from pensions or third-party guarantees still reliable? Have the issuing entities placed their assets in depreciating real estate, deflating bonds, devalued equities, or perhaps in low-interest-rate risk-avoidance assets? These questions are often tough to answer. The picture has never been totally clear, but deleveraging and the resulting deflation make that already-blurry picture dramatically worse.

The answer depends on the shape of the recovery to come. Will our future economy recover in a V formation, or a double-dip W, or suffer a long-term depression, in an L formation? I feel we are most likely looking at an elongated series of Ws (WWW) with the potential of some of the next lows to be lower lows. We have used up most quick-fix response remedies. The Fed's emergency ammunition kit of super-low interest rates, bailouts, and "quantitative easing" (easy money through bond-creation) is now used up. The only "emergency" item left is negative interest rate plans (NIRPs) on "safe investments" (i.e., you get charged a fee to store your money safely—invest $100,000 with the Treasury and get back $98,000 in nine months, for example).

Negative interest rates aren't very appetizing—offering a "guaranteed loss"—so they would likely push more money toward assets with more risk, like corporate bonds and stocks, real estate, or private investments such as businesses and commercial property. The global bond market won't accept low or negative rates, so demand for U.S. Treasury debt will dry up.

Derivatives: Weapons of Mass Financial Destruction

Derivatives can be prudent hedges or leveraged speculations. Sometimes they are called *swaps*, *forwards*, or *options*. Risk is not eliminated; it is just transferred to a different party. If that party can't pay off as promised, then the "insured party" can be harmed. A domino effect can be set off. We experienced that in 2008 with Lehman Brothers and AIG. Lehman Brothers was allowed to fail, as money funds were about to "break the buck," causing a financial panic.

Derivatives have grown in global market value to exceed $600 trillion (*Fortune*, July 6, 2009), up from $95 trillion in 2000. Compare those numbers with a total of just $11 trillion in all U.S. stocks and perhaps $60 trillion in all global stocks. Derivatives are at least 10 times larger than all global equities. Warren Buffett calls derivatives "financial weapons of mass destruction." They brought down Long Term Capital Management in 1998 and in the past two years, derivatives killed Bear Stearns, Lehman Brothers, Merrill Lynch, Wachovia, and others.

Hedge funds are not transparent. We can't see what's inside them. Many of these funds employ derivatives. Many have *lockup* periods (i.e., you can't get your money out when and if you want). That's why increased illiquidity can return so quickly in times of financial stress.

The Next Move: A Return to "Stagflation"

While asset deflation is our near-term threat, global currencies are still being printed around the clock in an effort to stop deflation from spreading. This will eventually result in rising inflation during a time of chronic stagnation, giving us a return to 1970s-style *stagflation.*

Fiscal stimulus is the universal answer to unemployment. Governments—whether China, Russia, the United States, Argentina, or Zimbabwe—want to stay in power through providing financial stimulus for their voters or constituents. Sooner or later, inflation will hit like a tsunami. When it does, interest rates will rise (bond prices will fall), and there will most likely be a scramble for inflation protection assets, like commodities, real estate, and inflation-adjusting assets.

Bond market crashes—like in the 1970s—can be just as bad as stock market crashes. When both happen at the same time, there seems to be nowhere to turn. When the warning signs of inflation approach, a different type of asset-protection strategy comes into play—one of seeking continued absolute asset value, while providing purchasing-power protection. Even "all cash" or short-term Treasuries may not be safe under these extreme conditions.

From today's low interest rate levels, a mere 1 percent rise in long-term rates can wipe out almost three years of bond income. That's why, for preservation of principle and purchasing power, tactical allocation becomes crucial in times of rising long-term interest rates.

There is still a lot of nervous money on the sidelines in América. About $3.3 trillion sits in near-zero-return money funds; another $4.7 trillion sits in savings accounts, plus $3.1 trillion in CDs. This

$11 trillion in cash could begin to slide with more confidence toward more risk in stocks.

Before you consider putting all your cash in stocks, remember that the $11 trillion currently in equities was once $15 trillion in late 2007. Stock values were cut in half, to $7 trillion in March 2009, before rebounding to $11 trillion a year later. If too much of the $11 trillion in cash is reentered into investments, it could quickly be reduced by 50 percent again, as it was in 2008–2009. Sad to say, most investors tend to reenter the stock market near a recovery peak, not near its lows.

A New Investment Strategy for New Times: The Evergreen Portfolio

To survive financially and hopefully even prosper in the next decade requires a different strategy for these new and unprecedented times. Most of us have two types of investment assets: liquid and illiquid. Our illiquid assets include real estate and private business interests. We can't usually calculate them with daily quotes, but in most cases they have taken big hits. Our liquid assets can be divided into four major categories: cash, bonds (including annuities), stocks, and hard commodities, especially gold. Let's take a quick look at each category:

1. *Cash.* Although cash currently provides little income, it can appreciate relative to illiquid assets and sometimes to liquid assets as well, during periods of deleveraging and deflation. Other than what's needed as emergency reserves, say for one or two years of expected expenses, excess cash can be parked in low-yielding domestic deposits, or you can shift to higher-paying foreign currencies. Many currencies not only pay more interest, but can possibly appreciate to the U.S. dollar.

   A *disciplined* approach to buying and selling other currencies is *essential.* You can attempt to do it yourself or find someone with a disciplined foreign currency program to do it for you. Over the next 10 to 20 years, some currencies will probably blow up (become worth a lot less), while others will appreciate as stores of value. That's where I'd prefer to invest most of a cash position.

2. *Bonds.* The same principles apply to bonds as with our cash allocation. Certain countries will get their finances in order and have better fiscal management or excess natural resources and competitive goods to sell to the world. Some will run surpluses, just as certain states in the United States will be better fiscally managed than others. We'd prefer those countries and states that can reduce our risk of credit default, as fear of such would cause bond assets to decline in value when fear and panic set in.

   Buy and hold applies only to short-term maturities of highest quality. Nobody is exempt from surprises, not even AAA-rated corporations. Prior to the most recent battle for solvency, there were only six U.S. companies rated AAA. One was GE. Triple-A implies that a firm can survive depressions, but GE had to get bailed out during a "mere recession." If in the future governments vowed "no more bailouts," then you can see why *diversity* becomes paramount in our portfolio.

   Many investors, in reaction to the first two battles for investment survival of the past decade, have hunkered down in the cash foxhole, with the rest in "safe" bond funds. In 2009, while the stock market advanced almost 60 percent off the bottom in less than a year, investors in general sold $35 billion of equity funds, but put $421 billion into bond funds. You know what the rule is about the masses, and the dangers of following them. Remember, if rates go up, bond funds go down. They have no specific maturity date and therefore no promised return. The bonds are collectively being rolled over continually—there's no given date to cash in your principal.

3. *Stocks.* These have long provided the greatest return, and I believe they still deserve a double portion (40 percent) versus the rest: cash, bonds, and gold. We like stocks, but only if they are part of a disciplined sell strategy (or similar protective system). "Buy and hold" at your own peril. Our stocks of choice are high-dividend stocks. We'd diversify through a separate, personal, un-comingled, liquid, transparent account. Downside protection will be essential in our perceived elongated WWW formation, just as it was in 2000–2002 and 2007–2009. If you believe that buy-and-hold is a preferred strategy for these times, please go back and

read the first half of this chapter, about the debts, deficits, deleveraging, deflation, defaults, and derivatives. Then imagine the unknown disasters that always surprise us—man-made, natural, and otherwise. We can't predict the unexpected, but we can better prepare for it.

Dividends have provided over half of the return of equities for the adult lifetime of any reader of this book (dating back to 1929). U.S. corporations are in a good cash position now, with over $1 trillion in cold storage. Maybe half of that can be regarded as "excess" cash—to be used for dividend increases, share repurchase, or fuel for mergers and acquisitions (*Barron's,* March 8, 2010).

Ned Davis Research shows that over the past 40 years companies with increasing dividends returned 40 percent more than the S&P 500. Professor Jeremy Siegel of the Wharton School of Business says that dividend-paying stocks offer "bear market protection and return acceleration." He points out that it took 25 years (1929–1954) for the market to return to its 1929 highs, but those who reinvested dividends earned 334 percent total return in that time span. Higher dividends allow for reinvested dividends to accumulate new shares at lower prices, and high-dividend-paying stocks gives us "birds in the hand" to help offset low cash (or high-quality bond) returns.

To a lesser degree, a portfolio of international exposure might be included in the equity mix, but only with a firm sell discipline. For instance, don't get overly caught up in the Asia miracle. A lot of that growth is fueled by government intervention. China's export market to U.S. consumers has shrunk drastically. Infrastructure and real estate spending are far ahead of themselves in China. Excess capacity in manufacturing and housing is almost global.

Passive investing, whether through indexing or a buy-and-hold strategy with other kinds of funds, is for suckers. Over the past 15 years, about 60 percent of the mutual funds that invest in blue-chip stocks failed to beat the S&P index. Managers of bond and foreign stock funds also struggle to beat their benchmarks. Twice in less than a decade, in fact, investors who did the easy thing—just owned "the market"—have seen huge chunks of their wealth destroyed by bursting asset bubbles. You need a strategy that shields you from the excesses of "irrational exuberance."

4. *Gold.* Starting from a base of only $255 in 2001, gold has averaged over 15 percent per year for nine years. Sure, gold is much more volatile than cash, but the returns have been rewarding. When gold started taking off, the bears said it couldn't last, because central banks had been net sellers of gold since 1988. They planned on a systematic unloading of their gold positions.

All that changed in 2009, when central banks became net gold buyers. As currency crises have struck in Iceland, Argentina, Greece, and some other developed countries of Europe and the Americas, we can see that no currency lasts forever. Gold cannot be printed, manufactured, or mined in enough quantity to expand the global supply of gold by more than about 2 percent per year. Gold has been a store of value and medium of exchange for 6,000 years. Probably less than 5 percent of Americans have owned or even held a real gold coin. It's an under-owned asset.

How much should you allocate to this fourth and final portion? Invest up to your comfort level. Some people feel comfortable with 5 percent or much more in gold. Others start with maybe 1 percent or 2 percent. Unlike other investments, gold is more of a buy-and-hold proposition, but continue to have a disciplined protection strategy for any gold or silver mining equities, for the time being. If gold goes substantially higher, which is my expectation, then gold miners will become substantially more profitable and perhaps disconnect from the general markets, as happened in the 1930s.

Will we have a repeat of the 1930s in our near-term future? A large part of the world won't like the answer. Come and join our contributing authors as we meet to discuss once again these and other questions at our next Chota Forum, April 15, 2011. (For more information, contact www.aicatchota.com.)

I hope to see you next April in the North Georgia mountains!

About the Authors

Martin Truax is a managing director of Morgan Keegan & Co., Inc. After starting his career teaching university investment courses, he joined what later was to become Smith Barney as a financial consultant in 1971. He is author of the book, *Building Personal Wealth.* He wrote a client newsletter at Smith Barney and continues to write that letter at Morgan Keegan today. With 40 years' investment experience, his primary role continues to be working with private individual investors in their investment planning and overall portfolio management implementation. For his most current outlook, you can visit www.ipmg.mkadvisor.com.

Ron Miller began his career as an aerospace scientist in 1962 after receiving BS and MS engineering degrees from the University of Kansas. He conducted basic and applied research at the Douglas Aerophysics Laboratory in California and the Lockheed Aerospace Sciences Laboratory in Georgia during the first decade of his career. He received an MBA in Finance from Georgia State University in 1971 where he earned membership in Beta Gamma Sigma, the honorary business school society. In the same year he put aside a successful career in aerospace research for the challenges of Wall Street by joining the firm of Shearson Hammill & Co., which eventually, through many mergers, became a part of Salomon Smith Barney. In 1977, he became a certified financial planner, a distinction he has maintained to the present. He joined the Salomon Smith Barney Portfolio Management Group in 1988 and twice received the Portfolio Performance Award for the top performance among over 250 portfolio managers at the firm. He was appointed a senior portfolio management director in 1994. In 2001, he and Martin Truax moved their Investment Planning and Management Group to Morgan Keegan & Co. Ron brings a wide variety of analytical and investment skills to his unique portfolio management philosophy as a result of his scientific background and extensive experience as an investor and a portfolio manager in all types of investment environments over four decades. The key to his portfolio management success is a focus on risk management in response to volatile financial markets. Ron's market commentary and portfolio action updates for the various investment strategies he manages are discussed regularly at www.ipmg.mkadvisor.com.

About the Contributors

Gary Alexander is senior writer for Navellier & Associates, with a weekly column at www.Navellier.com. For the previous 30 years, he was senior editor for many leading financial newsletters. He has also served as emcee or moderator at about 100 investment conferences since 1980.

Mark Skousen is a professional economist, financial advisor, university professor, and author of over 25 books. He has taught economics and finance at Columbia Business University, Barnard College, Mercy College, and Rollins College in Florida. In 2001–2002, he was president of the Foundation for Economic Education (FEE) in New York. From 1972 to 1975, Dr. Skousen was an economic analyst for the Central Intelligence Agency (CIA). Since then, he has been a consultant to IBM, Hutchinson Technology, and other Fortune 500 companies. He has been a columnist for *Forbes* magazine (1997–2001), and has written articles for the *Wall Street Journal, Liberty, Reason,* and the *Journal of Economic Perspectives.* He has appeared on ABC News, CNBC Power Lunch, CNN, Fox News, and C-SPAN Book TV.

Since 1980, Dr. Skousen has been editor in chief of *Forecasts & Strategies,* a popular award-winning investment newsletter published by Eagle Publishing in Washington D.C. (www.markskousen.com). He is also editor of his own web site, www.mskousen.com, and three trading services, Skousen Hedge Fund Trade, High Income Alert, and Turnaround Trader.

He earned a PhD in economics and monetary history from George Washington University in 1977. Since then, he has written over 25 books, including *The Structure of Production* (New York University Press, 1990), *Economics on Trial* (McGraw-Hill, 1991), *Puzzles and Paradoxes in Economics* (Edward Elgar Publishers, 1977), *Economic Logic* (Capital Press, 2010), *The Making of Modern Economics*

(M.E. Sharpe, 2009), *Vienna and Chicago, Friends or Foes?* (Capital Press, 2005), *The Big Three in Economics* (M.E. Sharpe, 2007), and *EconoPower* (Wiley, 2008).

His financial bestsellers include *The Complete Guide to Financial Privacy* (Simon & Schuster, 1983), *High Finance on a Low Budget* (Bantam, 1981; co-authored with his wife Jo Ann), *Scrooge Investing* (Little Brown, 1995; McGraw Hill 1999), and *Investing in One Lesson* (Regnery, 2007). He also was editor of the investment series, *Secrets of the Great Investors,* with Louis Rukeyser as narrator.

Dr. Skousen is the founder of FreedomFest, an annual gathering of the freedom movement from around the world, held every July in Las Vegas (www.freedomfest.com).

Dr. Skousen has lived in eight nations, and traveled and lectured throughout the United States and 70 countries. He grew up in Portland, Oregon. He and his wife, Jo Ann, and five children have lived in Washington D.C.; Nassau, the Bahamas; London, England; Orlando, Florida; and New York.

Robert R. Prechter, Jr., CMT, is founder and president of Elliott Wave International, the world's largest independent financial forecasting firm. He has been writing market commentary since 1976. In 1984, Bob set a record in the options division of the U.S. Trading Championship with a real-money trading account. In December 1989, Financial News Network (now CNBC) named him "Guru of the Decade" Bob served for nine years on the national Board of the Market Technicians Association and in 1990–1991 served as its president. He currently serves on the advisory board of MTA's Educational Foundation. During the 1990s, Bob expanded his firm to provide round-the-clock analysis on global financial markets. He has written 14 books on finance, beginning with *Elliott Wave Principle* in 1978, which forecast a 1920s-style stock market boom. His 2002 title, *Conquer the Crash: You Can Survive and Prosper in a Deflationary Crash and Depression,* which predicted the current debt crisis, was a *New York Times* best-seller. In 1999, Bob received the CSTA's first annual A.J. Frost Memorial Award for Outstanding Contribution to the Development of Technical Analysis. In 2003, Traders Library granted him its Hall of Fame award. In 2008 and 2010, the Georgia legislature invited Bob to testify before its Joint Economic Committee regarding the state's developing real estate and budget crises.

Prechter outlined a new approach to social science in *Socionomics: The Science of History and Social Prediction* (1999–2003). In 2007, the *Journal of Behavioral Finance* published "The Financial/ Economic Dichotomy: A Socionomic Perspective," a paper on financial theory by Prechter and his colleague, Dr. Wayne Parker. Prechter has made presentations on socionomic theory to the London School of Economics, Cambridge University, MIT, Georgia Tech, SUNY, and academic conferences. He has served as a reviewer for academic journals devoted to economics and finance. Read more at www.robertprechter.com.

Alexander Green is investment director of *The Oxford Club*. A Wall Street veteran, he has over 25 years' experience as a research analyst, investment advisor, portfolio manager, and financial writer. Under his direction, *The Oxford Club's* portfolios have beaten the Wilshire 5000 Index by a margin of more than 3 to 1. *The Oxford Club Communiqué*, whose portfolio he directs, is ranked in the top five in the nation for risk-adjusted returns over the past 10 years by the independent *Hulbert Financial Digest*. Mr. Green has been featured on *Oprah and Friends*, Fox News, *The O'Reilly Factor*, CNBC, MSNBC, and C-Span and has been profiled by the *Wall Street Journal, Business Week*, and *Forbes*, among many others. He is also the author of two national bestsellers: *The Gone Fishin' Portfolio*, and *The Secret of Shelter Island: Money and What Matters*.

Richard Maybury is a world-renowned author, lecturer, and analyst. He consults with business firms and individuals in the United States and Europe, is president of Henry Madison Research, Inc., and the editor of *U.S. & World Early Warning Report* newsletter. Mr. Maybury is widely regarded as one of the finest free-market writers in America today. His articles have appeared in the *Wall Street Journal, USA Today*, and other major publications.

Mr. Maybury has been compared to General Billy Mitchell (the army officer who foretold the Japanese attack on Pearl Harbor, to whom no one listened until it was too late), one of those rare individuals with the uncanny knack for seeing through the media and political smokescreens and spotting crucial trends—the kind that catch 99.9% of the population by surprise—and doing this well ahead of time, so it has the greatest benefit for his clients.

To learn more about Richard Maybury, including his easy-to-read books, the accuracy of his predictions, and his exciting newsletter, *U.S. & World Early Warning Report*, visit www.richardmaybury.com or call (800) 509–5400.

Adrian Day is a British-born writer and money manager, a graduate of the London School of Economics, who has made a name for himself searching out unusual opportunities around the world, with two books on the subject. His money management firm, Adrian Day Asset Management, specializes in global diversification and gold equities for individual and institutional clients. He is a frequent speaker at international seminars, is frequently a guest on CNBC and The Wall Street Journal Radio Network, and has been interviewed by *Money, Straits Times, Good Morning America,* and others. He is also the author of the upcoming *Investing in Resources: How to Obtain the Outsized Rewards and Avoid the Outsized Risks* (due in 2010 from John Wiley & Sons).

You may learn more about his services at www.AdrianDayAsset Management.com, or via e-mail at AssetManagement@AdrianDay.com.

Roger S. Conrad is editor of *Canadian Edge,* an Internet-based service directed at U.S. investors that tracks more than 130 Canadian income trusts. He's also editor of *Utility Forecaster,* the leading U.S. advisory on essential service stocks, bonds, and preferred stocks, was named Best Financial Advisory of 1999 and 1997, and has been cited for editorial excellence five times in the past seven years by the Newsletter & Electronic Publishers Association. He's an associate editor of *Personal Finance* and lead editor of *The News World.* He is the author of *Power Hungry: Strategic Investing in Telecommunications, Utilities and Other Essential Services.* To subscribe to his free weekly e-zines, go to www.utilityandincome.com and www.mapleleafmemo .com (the latter of which focuses on Canadian trusts).

Elliott H. Gue is editor of the long-running investment newsletter, *Personal Finance,* contributing his knowledge of global energy markets and growth investing strategies. For the past five years, Elliott has helmed the *Energy Strategist,* a semimonthly financial advisory that unearths the most profitable short-term and long-term opportunities in this space and outlines the interrelated economic and geopolitical forces that drive these markets. His latest endeavor,

MLP Profits, covers high-yielding master limited partnerships and includes sample portfolios for aggressive and conservative investors, advice on tax treatment of MLPs, and proprietary ratings of every name in the Alerian MLP Index.

A recognized expert on all things energy, Elliott appears regularly on Clean Skies TV to discuss developments in this fast-moving sector and has also appeared on CNBC and Bloomberg TV.

Prior to joining KCI Investing, Elliott lived and worked in Europe for five years, earning a bachelor's degree in economics and management and a master's degree in finance at the University of London.

Duane Poliquin is a geological engineer who has spent his entire career generating new mineral projects, first with major companies worldwide, and, since 1972, privately and for junior exploration companies. He has focused mainly on gold and gold copper prospects, and he has been involved in or directly responsible for the discovery of several prospects that became mines. Duane is still active as chairman of Almaden Minerals Ltd., which is exploring for gold in the western part of Canada, the United States, and Mexico.

Van Simmons is a lifelong entrepreneur, collector, and collectibles dealer. He has been a rare coin collector since age 12 and a rare coin dealer since 1979. Van has also been a dealer in sports cards, rare firearms, Western memorabilia, and collectible knives. His collecting interests include: English pottery, Bowie knives, American and French art glass, Western Americana, Indian baskets and weavings, and early Gold Rush memorabilia. In 1986, Van and his business partner, David Hall, created the coin-grading company, the Professional Coin Grading Service (PCGS), and in 1991, he created the sports card-grading business, PSA. In 1999, they took the company public under the name Collectors Universe (CLCT), and it trades on the NASDAQ exchange. Van serves on the Board of Directors of Collectors Universe. Today, Van is the president of David Hall Rare Coins. He is held in highest regard by both his peers and his clientele for his knowledge and his integrity.

David Hall is one of the world's authorities on the rare coin market. He became a full-time dealer in 1972 and was quickly one of the major players. In the 1980s he and Van Simmons were the driving force behind the major market innovation of the decade: guaranteed buy/sell markets, electronic trading for coins, and the Professional Coin Grading Service (PCGS).

In 1990, David Hall was named Orange County "Entrepreneur of the Year" by *Inc.* magazine. In February 1996, *Numismatic News* called him "the man who changed the coin market forever." In 1999, *Coinage* magazine named David Hall one of the top "Numismatists of the Century."

Frank Trotter is president of EverBank Direct. A founding partner of EverBank in 1998, he has acquired over 30 years' experience in banking and global investing. Mr. Trotter is a widely quoted speaker on financial topics, especially banking and the international markets. Publications recently quoting Mr. Trotter include the *Wall Street Journal, New York Times, U.S. News and World Report, Forbes, CBS MarketWatch, USA Today, Bloomberg, Fox News, CNNfn,* and the *Chicago Tribune,* among others. Mr. Trotter graduated from St. Olaf College and holds an MBA in finance and international finance from Washington University.

Gary Kashdan was a senior financial planner for Synovus Corporation for over four years prior to joining Morgan Keegan. Before joining Synovus, Gary was a financial planner for Robinson Humphrey Co./Smith Barney in Atlanta, Georgia for seven years. Gary's experience in financial planning runs the gamut from basic retirement and education funding projections to advanced estate planning, charitable giving strategies, and business succession planning.

Gary received a Bachelor of Science degree in accounting from the University of Tennessee and a Masters in Taxation from Georgia State University. He is a CPA in Tennessee (inactive) and has been a certified financial planner since 1986.

Gary holds a Series 7 securities license and a Series 65 Registered Representative license, and is licensed as a life, health, and variable annuity agent in Georgia. He is a member of the Atlanta chapter of the Financial Planning Association.

Index